BETWEEN THE LINES

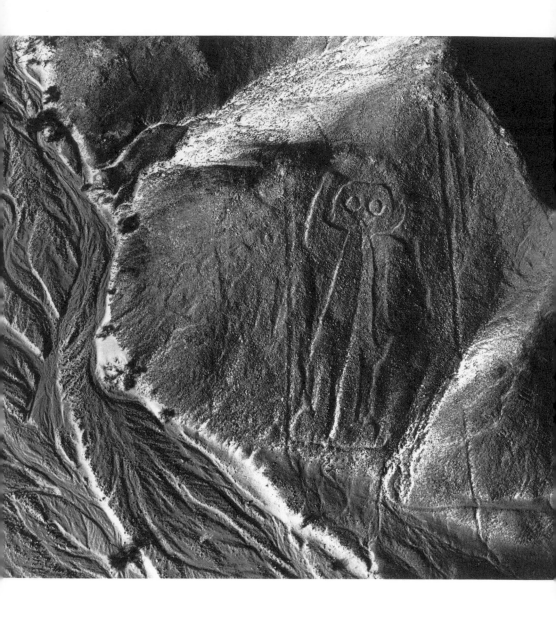

Anthony F. Aveni

BETWEEN THE LINES

The Mystery of the Giant Ground Drawings of Ancient Nasca, Peru

UNIVERSITY OF TEXAS PRESS, AUSTIN

First edition, 2000

Requests for permission to reproduce material from this work
should be sent to
  Permissions, University of Texas Press,
  Box 7819, Austin, TX 78713-7819.

⊗ The paper used in this book meets the minimum requirements of
ANSI/NISO Z39.48-1992 (R1997) (Permanence of Paper).

Frontispiece: *Owl Man, Nazca, Peru,* © Marilyn Bridges, 1979, courtesy of Felicia Murray.

Design: José Clemente Orozco

Library of Congress Cataloging-in-Publication Data
Aveni, Anthony F.
Between the lines : the mystery of the giant ground drawings
of ancient Nasca, Peru / Anthony F. Aveni.— 1st ed.
    p. cm.
Includes index.
    ISBN 0-292-70496-8 (hc : alk. paper)
    1. Nazca Lines Site (Peru)   I. Title.
    F3429.1.N3 A94   2000
    985'.27—dc21   99-050535

For Tom, Gary, Persis, Helaine, Clive, Gerry, Doug, Bill,

and all the others I have worked with at Nasca.

CONTENTS

PREFACE *ix*

ACKNOWLEDGMENTS *xiii*

PART ONE. PRELUDE

    1. Introduction: A Mystery on the Desert *2*

    2. Wonders of the World: Nasca in Perspective *9*

PART TWO. PROCESSIONAL

    3. Nasca before Columbus *44*

    4. Seeing Is Believing: Rediscovering the Pampa *76*

PART THREE. CEREMONY

    5. Sacred Landscapes: A Nasca for a New Millennium *118*

PART FOUR. RECESSIONAL

    6. Ley Lines to Labyrinths: Remaking the Earth
       beyond Nasca *212*

NOTES *235*

INDEX *247*

PREFACE

They have been called the eighth wonder of the world—archaeology's greatest conundrum—the Nasca lines. Ever since the first commercial aviators flying toward the high Andes spotted them in the 1930's, the giant ground drawings that cover 400 square miles of southern Peru's coastal desert floor have challenged all explanations. Acre-sized tracings of hummingbirds, foxes, and condors; a hundred-foot-tall man with owl-like eyes, his arm raised, beckoning to us from a hillside (see frontispiece); dozens of spirals, zigzags, triangles, and trapezoids; and a thousand miles of long straight lines crisscross the dry wasteland. Could these geoglyphs be effigies of ancient animal gods or patterns of constellations? Are they roads, star pointers, maybe even a gigantic map of the world? If the people who lived in south coastal Peru some 2,000 years ago had only a simple technology, how did they manage to construct such precise figures? Did they have a plan? And if so, who ordained it? It all seems so otherworldly.

In 1976, I invited a group of archaeologists, anthropologists, engineers, and surveyors to share their findings concerning the enigma on the desert (the pampa, as the locals call it, after the Quechua word for plain or space). Together with other investigators who were already studying Nasca, we spent nearly two decades trying to answer these questions. *Between the Lines* tells the story of what we discovered. We think we now know how these earth markings were made, even who made them and when, but the great mystery of Nasca that has always confronted us is why—why move tons of dirt and stone around on a desolate landscape for no apparent reason? To offer our collective solution to the puzzle we needed to learn more about the people who lived there at the base of the Andes from the beginning of the Christian era all the way up to the time of the Incas, the last great civilization to come to the river valleys that border the barren Nasca plain, just before the Spanish arrived in the sixteenth century.

Between the Lines puts our solution to the Nasca puzzle in perspective by chronicling the history of visits to and explanations about the mystery on the pampa, from colonial conquistador to modern astronomer, historian, artist, engineer, anthropologist, and adventure-seeking explorer of the contemporary age.

All those who travel to Nasca to decode the puzzle seem obsessed with finding their own meaningful answers to the problem. Artists have pronounced the figures artwork while some mathematicians and engineers believed they harbor a record of a lost culture's advanced knowledge of geometry. Astronomers have said the straight lines point to the stars and that the animals are constellations. Peering at the Nasca geoglyphs through many different eyes over the ages helps put my own view in place, a view based on the cultural and physical evidence I and my colleagues spent years collecting and interpreting. Finally, there may be an even more profound question worth considering from the Nasca achievement. What motivates people all over the world to sculpt their landscapes on a grand scale, from the dead-straight ley lines of Great Britain to the great serpent mound of Ohio, from the 150-foot figure of a man carved on the desert floor near Blythe, California, to contemporary environmental art?

Decoding the lines is a complex and changing puzzle, one that invites us to think about the many processes that influenced their construction and our interpretation of the Nasca phenomenon. I once pulled a copy of an early seventeenth-century astronomy text off a dusty shelf in a remote corner of an antiquarian bookshop. As I recall, it was a text on "pastoral astronomy"—it had less to do with how to watch stars in the field, more with how to understand the place of astronomy in religious endeavors. Surprisingly, the little tome still proffered the even then somewhat outdated idea of an earth-centered universe. Being pre-Darwinian, the text never employed the term "stellar evolution," and of course the Big Bang was never mentioned. In the margins of the book I found page after page of at least three sets of comments, two of them written in different colors of faded ink, by readers now long deceased. I surmised these once astute readers were students who used the book in a course taught at a nearby college. The third set was of very recent vintage, and it matched both hand and date inscribed on the inside cover. In the chapter on the solar system in the section that dealt with planetary orbits, one of the older commentators posed the question "Then how to explain the annual motion of nearby stars?" (first detected in 1838). This comment lay next to a sentence stating that God so created the universe with a fixed earth in the center. On the opposite margin, same line, the recent commentator simply inscribed "!!!" (which I translate as: "Are you serious?"). I marveled at what a different set of reactions to a text a couple of centuries could produce. Such is the case at Nasca.

I want my readers to think of the Nasca lines as a text in the landscape, a text whose marginalia have been writ over a long period of time, indeed over several centuries. We are but the most recent of several generations of readers and interpreters of this text. We make our notes in the margin in response to questions and problems we raise about the text, and our remarks shall forever reflect the times and conditions in which we live. This is not to deny that progress might be made in attempting to reveal cultural truths about the lines. In *Between the Lines* I aim to give a rational account of the processes that went into both the indigenous "writing" of the Nasca text and the marginal notes (including my own) that give insight into the minds of those who have given it a good read.

ACKNOWLEDGMENTS

Though I bear all responsibility for any errors of fact and interpretation, the collective "we" I shall use throughout *Between the Lines* includes a number of individuals and institutions I wish to thank, not only for their cooperation but also for their interest, encouragement, and participation in this work. I shared an early interest in the lines with anthropologist Tom Zuidema, with whom I had been working at Cuzco, the Inca capital, since 1976. In 1981 I was joined in my studies by another anthropologist, Gary Urton, who probably has had the most profound impact on the direction of my work at Nasca. In 1982 Gary and I initiated much of the survey work I describe in Part Three. We were assisted in the field by both Earthwatch volunteers and Colgate University students. The periods of study with Urton were supported by joint grants from the National Geographic Society, the Wenner-Gren Foundation (Grant No. 4175), the National Science Foundation (Grant No. BNS81-02336), and the Earthwatch organization. The OSCO Fund, administered by Walter Fullam, Colgate class of 1932, also supported studies I conducted with my students. Meanwhile, Urton resided in Nasca in 1981 and 1982, walking and taking magnetic compass readings on selected lines while he undertook his field studies of contemporary coastal peoples. Archaeologist Persis Clarkson worked with us on a number of these occasions as she explored and discovered dozens of new line centers since 1982, later actively exploring Nasca into the 1990's. During the 1984 season, the group from the University of Minnesota Remote Sensing Laboratory joined us in a program of aerial photography of the lines. Archaeologist Helaine Silverman's work at the nearby site of Cahuachi was conducted by separate grants administered to her. She was particularly instrumental in influencing the course of our research after 1982.

In addition, Gary, Persis, and Helaine were thoughtful reviewers of earlier drafts of *Between the Lines,* as was archaeologist Katharina Schreiber. Permission to work on the pampa was generously granted by the Instituto Nacional de Cultura, in Lima, while the Instituto Geográfico Militar and the Servicio Aerofotográfico Nacional generously provided maps and photographs. To all of those who provided me with must-see materials to illustrate the text, I also express my thanks: Gary, Persis, and Helaine, along with Evan Hadingham, Tony Morrison, and Donald Proulx. I owe special gratitude to artist-photographer Marilyn Bridges for allowing my book to display some of her beautiful pictures and to the skilled hand of artist Julia Meyerson, which has helped give *Between the Lines* a special visual quality. Lastly I am indebted to Jacqueline D'Amore, Lorraine Aveni, Dana Smith, and Diane Janney for assistance in preparing the manuscript; to Theresa May and her staff at the University of Texas Press, especially Carolyn Cates Wylie, José Clemente Orozco, and Lorraine Atherton; and as always to my agent Faith Hamlin for finding the right place for it.

PART ONE. PRELUDE

1 INTRODUCTION

A MYSTERY ON THE DESERT

> I did not imagine then, that it would be near the coast
> that the most important monument of Peru, and perhaps
> of the world, would be found.
>
> **Maria Reiche, in a popular early work[1]**

What makes a wonder of the world? Three things I think: First, it has to be one of a kind. Second, an almost inconceivable effort must have gone into building it. And third, it must leave a timeless message for all eternity. This is what puts the maze of football-field-proportioned animal figures and Fifth Avenue–sized straight lines etched on the desert of Peru's south coast squarely in the same class with Egypt's pyramids and the Hanging Gardens of Babylon. As a prelude to our in-depth encounter with the fabulous Nasca lines, I dedicate my opening chapter to the seven wonders of the classical world, to the spectacle and the attention paid them over the years. This ever-changing must-see list will give us a sense of how our culture defines a grand feat of human architectural achievement. To get at the issue of people's motives for building on a grand scale all over the world, I try to tap into what was going on in the minds of those who erected these unforgettable monuments and memorials that still dazzle the imagination hundreds, even thousands of years after they were built.

How can we begin to describe anything so vast as the lines of Nasca—more than 1,000 figures covering 400 square miles? I conclude Chapter 2 by soaring down from the air where the pampa looks like a giant blackboard at the end of a busy school day. Then we hit ground level, where I descriptively peel the figures off the desert floor one at a time. What do the lines look like from the builders' perspective? Piles of dark stone removed from the surface and carefully arranged along the sides give the appearance of wide pinkish avenues with borders. Some lines are as narrow as the width of a boot. At the other end of the size spectrum is a giant trapezoid over 900 yards long and 100 yards wide, perfectly formed and physically joined to half a dozen others.

But the real eye-catchers are the figural drawings of animals. We trace a monkey's labyrinthine profile by a single line that begins where it ends, taking the viewer's eye all the way into and out of the 75-yard-wide coiled spiral tail. The line that demarcates the shark or killer whale passes both inside and outside its body. A huge bird, 300 yards long, has a zigzag neck running half the length of its body. Our detailed study of the birds of South America confirms that it's probably an anhinga, a coastal fish-eater noted for diving in a zigzag pattern. In the "Scratchpad" section of the chapter I give a detailed description (with lots of illustrations) of exactly what lies on the pampa, based on materials the anthropologists and archaeologists saw, collected, and analyzed.

The identity of some figures yet eludes us—strange combinations of exotic imaginary creatures. One has a cat's head attached to the tail of a fish, and another is half plant, half animal. Who made them? What do the archaeological excavations tell us? How old are these peculiar figures? How do archaeologists date the lines? Both ceramics and radiocarbon dating of materials scattered on the lines indicate that some are more than 1,500 years old. One surprising result is that the lines and figures may have represented at least two separate and unrelated efforts portrayed on a single canvas.

In Chapter 3, "Nasca before Columbus," I turn back the clock and sketch out the history of exploration of coastal western South America. In 1532, explorer Francisco Pizarro docked his ship 500 miles up the coast from Nasca below the highland city of Cajamarca. There, having followed Columbus's discovery of the New World by just two generations, he captured the Inca emperor Atahualpa. Although his predecessors sought spices, Pizarro's New World quarry was gold, which was rumored to have lined the streets of the celebrated cities of the sun-worshiping Incas. The Incas ruled a vast empire from their highland capital of Cuzco. They conquered Nasca and left traces of a vast system of roads we can still faintly trace crisscrossing the pampa—roads that resemble many of the Nasca lines. Spanish chroniclers (priests sent to convert the natives) who wrote of these ancient New World people highlighted their intense interest in and considerable skills at road building and irrigation.

Testimonies from tattered texts offer clues to why the Nasca lines were built, clues based on the Incas' ideas about the landscape. As we explore the Inca culture, we discover that they conceived of their capital city in a spoke-and-wheel plan resembling the faintly etched straight features we traced out on the pampa. In Cuzco 41 invisible radial lines (the Incas called them *ceques*, variously translated as "rays," "lines," or "paths") extended outward from the Temple of the Ancestors in the city center, dividing the landscape into pie-wedge irrigation zones, each assigned to a different kinship group. These lines interconnected with ceque systems from neighboring communities. Ceques were a mechanism of expressing the social order by partitioning the urban landscape. But the Nasca lines were visible, etched out on the pampa, and we would soon discover they, too, exhibited order. Practically every line we walked, measured, mapped, and photographed—more than 800 of them—emanated from one of some five dozen ray centers that connected with one another like a giant mosaic of spiderwebs spread across the pampa. Despite the fact that the line builders preceded the Incas by a thousand years, Nasca ideas about how to configure the pampa seemed to us to relate in a subtle way to Inca concepts of construction. The ideologies of these two cultures, though spread wide apart in space and time, may have been closer than we thought. Here was a continuation of ethnic identity of Native American people transcending more than a millennium!

As attention turned from conquest to colonization and the slow erosion of indigenous societies proceeded through the seventeenth and eighteenth centuries, a kind of forgetfulness of native folkways descended over all of the Americas. Populations were redistributed; crops and natural resources were exported to mother Spain. Interest in the ancient history of Peru and its wonderful remains was not a part of the picture. Nasca, too, would slumber.

In Chapter 4, "Seeing Is Believing: Rediscovering the Pampa," the age of aviation suddenly reopened the world's eyes to the spectacle on the pampa. Recognized in the 1930's, the lines on the pampa began to attract a steadily increasing stream of visitors and curiosity seekers. Explorers of the early twentieth century viewed the geoglyphs of plants and animals as totems, giant effigies of living things worshiped by superstitious natives. Still, nobody had bothered to look into the history of the early peoples who had lived in the river valleys bordering the Nasca plain. Tourists who flew over the lines for the first time focused their eyes only on the lines. But then, we *are* a visually oriented culture. We watch the history of the world unfold on a two-dimensional TV screen, we live out our fantasies through images projected onto a flat silver screen in a darkened theater, and we pay admission to gain access to a feast for the eye hung on the walls of an art museum. Can the lines be anything other than something to see?

When Peruvian archaeologist Toribio Mejía Xesspe ascended the pampa and discovered the lines for himself in 1927, he imagined a different scenario. His sense of the lines was tactile; they were places to walk upon rather than sights to see. You sense what Mejía was thinking when you tread the periphery of an animal figure—you move, you run, you dance. As we chronicle Mejía's and others' attempts to trace through once practiced folkways, this chapter tells about the wealth of fascinating information we recovered from the ancient records in the Spanish chronicles about how people moved over their landscape.

If Toribio Mejía Xesspe was the forerunner of today's decoders of the desert mystery, Maria Reiche—a frail, eccentric Nascaphile, recently deceased at 95—would bask in the late-twentieth-century limelight of the pampa. The tale of Maria is almost as fascinating as the story of the lines themselves. A German-born teacher of mathematics who emigrated to Peru in the 1930's to escape Hitler's Third Reich, she would become captivated for life by the mystery on the pampa. Maria ended up spending over 50 years single-handedly mapping, preserving, and offering her own explanation for the figures. Her lab and residence started as an adobe hovel astride the Pan-American Highway bordering the pampa where she worked with antiquated equipment. (Today this humble abode has been converted into a small museum complete with an effigy of Maria.) Reiche unwittingly popularized the most famous of all the explanations for the lines: for her they were a page out of the "biggest astronomy book in the world." She fervently believed that the lines pointed to the sun, moon, and stars at the horizon and that the appearance and disappearance of these luminaries was used to demarcate the precise passage of time. If she could solve the Nasca puzzle, Reiche believed, she would discover the ancient Nasca measuring unit, along with a compendium of secret knowledge that would prove once and for all that the mathematical and scientific prowess of ancient Peruvians was second to none on this planet. Charismatic in her manner (schools still close on her birthday and a postage stamp honors her accomplishments), Howard Hughesian in her eccentricity (she ate the same meal, a concoction of bananas, jam, and milk, three times a day, seven days a week), the reclusive Maria kept most of her data squirreled away in boxes stashed beneath her bed in the local hotel that later housed her. She shunned all would-be Nasca decoders, from serious-minded astronomers like Gerald Hawkins, who arrived in the late sixties fresh from having interpreted Great Britain's Stonehenge as a Bronze Age observatory and computer to analyze the geometry of the pampa with his own computer, to publicity seekers like Erich von Daniken, who promoted the idea that the gigantic trapezoids were runways on which the forerunners of today's alien abductors once landed their spacecraft. I, too, would become suspect when I began to challenge Maria's theory of why the lines were made.

In step with social upheavals that dogged the outside world, the sixties and seventies became a heyday of wild theories about the Nasca phenomenon. Aviators flew over the lines in hot-air balloons, theorizing that the builders had done exactly the same 2,000 years before. Fitness nuts jogged on them to test the

Olympic running track theory: had ancient athletes constructed the lines for competitive foot races? Still other New Age fantasizers variously proposed that the geoglyphs represented a memorial to a forgotten atomic war, a tidal calculator, or an ancient global trade-route map.

Today, cultural pluralism impacts just about every phase of our lives, from the laws we legislate to the history we rewrite. The Nasca geoglyphs are no exception. As we discover in Chapter 5, "Sacred Landscapes: A Nasca for a New Millennium," my collaborators and I began to recognize that the Nasca lines might have served a multitude of purposes. They may have persisted over a long period of time and through many cultural transitions. Nasca wasn't built in a day! Even today, straight lines discovered in Chile have been linked to mountain worship. One anthropologist tells of a remote Bolivian people who still build *mallku,* cone-shaped piles of stones and dirt, to represent the effigies of various earth spirits, each with its own name. These structures lie on straight lines 5 to 15 miles from the nearest village, and they radiate outward "like spokes on a wheel." Pilgrims still journey there to place offerings to the gods in chambers at the bases of the mallku. Could the Nasca lines have been places to convene upon—a medium through which people gathered, perhaps to invoke the rain god? This idea makes sense in an environment that receives 99 percent of its precipitation from highland runoff, for it almost never rains on the pampa.

We also learned that underground aqueducts ring the desert land adjacent to the pampa. When archaeologists descended into them to explore their construction, they discovered evidence that these irrigation tubes were as old as the Nasca lines themselves. As our work proceeded, the air and ground surveys we conducted revealed the surprising conclusion that most of the straight lines on the pampa are tied to water sources. Then another archaeologist, Helaine Silverman, excavated among the pyramids of Cahuachi, a huge ceremonial center near the crisscrossing line pattern, and formed the surprise hypothesis that the lines were linked to ancient long-distance pilgrimages.

People once did walk the Nasca lines, perhaps for a variety of reasons, among them to pray to the mountain gods for water. Different groups of people may have walked on different lines. Living in contemporary highland communities, Gary Urton discovered that dividing up public space into long, narrow cleared strips, like the Nasca lines, still serves as a medium for expressing and negotiating social status. Each kinship group that makes up the small community of Pacariqtambo still sweeps, decorates, and cares for its own assigned strip of the partitioned town square every time a festival takes place. The anthropologist's tale reminds me of the way we divide up a sports stadium into centrally located private boxes for the wealthy down to general-admission seats for the masses, who sit far from the action. By seeking many answers from a multitude of perspectives, we slowly begin to peer between the cracks of the mystery of the Nasca lines. People used the lines for very practical purposes, and building runways for fictitious alien visitors surely wasn't one of them.

How much skill does one need to make a Nasca line? Was there an overall precise plan? If so, how precise was it? Chapter 5 chronicles our own efforts at etching geoglyphs in a remote region of the pampa to see what sort of engineering is involved. Those efforts would be resisted and dogged by difficulty, for we needed to deal with a few powerful Nasca locals who were protective of their turf and their ideas about who made the lines and why. At one point we found ourselves arrested and detained on charges of "looting the graves of the Incas' ancestors"—so read the headline in one Lima newspaper. While this diverted our attention from the Nasca pampa, it led us to the serendipitous discovery of exciting new information about what the lines mean, from another pampa near Nasca and just out of local jurisdiction.

Maybe Nasca isn't so unique after all. In the closing chapter, "Ley Lines to Labyrinths: Remaking the Earth beyond Nasca," we leave the pampa and re-image the Nasca phenomenon in world perspective once again, this time by looking specifically at other human attempts to move and shape earth on a grand scale. This chapter recovers many of the themes and motives that might have played out on the pampa: visual sighting, walking and movement, pilgrimages, labyrinths, and a concern about environmental essentials. I compare the geoglyphs to Britain's controversial ley lines (straight invisible connectors believed to tie together key points in the landscape) and Ohio's effigy mounds, multiyard octagons connected to circles. Nearby, a huge ancient earthen serpent flanks the entire fairway of a par-five hole of a modern golf course. Sculptured on the chalky downs of the south of England, Uffington's great white horse dates all the way back to the Iron Age, and Death Valley's hundred-foot-long stick figure of a man, hands raised, brings the carved Nasca Owl Man to mind. *Spiral Jetty,* by modern earth sculptor Robert Smithson, located on the periphery of the Great Salt Lake, comes off as a contemporary bulldozed labyrinth, reminiscent of so many Nasca spirals our team had mapped and walked.

The question persists: Why have people insisted upon making massive environmental works of art ever since they learned to farm and make tools? Is it for power or for show? Are we boasting of our conquest of the forces of nature? Perhaps we're seeking mysteries we imagine lie hidden within the body of mother earth, tapping her energy, questing after the source of her fertility. To comprehend Nasca we need to escape from the straitjacket of our own universe of discourse. Exploring examples of earth sculpture in a variety of contexts helps open our minds to the complexity of motives that dwell in the minds behind the hands that continue to alter the surface of our world on a grand scale.

2 WONDERS OF THE WORLD

NASCA IN PERSPECTIVE

> I have gazed on the walls of impregnable Babylon, along
> which chariots may race, and on the Zeus by the banks
> of the Alpheus. I have seen the Hanging Gardens and
> the Colossus of Helios, the great man-made mountains
> of the lofty pyramids, and the gigantic tomb of
> Maussollos. But when I saw the sacred house of Artemis
> that towers to the clouds, the others were placed in the
> shade, for the sun himself has never looked upon its
> equal outside Olympus.
>
> **From an ancient guidebook[1]**

We are a culture of lists. Music ranks its Top 40, and the *New York Times* has its 20 best-sellers, fiction and non. Football sports a Pac Twelve and a Big Eight; basketball has the Big East, golf and Nascar the ten top money winners. The hierarchy of Olympic medalists consists of three gradations of ore from the precious to the common. In the entertainment world it's the movies' top box-office moneymakers, TV's Nielsen picks, and Mr. Blackwell's ten worst-dressed. But to the antiquarian goes the honor of the oldest and the most enduring list of all.

In the second century BC, a travel writer named Antipater, who lived in the Palestinian city of Sidon, authored a famous guidebook. Just as in Europe's great eighteenth-century Enlightenment, tourism flourished two thousand years earlier in an age of sustained exploration and expansion of the relatively peaceful Aegean world under Rome's domination. New territories were being mapped into the geography books, and they harbored marvels to be seen by any who would consider themselves knowledgeable about the world. Antipater's must-see list of human-made colossi in the world numbered a sacred, lucky seven, the same as the number of the ages of man, days of creation, deadly sins, virtues, liberal arts, and days of the week. For the ancient Greeks, the virgin number seven spelled magic. (Mathematically speaking, it is the only one of the first ten that is neither a factor nor a product of any of the others.)

Antipater's seven wonders consisted of a garden, a temple, a lighthouse, and a pair each of tombs and statues. Though their locales straddled three continents, all lay in the eastern circum-Mediterranean area between the Peloponnese and the Nile delta, and with a single exception, they all dated from the sixth to the third century BC. But you can't blame antiquity's Michelin guide for being temporally and spatially prejudiced. There simply wasn't much more to the known civilized world in the early days of the Roman Empire.

Though history has assigned him full credit for the special seven, Antipater is said to have copied his list from Callimachus, a librarian in the great library of Alexandria who lived a century before him. I believe the idea for a list of any numbered wonders probably goes back beyond both Antipater and Callimachus. It may have been dreamed up by Herodotus, the Greek historian, who preceded Antipater by two centuries. flushed with the grandeur of the blossoming Greek civilization in the wake of her victory over mighty Persia, Herodotus looked back to the surviving relics of the Middle East, upon the ruins of the Minoans and the Myceneans, to whom the pan-Hellenic cultures who would come to control the Aegean for three centuries owed so much for their origins—especially for the great architecture they would erect upon their acropolis. When Alexander the Great united the East and West in the fourth century BC, he linked Greek culture to even more faraway exotic places, like Egypt and Babylon, thus adding both to the historical motivation for list-making and to the choice of objects that would ultimately make up the wondrous roster. But it wasn't until the Renaissance, that time of renewed appreciation and admiration of the world of classical antiquity, that the list of masterpiece monuments became fixed as a standard of Western history.

Few are those who can name all seven undisputed masterpieces (the Parthenon and the Colosseum never made the original list), though practically everybody knows the oldest and the only one of them that remains standing. It is tucked away in the list of the magnificent seven originally introduced by Antipater in a poem, my epigraph to this chapter. "The great man-made mountains" refer specifically to the pyramids, especially the Great Pyramid of Khufu, or Cheops. It was built about 2500 BC in Egypt's Old Kingdom. The lithic essence of Egyptian rulership, the pyramid was intended as a burial place through which the soul of the divine ruler could access the world beyond the living.

From Teotihuacan to Cahokia to Cairo, I have never been able to get away from the notion that all pyramids are man-made mountains. At least that's what the Egyptians called them, the Mountains of the Pharaoh. Making your own mountain is just about as audacious a technological feat as anyone can imagine. Pyramid building, whether in Mexico, Peru, or Egypt, has always been a highly competitive enterprise. Each pharaoh sought to erect a mausoleum more magnificent than that of his predecessor and more innovative as well; for example, Zoser's stepped pyramid, Sneferu's bent pyramid, and architect Imhotep's invention of building pyramids in stone only indicate how high a premium Egyptian people once placed on the afterlife. Khufu's, of course, is the greatest—the Great Pyramid with a capital G—and it comes with the added bonus of a reclining sphinx adjacent to it. No wonder it attracts such a huge volume of tourists.

How colossal *is* Egypt's Great Pyramid? It covers over 13 acres, and it rests on a precisely leveled perfect (to within 8 inches) square oriented exactly on the cardinal directions; it measures 756 feet on a side, which amounts to a half-mile walk around its perimeter. At 481 feet in height, it was, for nearly 4,500 years (until 1900), the tallest building on the face of the earth (compare 555 feet for the Washington Monument). The 2,300,000 stone blocks that comprise it range between 2 and 15 tons and average 2.5 tons in weight. They are fitted together so tightly that only paper-thin layers of mortar lie between them.

Historian Diodorus of Sicily, who visited it in the first century BC, says it took 360,000 men 20 years to put the Great Pyramid together. Even after 5,000 years there is no universal agreement on how it was built, though University of Chicago Egyptologist Mark Lehner gets my nod for the sanest proposal.[2] Lehner believes the builders constructed a series of wraparound ramps of progressively increasing grades (from 6 to 18.5 degrees) as they approached the top, all accessed from a main supply ramp 320 yards long. Lehner's on-site research has demonstrated that lifting the blocks was made possible only by greasing the ramp with wetted-down, slick clays. A thousand highly trained craftsmen supervised the job, assisted by a rotating workforce of 5,000 to 7,000 men to do the heavy lifting.

The Great Pyramid's interior is pierced with more than half a dozen shafts and chambers, including the 153-foot Grand Gallery, whose 28-foot-high polished limestone walls connect to the Queen's Chamber at one end and the King's Chamber at the other, along with half a mile of ascending and descending corridors designed to baffle tomb robbers in quest of the king's hidden ransom. Can you blame a thief for being attracted to such an obvious treasure marker?

Impossible-to-imagine feats of engineering like the Great Pyramid serve as grist for the mill of ideas that giant pyramids all over the world hold the secret of technological know-how now lost to posterity. Some wonder, have scholars conspired to keep this secret knowledge to themselves? Is there a way to harness this know-how by studying the meticulous details of the pyramid's construction, details that might conceal additional information? Perhaps they evolved a pyramid inch, a precise unit locked into the construction and layout of their edifices, a unit that encapsulates other universal standards of mensuration in the world including pi, the golden mean, maybe even the diameter of the earth and the radius of the solar system. One of the more imaginative pyramid theories alleges that there is a time scale for Armageddon encoded in measurements in pyramid inches between wall marks found in various corridors. There are plenty of other mysteries yet to probe, such as the site of the missing pit where one of the king's wooden boats designed to transport his soul to the underworld lies interred, and the clinging suspicion that despite every high-tech scanning technique employed on it, a concealed chamber holding a wondrous treasure yet resides undiscovered within the bowels of the pyramid.

The walls of the city of Babylon, or more specifically a rooftop garden lying at their summit, constitute the only other one of the seven wonders that predates classical Greece. Some say the garden never existed, but royal gardens were often an element in the structure and layout of Mesopotamian palaces, and since travel writer after travel writer down through the ages speaks of it profusely, it is hard to imagine that this lush royal garden was not a part of antiquity's largest, most impressive city. Several rubble heaps vie for consideration among disputing contemporary archaeologists. The walls that once circumscribed the city have been both partially excavated and fully described by Herodotus, among others. The city is surrounded, he says, "by a broad and deep moat, full of water, behind which rises a wall fifty royal cubits [about 27 yards] in width and 200 in height. . . . in the middle of the precinct there was a tower of solid masonry, a furlong [220 yards] in length and breadth, upon which was raised a second tower, and on that a third, and so on up to eight. The ascent to the top is on the outside, by a path which winds round all the towers."[3]

To judge by the old historian's description, this garden was a terraced affair, each layer of terrace weighing down the vaulted architecture beneath it. The roofs of the royal apartments below were protected with sheets of lead to keep moisture from penetrating to the next layer; in other words, the whole affair was an aboveground or hanging garden. So lush was the tropical vegetation adorning it (including rushes and fruit and nut trees from all over the world) that from a distance, one chronicler wrote, anyone would suppose the garden to be a veritable woods on the side of a mountain.

Who would build something so unnecessarily elaborate? Love ranks alongside death as one of the great mysteries of life; so tradition spilled down from classical times has it that King Nebuchadnezzar had erected the garden in the seventh century BC for his foreign wife, who came from the wooded mountains of Medea. Amid the oriental vegetation in this lush man-made mountain environment his queen could feel at home while she held court.

If Khufu's pyramid is a marvel in stone, Nebuchadnezzar's Hanging Gardens might more appropriately be termed a water wonder. The Babylonians were masters of hydrology. Had they not been able to irrigate the lands between the

Tigris and the Euphrates (flooded marshes in the wet season and desiccated, baked clay surfaces in dry periods), they never would have been able to evolve the high culture that would pass down to us our learned proficiency in the astronomical sciences and the mathematics of arithmetic. An inscription on the stela of Assurnasirpal tells of canal water that came flowing down the intricately winding artificial stream, waterfall, and cascades along pathways scented with flowers and "sparkling like the stars in heaven."

The world's greatest work of art? A statue of the king of the gods carved by a world-famous sculptor in the city that originated the Olympic games ranks as one of the five remaining marvels, all of them from the Greek sphere. The statue of the Olympian Zeus was destroyed several centuries after it was carved by Pheidias, when Christians, who forbade worship in the pagan temples in which it was situated, had it removed to decorate a church in Constantinople. Within a century the church perished in a fire that also consumed the statue. flecks of stone in the temple that once housed it still attest to its roots, and a representation of it has been unearthed on an old Greek coin. Pheidias, who already had acquired a reputation from his two great statues on the Athenian acropolis, was commissioned by his friend, the Athenian ruler Pericles, to create the primary cult image in the temple dedicated to the worship of Zeus.

The seated figure, clad in a golden robe below the waist, an olive spray about the head, and wearing golden sandals, held a staff in one hand and a gold and ivory winged Victory in the other. The statue's base alone measured nearly seven yards wide, ten yards deep, and a yard high. Gaudy and oversized by present-day standards, the Olympian Zeus was made mostly of ivory-covered wood. It was over 40 feet tall, as high as a three-story commoner's house. The second-century Greek traveler Pausanias tells us that the throne was decorated with gold, precious stones, ivory, and ebony. Tools cast out from the temple excavated by archaeologists and dated to the same time period seem to be consistent with those suitable for work with such materials. A broken jug found amid the rubble bears the inscription "I belong to Pheidias."

The site of Antipater's favorite wonder (to judge by his poem in the epigraph) lies in Ephesus, one of the most popular tourist venues of antiquity. Located along the central Aegean coast of Turkey, a region now being actively reexploited for tourism by vacation cruise liners and museum lecture tours, this ancient Greek colonial city is frequently highlighted in Sunday supplements, where it is justly touted to be even more impressive than Pompeii. The Temple of Diana or Artemis, a huge shrine built on a scale never before attempted, is positioned today on waterlogged turf below the hilltop city. Only a single (reconstructed) column gives testimony to its ancient architectural grandeur. If the Egyptian temple is the house of the God and the Christian cathedral the house of the people, then the Greek temple, writes classicist Bluma Trell, is the house of the soul. Her reconstruction of a model of the Temple of Artemis for the British Museum makes it out to be a rectangular colonnaded marble building positioned in a huge open courtyard. From different locations within it one can view its exquisite geometric proportions from every conceivable angle. Marble steps lead up to the high platform (425 by 255 feet). Devoid of the elaborate overdecoration and sculptural detail that would impress a later age, the Temple of Artemis exhibited slender, fluted Ionic columns and a figureless frieze. It had windows in its pediment, and its doorway was flanked by statues of Amazons surrounded by a forest of more than ten dozen columns.

Although experts disagree on precisely where the image of Artemis was actually positioned, Greek and Roman historians tell us that pilgrims came from far and wide into the port city for sanctuary and to make offerings to her, for she was one of the oldest cult deities in the Middle East. In a scene reminiscent of Lourdes or Notre Dame, we can imagine the merchants who once plied their wares outside the crowded courtyards, peddling miniatures of the cultic statue, oracles, even hunks of sacrificial meat "hot off the altar."[4] "Great is Diana of the Ephesians," cried the devotees of the temple when it was thought to be threatened with destruction by the preaching of the Apostle Paul (Acts 19).

Our word "mausoleum" has become a generic term thanks to old King Maussollos, who ruled Caria (a small state just south of Ephesus) in the fourth century BC. His tomb at Halicarnassus (today Bodrum) also made the top seven, I think at least in part because it was so huge. Today there is nothing left of it but a hodgepodge of chunks of the frieze in the British Museum, in addition to a few on-site scattered drums of marble and the outlines of a tombed chamber and its adjacent blocking stone. Pliny, the Roman historian of the first century, describes the magnificent place (made by Queen Artemisia, with the expertise of five supervising artists and architects, to house the remains of her deceased husband) as 63 feet long, 4,440 feet in circumference, 25 cubits [37.5 feet] high, and ringed by 36 columns, the top of it crowned by a marble four-horse chariot 140 feet above ground level and accessed by a 24-step stairway. So it stood for more than a millennium, until a thirteenth-century earthquake toppled the structure and its remains were quarried to build the nearby castle of the Knights of St. John. Still, most of Pliny's description is borne out by the archaeological excavations.

The Colossus of Rhodes, an island off the southwest coast of Turkey, is the third of seven wonders situated within a 1,500-square-mile area of the eastern Aegean's Turkish coast. It dates to 280 BC, just about the time the spoils of

Alexander the Great's vast empire were being subdivided. Rhodian warfare was involved in the construction of this must-see sight. The brave citizens of Rhodes had defended their city—a symbol of freedom of trade—against all odds by withstanding a year-long siege. To memorialize the occasion, the citizenry sold the equipment abandoned on their shores by Demetrius the Besieger and spent the money on creating a bronze statue of Helios, the sun god, 100 feet tall (compare it with the 152-foot Statue of Liberty, whose sculptor is said to have had the Colossus in mind when he made it). We know less about the Colossus of Rhodes than the other six wonders of the world, for there are no remains whatsoever to be sifted for clues, just scant descriptions by the historians of antiquity (Figure 1).

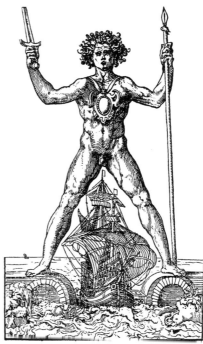

Figure 1. Our impressions of all the wonders of the world change with time. Compare the early-twentieth-century Statue of Liberty-like sketch of the Colossus of Rhodes *(left)* with the view imagined by a sixteenth-century artist *(right)*. Left: E. Banks, *The Seven Wonders of the Ancient World* (New York: Knickerbocker, 1916). Right: Jean Cousin's woodcut originally published in André Thevet's *Cosmographie de Levant*, 1556; reproduced in John and Elizabeth Romer, *The Seven Wonders of the World: A History of the Modern Imagination* (London: Michael O'Mara Books Limited, 1995). Cousin and other sixteenth-century artists show the Colossus astride the harbor, with ships sailing between its legs, which would not have been possible.

The complicated method for casting such a huge statue in bronze is, I think, what impresses us most today. As the historian Philo of Byzantium describes the process:

> Having built a base of white marble, the artist first fixed upon it the feet of the Colossus up to the height of the ankle-joints, having worked out the proportions suitable to a divine image destined to stand to a height of seventy cubits; for the sole of the foot already exceeded in length the height of other statues. For this reason it was impossible to hoist up the rest of the statue and place it upon the feet, but the ankles had to be cast upon the feet and, as when a house is built, the whole work had to rise upon itself.
>
> And for this reason, while other statues are first modeled, then dismembered for casting in parts, and finally recomposed and erected, in this case, after the first part had been cast, the second was modeled upon it, and for the following part again the same method of working was adopted.   .   .   . In order to prosecute the plan of operations on a firm basis throughout, the artist heaped up a huge mound of earth round each section as soon as it was completed, thus burying the finished work under the accumulated earth, and carrying out the casting of the next part on the level.
>
> So, going up bit by bit, he reached the goal of his endeavor.[5]

The Colossus also holds the record as shortest lived of the magnificent seven. The earthquake that hacked off the solar deity at the knee and toppled him in 226 BC, barely two generations after the statue was built, is said by Strabo to have left it still as impressive a sight prostrate as when it was standing. Leading kingdoms around the Aegean were so respectful of the metal mammoth that they pitched in with the intention of having it resurrected, though a Rhodian oracle later forbade them to put it back together. There lay the giant for nearly another thousand years for tourists to admire and poets to romanticize about, until the Arab occupancy of Rhodes in AD 654, when the whole of it was melted down for scrap.

Since the city of Alexandria, the rival of Athens positioned on the south coast of the Mediterranean on the continent of Africa, became the seat of Greek grandeur in later times, it fittingly deserves a wonder of its own. Any number of Alexandria's buildings could have qualified: for example, the famous library and the Temple of the Muses (from which we derive our word "museum"). But its lighthouse, or Pharos, was the crown jewel of the city that was founded by and named after the great liberator of Egypt from Persia. Based on an amalgamation of historical descriptions, some more reliable than others (one travel writer inflates its height to an impossible 1,836 feet), as well as its appearance on a number of coins, the Lighthouse of Alexandria seems to have been a three-tiered structure over 350 feet high: approximately 180 feet for the first cylindrical (or square?) stage, 90 for the second octagonal, and 45 for the third, again cylindrical. It was originally crowned with a statue of Zeus 15 feet high and perched on an island tucked close in to the harbor, so that every boat traveler entering the narrow mouth of the harbor could be awed by its skyscraping magnificence. This wonder too was done in by earthquakes, the first of them in the middle of the ninth century, and then finished off by another pair early in the thirteenth. Today a fifteenth-century Islamic fort occupies the site.

Both material and motive ring clear in this list of the original top seven handiworks so long admired by the West: mastery of stone and mastery of water, figural works of art in decorated wood and bronze, and works of architecture that reveal a subtle, exquisite geometry; a work for a husband and one for a wife; gifts of love to honor the dead and to exalt the gods; a pleasure dome, the symbol of a city, and a war memorial. The central role of religious worship that underlies the canon of marvelous achievements cannot be overstated. Pilgrims and patriots once came to revere these bigger-than-life one-of-a-kinds not to be missed by the eye of the informed traveler. They still do. To really understand the grandeur of human achievement, you too must experience all of them at least once.

Updating the List: From the Colosseum to Mount Rushmore

Since Antipater, the list of wonders—like all select canons—has changed with the times. Other wonders, even other lists, have appeared, especially during the Roman Empire, when tourism and list-making became exceedingly popular, as they are today. For example, the historian Diodorus lobbied to get the obelisk of Babylonian queen Semiramis included, and the Roman poet Martial thought the Colosseum to be easily the equal of any of the original seven. Likewise, the Great Hypostyle Hall in Rameses II's Temple of Amun at Karnak (Thebes) has often been mentioned.

Criteria changed too. A list by the sixth-century bishop Gregory of Tours included Noah's Ark and the Temple of Solomon at Jerusalem, both important to the history of early Christianity, even if they had vanished from the face of the earth. A ninth-century list reveals the loss of worldliness and the ancient past characteristic of the Dark Ages. It included the Lighthouse, the Colossus, and the Temple of Artemis, but it replaced the other four in favor of the Capitolium, a statue of Bellerophon (the Greek hero), a stadium, and a bathhouse—all located in the city of Rome.

By the Renaissance, when remains of practically all the hallmarks of antiquity had disappeared, imaginative writers, poets, and painters found the need to re-create them. The French artist Jean Cousin the Younger and the Dutch sixteenth-century painter Maarten van Heemskerck made engravings, and in his *Outline for Historical Architecture* (1721), the Viennese architect Johann Fischer von Erlach reproduced from historical descriptions his own "true versions" of the Seven Wonders (I think they all look rather dated; see Figure 1). Other nominees from among buildings that still exist include the Great Wall of China, England's Stonehenge, and Italy's Leaning Tower of Pisa.

What would a new millennial list of seven wonders comprise? One might begin by asking: What great marvels of construction technology attract today's tourist? A review of the travel sections of modern Sunday newspapers gives some answers. A winner that would surely enter my select circle is the world's best-known mausoleum, the Taj Mahal, yet another epitome of a man's love for a woman. Built by the seventeenth-century Mogul emperor Shah Jahan in Agra in the north of India to honor his queen Mumtaz Mahal, the onion-shaped domes of the Taj are today imitated all over the world. Inspired by the premature loss of his wife (she died in childbirth), the king chose an architect to supervise 20,000 men and women who worked night and day on the building for 22 years. So approving was Shah Jahan of their work that he chopped off the hands of the master builders and blinded the calligraphers so that they could never build another building to rival the Taj—or so goes the legend.

The Taj Mahal is a monument to lavishness built in a romantic age by an extravagant, extraordinarily wealthy individual. When they conquered India, the British were so impressed with the building that they made plans to dismantle it stone by stone and reassemble it in England. The Taj's main gate measures over 100 feet high; it is arched and studded with knobs made of different metals. Viewed through the gate, the distant main building looks small, but when ap-proached along the straight, parallel paths flanking the walled garden and reflecting pool whose axis bisects it, the 220-foot-high main dome inflates like a colossal balloon. Its bell shape is said to have been variously inspired by the tents of the Tartars, the Himalayas, the clouds, a ripe pear, a woman's milk-filled breast, even the lowly haystacks found in the countryside surrounding Agra.[6] Approaching the building that houses the queen's remains (later the king would be entombed there as well), the eye catches sight of the inlaid precious stones that adorn the facade. An octagonal marble screen carved in filigree surrounds the polychrome caskets, elaborately decorated with calligraphy. In a country divided by religion and class, the Taj, so dedicated to the ideals of love, stands as the singular endur-ing work that unites a love in all Indian people.

Though I described the Pharos at Alexandria as a skyscraper, the penchant for building really tall towers didn't take on a competitive air until late in the nineteenth century. The Eiffel Tower held the record for tallest human-made edifice from 1889, the year it was completed, until 1929. It exudes that unparalleled charisma that comes from the notion of building big just for the sake of big. This Paris tower was a monument built to progress and posterity, the potential of the Western world's Industrial Revolution and engineering prowess. The skills of engineer Gustave Eiffel would inspire Frédéric Bartholdi's design of the statue of "Liberty Enlightening the World." Commissioned as the centerpiece for the Paris World's Fair of 1889, specifically to be a tower a thousand feet tall, Eiffel's tower would show the world that Belle Epoque France in its Third Republic had not only survived humiliation at the hands of the Prussians in 1870 but had also escaped with a resurgent economy and a fully paid-up war debt, emerging as the leader of industrial Europe. It took years to erect the 986-foot iron-frame structure. A testimony to improvements in refinement and smelting in the iron industry of the nineteenth century, it cost 6 percent less than the allotted $1.6 million budget, all of this despite expert opinions that any structure so tall would collapse, sink, or be blown over by wind gusts.

In 1929 the Chrysler Building in New York City, at 1,046 feet, was ranked number one, but within two years it would be surpassed by the Empire State Building, which topped out at 1,250 feet, from sidewalk-level main entrance to the structural top. Disqualifying factory chimneys and antennae (which are not permitted by the Council on Tall Buildings and Urban Habitat, the official organization for determining the heights of buildings), the record was toppled in turn by the World Trade Center (1,350 feet), the Sears Tower in Chicago (1,450 feet), and the Petronas Towers in Kuala Lumpur (1,483 feet). Proposed future record setters include Seven South Dearborn in Chicago (1,537 feet) and the São Paulo Tower (1,622 feet).

"To make over a mountain into the form of a human head," writes art historian Simon Schama, "is perhaps the ultimate colonization of nature by culture, the alteration of landscape to manscape."[7] Such an invasion, especially on a grand scale, is warranted only by the most audacious and accomplished culture.

Along the same line, sculptor Gutzon Borglum wrote, "A monument's dimensions should be determined by the importance to civilization of the events commemorated."[8] For Borglum, the Idaho son of a Danish Mormon immigrant who would shape mountains, nothing could be too great to symbolize the spirit of America. When he single-mindedly set out to carve the faces of four great presidents on Mount Rushmore's granite cliffs in the late 1920's, the Seven Wonders of the World gleamed brightly in Borglum's mind's eye. All other monumental sculptures would be mere pygmies beside the countenances of Washington, Lincoln, Jefferson, and Teddy Roosevelt, who would symbolize not only the greatness of four men but also the endurance of a political social philosophy, as the outspoken superpatriotic Borglum put it. Borglum's view from the twenties envisioned a nation that had struggled through wars of independence and the interpretation of the word "freedom" in its hard-won constitution to emerge by saving Europe and all of Western civilization from the tyranny of Prussia.

What better place to celebrate America's grandeur than in its newly expanded heartland, on the spine of a body of land being possessed, mastered, and tamed by the frontier spirit, far from the decay of eastern urbanity. What better material than the solid rock that made up the foundation of the nation's expanded continent. What an original stroke of genius, thought Borglum, when compared to mere copies of standards of antiquity typical of America's other great architectural symbols, such as the Washington Monument and the Jefferson Memorial.

The idea to carve faces on the Needles, the granitic spires that make up South Dakota's Black Hills, was inspired as early as 1924 by Doane Robertson, the state's historian, who had heard of Borglum's terra-sculpture at Stone Mountain in Georgia. There Borglum, the budding earth sculptor, had been chiseling away on a 20-foot head of General Robert E. Lee (it was never completed because of a dispute over funding). Looking for a way to attract tourists along the newly built highways of mid-America, Robertson invited Borglum to inspect a variety of sites. Full-scale operations began three years later, thanks to private donations, which turned out to be a pittance given what Borglum had in mind. An ardent self-promoter with messianic ambition, Borglum would frequently lobby Washington to seek support for the project. He succeeded in attracting penny-pinching President Coolidge to the site and exacting some funds from him, finally eliciting full federal support from the Roosevelt administration in 1934.

Every day Borglum would appear with his assistants suspended from cables attached to hand winches on the contoured profiles of his subjects. What had been shaped roughly with carefully placed charges of dynamite was now gradually smoothed by drills of decreasing size to resemble faces familiar to all. A crack here, a blemish there slowed the laborious path to perfection trod by the genius stonemason. By the end of the project 400,000 tons of granite rubble had fallen away into a heap at the foot of the cliff below the memorial, liberating the four artificially lighted male countenances. How big is the Colossus of Rushmore? If Washington's 60-foot-long face had a body of proportionate size, he would be 470 feet tall; he could cover a mile in 20 paces and wade knee deep across the Mississippi. He could do the limbo under the Brooklyn Bridge, reach the tip of the Washington Monument, and touch the top of the Saint Louis arch as he passed two head lengths beneath it.

After the American flag was lifted from the face of the final figure at the 1938 unveiling, an awed President Roosevelt, who had not planned to speak, abruptly changed his mind and uttered these words:

> On many occasions when a new project is presented to you on paper, and then, later on, you see the accomplishment, you are disappointed, but it is just the opposite of that in what we are looking at now. I had seen the photographs, I had seen the drawings, and I had talked with those who are responsible for this great work, and yet I had no conception, until about ten minutes ago, not only of its magnitude but also of its permanent beauty and importance.[9]

I cannot imagine a list of seven modern wonders without at least one bridge. Like the tallest tower, the longest bridge need not necessarily be the most spectacular today. I think what matters more is when the mark was set and for how long the holder held the record—the same sort of magic that still keeps Babe Ruth towering over Mark McGwire and Roger Bannister ahead of all those nameless record-breaking milers. Viewed in their own time, two such bridges come to mind: the Brooklyn and San Francisco's Golden Gate, the mid-thirties' longest and tallest suspension span that tamed a turbulent tide-turning channel second only to Sicily's Straits of Messina in unpredictability.

This west-coast Depression miracle, engineered by Joseph Strauss, took four and a half years to build and cost two dozen lives. The pits that house its bases were dug deep enough to swallow a twelve-story building. Its 80,000 miles of wire were plied into bundles to cover a 4,300-foot span. Towers 746 feet above sea level required 22,000 tons of steel held together by 600,000 rivets. Better known today as a prime site for gravity-assisted suicides (and built in a city that tallies more than its share), the Golden Gate vies with Eiffel's tower (which is actually a distant second) for the top spot in that dubious category of places to die from (13.1 per year vs. 4.2; however, the many bridges of the Seine offer multiple convenient alternative venues for despondent and downtrodden Parisians).

Along with bridges and towers, my nominations for the list of other wonders of engineering include two canals, the Suez (opened in 1869) and the Panama (completed in 1914). Motives for constructing canals were as practical as those that resulted in great bridges, and they were at least as challenging to build. Panama's malarial swamps utterly defeated the French and exacted a severe toll on the American workforce that ultimately took over and completed the project.

Dams should belong on the list too: Italy's Vaiont, America's Hoover, and Egypt's Aswan, probably the most impressive since it necessitated moving the colossal statues of Rameses II and reassembling them piece by piece in an artificially constructed environment. That feat in itself is a wonder of the world.

The Palace of Versailles, on the other hand, belongs not so much with wondrous works that stagger the techno-imagination but rather with those that inspire the soul. Like the Eiffel Tower, it falls into the "elegant, but is this really necessary?" category. Still, like his contemporary Shah Jahan, Louis XIV was an archetypal seventeenth-century monarch of extravagant tastes. His baths, beds, even his clothing, were decorated with gold and precious stones, and he was often said to have received leaders of foreign states weighed down and stoop shouldered in a diamond-encrusted robe. Being a connoisseur of architecture, among many other crafts, he also elaborately decorated his famous palace at Versailles. (London's Crystal Palace and Chicago's 1893 Exposition belong in this ostentatious category too.) Louis XIV's line, a symbol of the extraordinary concentration of wealth and power, would collapse under the bloody French Revolution within a hundred years of his death.

When we think of today's wonders, those of nature such as the Grand Canyon, Niagara Falls, and Old Faithful usually take center stage. We often apply the word itself to life-saving drugs. We speak of the wonders of laser surgery, gene manipulation, and space exploration. All are marvels of modern technology, absolute necessities in promoting progress. And let's not forget the wondrous fantasy of Disney World.

The lists of great works any culture would deem marvelous go on and on, and they will forever change. Anthropologist Claude Lévi-Strauss once remarked that secular modern man worships nothing more than his own development, especially the things that have marked its pinnacles through time.[10] As long as the appetite for building on a grand scale remains alive in us, the concept of Wonders of the World as it was originally conceived in antiquity will endure. "Volume, great mass   .   .   . this is what has the greatest emotional effect on the observer. While quality of form affects the mind, volume shocks the nerve or soul centers," wrote Gutzon Borglum.[11] Eiffel himself said as much. So we single out archaic antiquity's pyramids, Europe's soaring Gothic cathedrals, and young America's statues. In an age of cultural diversity, as we run the lists of colossi, both past and present, of foreign and domestic lands—China's Wall, India's Taj, Mexico's Teotihuacan, and a mountain carving of Chief Crazy Horse sure to dwarf the neighboring white men's heads of Rushmore (if it is ever completed)[12]— I wonder, is the appetite for sheer scale and magnitude timeless as well as transcultural?

Why place such eternal and grandiose thoughts in the minds of my readers if not to set the stage for the wondrous work that I intend to probe in this book, for everything that has ever been said about the Pyramid of Cheops and Borglum's faces has been applied to it. With big ideas in our heads we turn to a wonder oft described in pictures in magazines and travel supplements, a spectacular achievement of the human hand accorded regular appointments in *National Geographic* and other popular pictorials, more than once assigned the label "Eighth Wonder of the World."

The Nasca lines constitute one of the greatest human ventures in earth moving. Without question they are spectacular, these multimile-long straight lines, geometrical figures, zigzag scrawls, spirals, and animal figures the size of a football field—all of them laid out on the warm, hazy desert between the Ingenio and Nasca river valleys on the south coast of Peru. Their mammoth size and sheer number attract our attention. We are surprised by their widespread distribution over an area that looks so inhospitable, a lifeless place where it almost never rains. The Nasca lines raise questions that beg for rational answers: Why move thousands of tons of dirt around on a barren desert to create such fantastic drawings for no apparent reason? Why invest the vast amount of time that must have been required to construct such enormous figures, especially if nobody could appreciate looking at them from the ground? How could the construction on such a grand scale of such perfectly proportioned earth pictures actually have been accomplished? Was there a plan, a blueprint? What technology was needed to erect them? Were they, like the marvels created by Borglum and Eiffel, conceived by a single monomaniacal individual?

Surprisingly, few of the world's most famous wonders have been less well understood than the Nasca lines, the last of which we now know was constructed about a thousand years ago. Runways for visiting astronauts, a map of the world, the site of pre-Columbian Olympic games: such have been the fanciful interpretations of these ruins, now being threatened by the onslaught of tourists who make their way to this part of the pampa, as the locals call the desert here.

As with the Seven Wonders, there are so many ideas about motive and meaning underlying the mystery on the desert, so much old information about the place that needs to be corrected, and a flood of new information not many people actually know about the Nasca lines, including informed tourists who have flown over them and gawked at them.

If we dig deep enough, persist long enough, there's a fair bit of history to read between the lines, and when it is put in chronological order we can begin to appreciate what Frederick Jackson Turner meant when he said that history is written by the eye of the viewer set in its own time frame far apart from the object it views. To read the complex story written in these enigmatic earth sculptures spread over hundreds of square miles of barren desert, we must trek through the history of Nasca as seen through the eyes of many beholders over a multitude of ages—and so we begin our journey over, around, and beneath the surface of one of the great wonders of the world.

The Great Scratchpad on the Landscape

What tornadoes are to Kansans and Mount Kilauea is to Hawaiians, the slow process of mountain building was to the inhabitants of Nasca. People become victims of the forces of nature. The high Andes are relatively young as mountains go, raised a mere 200 million years ago by the Nasca continental plate, the eastern edge of which is located off the coast of South America's continental landmass. Contact with the upthrusted edge of the plate amounts to a seemingly insignificant tenth of an inch of lift per year on the average. As the mountains steadily rise higher and higher, the action of rivers slowly erodes away the deeply sloping landscape. The result is a set of gorges running east to west down which mountain rains and other nutrients plummet to the narrow coastal strip.

Anthropologists have characterized the Nasca area as a crossroads because so many resources capable of sustaining sedentary civilizations come together in the narrow coastal strip where it is located. First of all, thanks to the Humboldt current, Nasca lies in the heart of one of the greatest fishing areas in the world. Second, the fertile valleys of the floodplains are ideal for growing maize, manioc, and sweet potatoes. Third, the vertical ecological environment of the mountains that can produce a variety of crops at different levels is not so far away.[13]

In ribbonlike lush valleys such as Nasca, the first sedentary people began to farm as early as the second millennium BC. Had they not invented irrigation canals to extend the sporadic rapid flow of water across the space of the valley, they could not have survived, for rain is scarce on the south coast. Constantly battling the erosive action of the rivers that worked their grinding power on the lifting landscape (some levels have risen faster than others, up to 20 feet in the past two thousand years), farmers slowly retreated toward the ever shrinking coast in search of irrigable land. This battle waged for land and water would emerge as a constant theme in shaping the three or more millennia of social contact among peoples of the coast, and as we would discover, it would ultimately figure in the construction and use of the Nasca lines. Here people truly were victimized by nature, and there is evidence to prove it.

Our wonder of the world lies neither in the high mountains nor in the rich low-lying, ever shifting farmlands that hug the rivers but in the delicate watershed of the space between coast and highlands. Today the western portion of the continent of South America beyond the Andes is outlined by a narrow coastal strip 2,500 miles long and up to about 100 miles in width. Geographers call it a foggy desert. The most arid portion of this region runs from northern Chile (the Atacama Desert) to southern Peru, where moisture from the Pacific Ocean is blocked by a thin mountain chain between desert and coast. This explains the low measurable rainfall, which occurs on the average of once in several years.[14] The desert terrain is the pampa, rough tablelands carved by those deep, lush gorges that connect the high Andes with the coast. These interriverine lands are scarred by *quebradas,* shallow streambeds and gullies that have lain dry for centuries.

One such gorge is carved by the Río Grande, 250 miles south of Lima. About 30 miles from the Pacific and 1,000 feet above sea level, several tributaries join to form the Río Grande de Nasca drainage system: the Vizcas, Santa Cruz, and Río Grande from the north, the Ingenio from the east, and the Nasca and Trancas from the southeast. Each runs in the summer months from November to Febru-

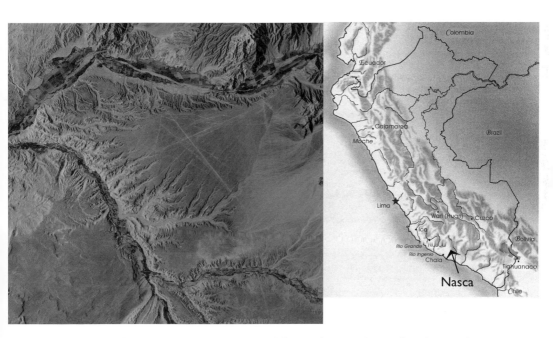

Figure 2. Nasca's desert scratchpad crisscrossed with lines is shown in this satellite photograph. The Ingenio River is at the top. The inset map shows Nasca's location on the South American coast. Map by Julia Meyerson.

ary, offering a verdant contrast to an otherwise dry landscape. It is in this region that the Nasca culture flourished some 1,250-2,000 years ago.[15] Between the valley strips irrigated by the Ingenio and Nasca rivers lies one of the many elevated dry plains. Crisscrossed by quebradas running generally northeast to southwest, the 100-square-mile, triangular Nasca pampa is bounded on the north by the Ingenio River, on the south and west by the Nasca River, and on the east and northeast by the foothills of the Andes, at the base of which the Pan-American Highway runs (Figure 2).

Smaller subpampas that make up this region all have different names, most of them of modern origin. For example, the northern zone—the one with all the famous animal figures—is variously called the Pampa de los Incas, the Pampa Jumana, the Pampa del Calendario, and the Pampa San José on older maps. The western zone is called the Pampa Majuelos, and the southeastern zone, which is nestled up against the Andes and bordered by the Pan-American Highway, is termed the Pampa Cinco Cruces, or the Pampa of the Five Crosses. Sometimes these names tell us a lot about who has been to the pampa and for what reason. My friend Ralph Cané, an engineer from Santiago, Chile, and a longtime explorer and aficionado of Peruvian antiquity, believes the latter derives from the crosses that mark the burial place of five criminals who were captured there after

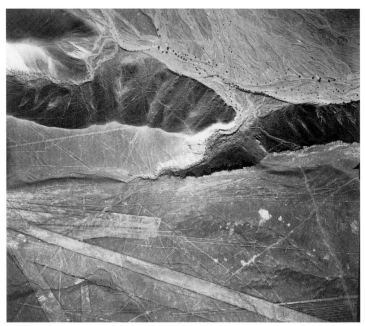

Figure 3. Like a classroom blackboard at the end of a busy day—when the janitor was out sick—the pampa is covered with a maze of intersecting straight lines and geometrical figures as well as animal and plant drawings. Photo Servicio Aerofotográfico Nacional, Peru.

Figure 4. Yes, you *can* see many of the Nasca lines from the ground. Here is a six-mile avenue as it appears from the top of a ray center. Note the dark border created by the neatly piled desert-varnished fragments. From *The Lines of Nazca*, ed. A. Aveni, 1990, courtesy of American Philosophical Society, Memoirs, vol. 183.

repeatedly assaulting travelers along this lonely stretch of highway. He wrote me in 1990, "The original burials were marked with Huarango [tree] crosses. These crosses broke down over the years, and one of my first excursions onto the pampa with Duncan Masson was to look for and retrieve one of the remaining original crosses. We found it and it should be still at Duncan's home in Ica." (Masson, who had explored the pampa since the thirties from his quarters at the Dunes Hotel, died in the late eighties.) Five crosses still clearly visible from the Pan-American Highway mark the spot today.

On this ancient alluvial plain appear the celebrated Nasca geoglyphs, also variously called ground drawings, markings, or simply the Nasca lines. From an airplane, they look like a tangled mass, overlapping and intersecting one another (Figure 3). My first impression was of an unerased blackboard at the end of a busy day of classroom activities. As an astronomer, I also thought of the surface of the moon, an area totally unfit for life in any form. The pampas are strewn with angular broken pieces of stone—flat, angular rock fragments ranging from thumb size up to chunks as large as a foot in diameter. Most of these rocks got there when ancient flooding tumbled them down from the Andes.

Trapezoids, rectangles, straight lines, spirals, concentric ray systems, and animal, plant, even humanoid shapes dot the pampa. Tourists can fly over several birds, a few fish, a monkey, a spider, and a flower, as well as several other life forms; there is no universal agreement on their identification. (We will probe them all in detail in Chapter 5.) Some of the trapezoids are immense, up to a quarter-mile on their longest side. The animal geoglyphs are much smaller, usually tens of yards in dimension, or less than a football field in area. But it is the lines, many up to a few miles long and ranging in width from a narrow footpath up to hundreds of yards, that form by far the largest share of the drawings.

Although the Nasca geoglyphs generally appear as stark, light-colored features on a dark background in aerial photographs, it is not widely known that some of them can be seen, if with some difficulty, by ascending any of the small peaks or dunes that circle the pampa, particularly on the north and west. Have a look at Figure 4 for an example.

Ever since I laid eyes on them more than 25 years ago, I have felt that the Nasca figures should really be thought of as etchings. They were, after all, constructed by a subtractive or removal process. The etching proceeded by taking away the dark rock fragments that coat the floor of the pampa. Long before human occupation, these broken, angled pieces had been covered over several millennia by desert varnish, a dark oxide layer deposited there by airborne microorganisms.[16] The difference in darkness between the exposed and unoxidized sides of a piece of pampa rock can be quite noticeable, as Figure 5 shows. Once this dark surface material is removed, the underlying unoxidized layer, which is

Figure 5. Easily held in the palm of your hand, this desert-varnished rock is typical of the fragmented material carried down from the mountains in floods that occurred up to half a million years ago. The dark side *(left)* has been varnished by exposure to air. The light side *(right)* lay protected in contact with the ground until I turned it over. The Nasca lines are so easy to spot from above because line-building removed much of this dark material. Photos by author. From *The Lines of Nazca*, ed. A. Aveni, 1990, courtesy of American Philosophical Society, Memoirs, vol. 183.

composed of light-colored alluvial soil, is visible. The contrast can be even more dramatic when viewed from an airplane; it is further heightened by the black rim or border created by the detritus neatly deposited there by the builders of the lines. These hummocks of rock fragments range in height from an inch or so up to a yard.

How did the ancient inhabitants of Nasca create the lines? Who was their Gutzon Borglum? Clues to the method of construction come from some lines that for unknown reasons seem to have been abandoned in an unfinished state more than a thousand years ago. On our many visits to the pampa we often

Figure 6. How were the Nasca lines made? Archaeologist Persis Clarkson demonstrates the arm's-length spacing between neat piles of fragments that the builders never removed from the unfinished trapezoid shown at the top. Photos by author.

Figure 7. This drawing by *National Geographic* artist H. Tom Hall shows a scene I think might have taken place on the pampa 2,000 years ago. One team of workers collects and stacks the stones; another removes them to make sharply defined black borders. A construction foreman atop a line center assures the edges will be straight by directing workers who hold sighting sticks. We found no bulldozers or brooms on the pampa. H. Tom Hall/NGS Image Collection.

found numerous piles of stones in the middle of partially cleared wide lines. These piles always seemed to be conveniently located about an arm's length from one another (Figure 6). I suspect the fragments had been gathered one by one into these neat piles by teams of workers who squatted there. The piles were then likely removed to the borders, where the edging process (the careful lining up of cleared stones to form the outlines) would then proceed (Figure 7). Today, native farmers in the adjacent valley still clear their cotton fields by this orderly method of removing and neatly piling stones. (An alternative possibility for such arrangements is that they are mock fields dotted with stone crops used for agricultural rites.)

Though etched more than a dozen centuries ago, the lines have remained pretty much in their original condition. This is because the pampa has remained relatively stable; there has been little natural reworking of the materials on it since the first human-made deposits were laid down more than 2,000 years ago. Wind erosion is minimal and water erosion practically nonexistent, except for the rare occasions when El Niño brings rainfall to the area. Even then, as many of the figures are laid out on small mesas above the pampa, they remain out of the reach of most floodwaters. While wind-blown sand constantly passes back and forth over the lines, keeping the angled fragments that define the lines well exposed, the light-dark contrast between the interior of a Nasca figure and the surrounding desert gradually diminishes through time. Human erosion over the past half-century from inquisitive tourists motoring on and about Nasca pampa has wrought considerable damage to the drawings, more than nature has accomplished in the centuries that have elapsed since the Nasca lines were created. To add to this, occasional Peruvian army maneuvers have been held on them, and power-company workers recently obliterated a figure near the Pan-American Highway.

The vast majority of desert features at Nasca are lines, geometrical figures such as trapezoids, and abstract spirals and zigzags, but the eye-catchers, the geoglyphs everybody always seems to want to know more about, are the figural flora and fauna. (Figure 8 shows an assortment of them.) Practically all of them cluster along a 10-square-mile strip hugging the southern bank of the Ingenio, which always had led me to think they were a local phenomenon. On my first visit alone I counted eighteen birds (among them condors, pelicans, cormorants, and two hummingbirds), two lizards, a fox, a monkey, a spider, four fish, and an insect, along with a handful of weird composite creatures (half bug-half bird and half cat-half fish). Each of these figures was executed with a single continuous line that outlines the contour of the body. Largest of them all is a bird profile situated at the far east end of the pampa (Figure 8a). Its puffed-out chest covers five football fields. This avian denizen of the pampa has a beak 300 yards long, and the largest feather in the three feathered comb atop its head measures 80 yards in length. The condor, with a wingspan of more than 150 yards, and a hummingbird, 100 yards long with a 50-yard beak, are easier to identify (Figures 8*b* and *c*). Some of the figural drawings are so weirdly abstract that they defy all reason. Take the second largest figure on the pampa. At 180 yards in length, it has the pincer jaws of an insect framed in a goggle-eyed bird head attached to rectangular wings by a concave neck. A ponderous appendage hangs from its head like an elephant trunk (Figure 8*d*). Then there's the cartoonish tweety-bird geoglyph (Figure 8*e*). Its head starts out like the monkey with the coiled tail. It has protruding ears, but then it degenerates into a smooth curve on one side and a notched rectangular shape on the other. Stick limbs and dangling gargantuan feet, five toes on one and four on the other (just like the pampa monkey in Figure 8*f*), complete the figure. If you're still looking for weird birds, check out the aerodynamic pelican in Figure 8*g*.

Zigzags are epidemic on the pampa. They seem to run chaotically across the desert, bouncing off the quebradas and back to midpampa, or in saw-toothed fashion adjacent to or over a major figure (again, see the monkey in Figure 8*f* or

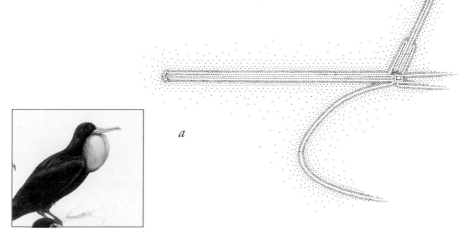

a

Figure 8. Birds seem to be the most common forms of life etched on the pampa.

    a: This bird with a puffed-out chest is one of the largest; it occupies an area of 80,000 square yards. We identified it with a frigate bird (see inset). Drawing by Julia Meyerson. Inset drawing from *Grzimek's Animal Life Encyclopedia* (New York: Van Nostrand, 1972), vol. 7, p. 176, no. 2. Courtesy of Guy Tudor.

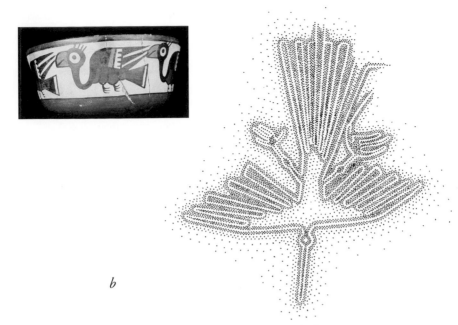

b

b: This condor looks like a shadow of its real counterpart, often seen soaring above. *Solstice Bird, Nazca, Peru,* © Marilyn Bridges 1979, courtesy of Felicia Murray; drawing by Julia Meyerson; photo of ceramic pot courtesy of Donald Proulx.

the "fishing rod" in Figure 9). Often the zigs and zags are squared off into contours that remind me of the opposing parallel lines farmers make when they plow a field (Figure 10). Explorer and anthropologist Johan Reinhard is convinced that these zigzags are related to a water cult. He points out that many of the pre-Hispanic canal systems found on the coast possess an undulating quality.[17] Still others have suggested that they have to do with weaving. Weaving and textiles cannot be left out of the picture here, and one of the most significant discoveries in the minds of Nasca people may have had to do with the way weaving patterns depict other kinds of movement in the world of nature. Local Nasca priest Alberto Rossel Castro ties zigzagging to textile art. He contends that the back-and-forth component of certain figures represents the warp of textile weaving. A good example is the figure on the Pampa Sacramento just north

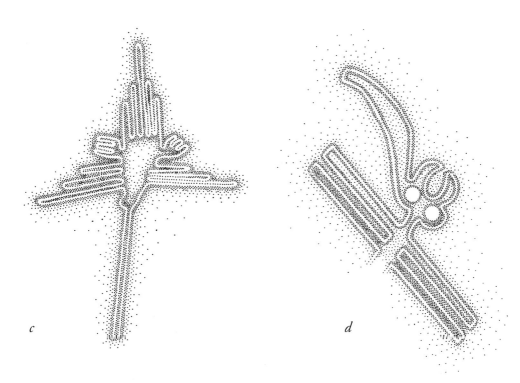

c: A hummingbird sucks imaginary nectar from a linear feature (not shown) that was probably constructed at a later time. Drawing by Julia Meyerson. Compare the hummingbird on a Nasca pot in Figure 17.

d: The pincer jaws of this pampa creature suggest an insect, but the gular sac and the stylized wings may indicate a pelican. Drawing by Julia Meyerson.

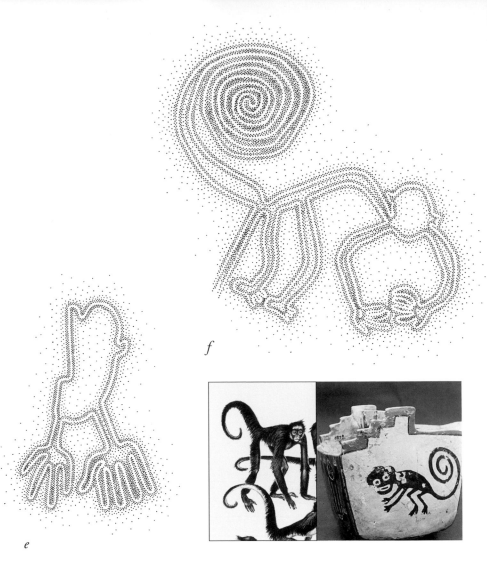

e: Tweety bird, or is it a plant upside down? Compare the head and hands with those of the monkey in *f.* Drawing by Julia Meyerson.

f: The monkey is the most famous of all the Nasca figures. Can you follow the single line (over a mile long) that takes you into its body, around its double-spiral tail (which, if compared with that of a real monkey, coils the wrong way), and back out to the pampa where it began? Spider monkeys come from the Amazon jungle over the mountains; they are not native to the coast. Drawing by Julia Meyerson; photo of ceramic pot courtesy of Donald Proulx; monkey drawing from *Grzimek's Animal Life Encyclopedia* (New York: Van Nostrand, 1972), vol. 10, p. 341.

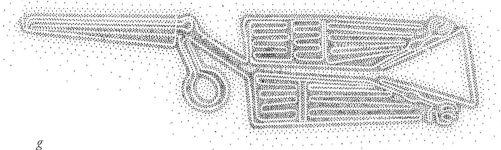

g

g: This aerodynamic pelican is made from triangular forms that flank a rectangular body. Again a single line carries the viewer's eye through the body and neck pouch of the bird to the beak without ever crossing itself. Drawing by Julia Meyerson.

h: Another insect-pelican combination; this one differs from *d*. Drawing by Julia Meyerson.

h

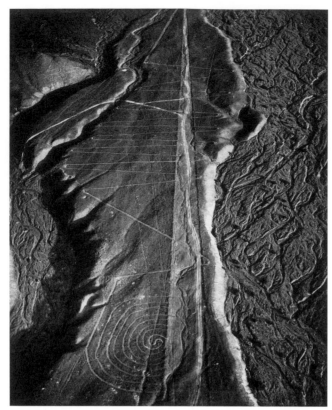

Figure 9. Three earmarks of the Nasca figures appear in the 2,000-foot-long fishing rod, or yarn and needle, on the adjacent pampa of Cantalloc: a long triangle, a zigzag, and a spiral. *Yarn and Needle, Nazca, Peru,* © Marilyn Bridges, 1979, courtesy of Felicia Murray.

Figure 10. The zigzag motif: could it symbolize weaving, plowing, or the meandering dance performed in celebration of rites to the water god? Whatever the explanation, it is spread all over the pampa. Here a box labyrinth is sandwiched between zigzags. Photo Servicio Aerofotográfico Nacional, Peru.

of the neighboring town of Palpa, where sets of parallel zigzag lines are etched across the pampa in two directions at right angles to one another. There's a conceptual unity between textile art and Nasca figures on the pampa (Figure 11). In early Nasca textiles, cross-knit looping, which uses a single thread for knitting an entire textile, is reminiscent of the single line used to draw the animal figures and many of the labyrinths.

Pythagoras on the Pampa?

One look at the section of the pampa shown in Figure 12 is enough to convince most people that the ancient Nascas were skilled and enlightened mathematicians. To quote one admirer of their imagined geometrical prowess:

> Everything is laid out with an impressive mastery of geometry. The few rounded lines are drawn with a skill that indicates the disorder is only apparent, that though the whole is incomprehensible to us, for brains conditioned differently there is a logic.
>
> The people who laid out Nasca could not have been careless architects; they must have been enlightened mathematicians and talented planners capable of producing designs so large and complex that they could not be seen in their entirety, but had to be laid out on the basis of a precise mental image.[18]

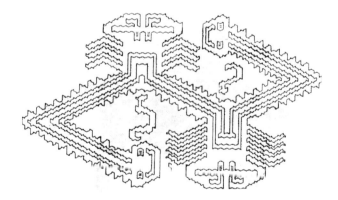

Figure 11. This zigzag snake and spider design, resembling motifs found on the pampa, appears on a textile from the site of Huaca Prieta at least 1,000 years before Nasca. J. Bird, "Preceramic Art from Huaca Prieta, Chicama Valley," *Ñawpa Pacha* 1 (1963): 29-34, fig. 4 (Berkeley: Institute of Andean Studies) Courtesy of Betty J. Meggers.

More likely mad geometricians than sane mathematicians, to judge from the tangled maze of quadrilaterals. The perfect double spiral overlooking the Ingenio basin is positioned at the end of a long trapezoid that covers over the figure of an archaic bird. Let your eye follow the single wide line that winds its way to the center, then snakes around in the shape of an **S** as it leads you back out onto the open pampa where it originated. There are at least a hundred other spirals on the pampa just like it, some square, others single (ending at the center), but this one seems particularly well demarcated.

How did the ancient people of the pampa manage to construct such a perfect spiral? Nasca researcher Maria Reiche theorizes plans were first executed in chalk on starched cloth; some trial figures may even have been laid out in small scale on the pampa before proceeding to the gigantesque phase (Figure 13). As she told one interviewer, "Some [plans] would have had to be quite large to be detailed

Figure 12. When visitors to the pampa theorized that the Nasca lines were testimony to the geometrical and mathematical skills of their builders, they probably had this area of the desert in mind. The giant, 89-yard-wide spiral and the pair of trapezoids that accompany it seem very precisely constructed. Surely careful measurements and an exact plan must have been necessary. That would point to a technologically highly advanced culture, but our results would prove otherwise. Note the early bird underpinned by the giant trapezoid. Note, too, the way the pampa falls off into the Ingenio Valley below (bottom of photo), through which the Pan-American Highway runs. Photo Servicio Aerofotográfico Nacional, Peru.

enough. The body of the monkey, for example, would need to be at least two meters long to be inlaid with accuracy."[19] According to Reiche, the transcription of the planned figures from cloth to pampa would have proceeded by swinging compass arcs of various multiples of a fixed measuring unit (she has often suggested 38 centimeters, or 15 inches) using poles and ropes. These units, she believes, are derived from body lengths, for example, the distance from the tip of the nose to the tips of the fingers with the hand held extended or from thumb and index finger to elbow. In my opinion, this is plausible. Many of our own measuring units, such as the digit, cubit, foot, and pace, derive from the proportions of the human body. As we will learn in Chapter 5, however, the archaeological record does not entirely bear out her hypothesis.

Unlike the animal figures, the purely geometric geoglyphs seem to be scattered all over the pampa, though the densest concentration lies on the south bank of the Ingenio (Figure 12). The ancient Nascas' love affair with the trap-

Figure 13. Maria Reiche demonstrates why she thinks spirals like the yarn and needle in Figure 9 were made by moving the point of a huge compass and connecting arcs drawn with radii made up of multiples of a precise measuring unit. She theorizes that the Nasca people made careful blueprints on cloth before venturing up onto the pampa. Instead, we argue that the spiral in Figure 9 was probably made by attaching straight and curved segments together and that the whole figure was shaped in the field by eye. Photo by author.

ezoid even transcends their passion for zigzags and seems to have been pan-Andean. The trapezoid is central to the architectural design of many an Inca site. Ollantaytambo in the highlands and Tambo Colorado on the coast boast huge trapezoidal plazas, and most Inca buildings exhibit trapezoidal windows. Of the largest geoglyphs, 62 percent are trapezoids, the rest rectangles or triangles. These figures cover more area of the pampa than all the other types of drawings combined. Our low-altitude aerial survey of the pampa tallied 227 geometrical

Figure 14. Giant trapezoids abound close to the riverbeds of the Ingenio and Nasca drainage. Photo Servicio Aerofotográfico Nacional, Peru.

Figure 15. Some trapezoids, like this one that abuts a quebrada, have lines shooting like laser beams out of their tapered ends and extending all the way to the other side of the pampa. Photo Servicio Aerofotográfico Nacional, Peru.

geoglyphs larger than 15 square yards. That alone amounts to the removal of nearly 4 million square yards of broken stone, about 29 percent of the entire pampa, assuming no overlap. A typical geometrical feature would scrape out an area of pampa rubble somewhat in excess of 10,000 square yards. Since the average trapezoid is about ten times as long as it is wide, its dimensions would be approximately 40 by 400 yards. The mother of all geometrical figures, by the way, is 160,000 square yards in extent. It lies among 13 others that overlook the southern bank of the Ingenio, a place aptly termed the "Land of the Giant Trapezoids" (Figure 14). Some trapezoids stand alone, but frequently a narrow line seems to shoot out a skinny end (Figure 15). Habitually it will run for half a mile or so before terminating in a complex of lines or in another geometrical figure. Sometimes the line oddly plugs back into the rear end of the trapezoid from which it emanated.

The smaller figures lie a bit farther out into the pampa. From the practical standpoint of efficiency, I think it makes sense that both the density and the size of the figures would dwindle as the builders moved out toward midpampa; it would have been more difficult to sustain a workforce there for an extended length of time, especially in the blistering heat. On the other hand, were the most ambitious clearing projects undertaken closer to the habitation areas purely out of convenience, or was it because of the importance given to the region where precious water is overtaken by the desert?

So ends our brief introduction to the wonder-of-the-world mystery on the desert. Our acquaintance with the pampa would span three decades, and it would reveal just how different this space can be when experienced from ground level, the way the Nasca line builders knew it, rather than as it is so often described and experienced from the air. Walks, along with photography, sketching, drawing, and recording samples of the ceramics and other artifacts, together with surveying and mapping, would occupy the efforts of all the people I worked with, most closely anthropologist Gary Urton, archaeologist Persis Clarkson, and our many volunteers for all the field seasons and visitations conducted in the late seventies, eighties, and nineties. Clarkson's studies of the ceramics and other remains would continue beyond this period, as would archaeologist Helaine Silverman's revealing excavations at Cahuachi. So too would my own thinking and rethinking of the Nasca enigma, but that gets us ahead of our story. We are not quite yet prepared to focus on Nasca in the context of twenty-first-century anthropology. First we need to learn the lessons of history. So let us back up the clock and meet the people who paraded out to the pampa before us—all of them with different motives.

PART TWO. PROCESSIONAL

3 NASCA BEFORE COLUMBUS

> The Pampa is willfully used and misused by a variety of
> forms and players in contemporary Nazca but it is never
> understood.
> ### Archaeologist Helaine Silverman[1]

Nasca is a culture, a style, and a place. It gets its name from the modern
town on the south coast of Peru, the nearest civilized outpost to the famous
geoglyphs on the adjacent desert floor. The ancient culture is known to us only
through its ceramic sequence, which dates it from approximately 100 BC to about
AD 800.[2] Colorful ceramics, exquisitely woven textiles, monumental architecture—these are the hallmarks of the people who constructed the Nasca lines, the
Nasca civilization that thrived on the south coast of Peru in the early centuries
AD. But the archaeologist's spade proves that the underpinnings of settled life on
the south coast go back at least 9,000 years before that time.

A schoolchild of 200 years ago would have been taught that there was but one
root culture in all of civilization. Because the only documented primitive way of
life was writ in the Old Testament, many antiquarians of the nineteenth century
thought all the Americas became peopled when the biblical lost tribes of Israel
arrived from the east. Classicists engaged in digging up Troy and Pompeii would
offer parallels for the art, architecture, and language of the Maya, Aztec, and
Inca high cultures of the New World that would be unearthed a century later.
Modern archaeology suggests something quite different: the influx of culture in
fact funneled in from the west, probably in periodic surges by Paleolithic hunters in pursuit of mammoths and other herbivores across the occasionally exposed Bering land bridge toward the end of the last glacial epoch.

For archaeologists the doorway to the past always opens in the present, to
turn a Darwinian phrase. Digging downward and backward, they have dated
crude stone tools, flint points, and remains of charred wood in cave sites to
possibly earlier than 24,000 years ago in Texas, and distinctive types of spear-
heads known as thinned points were being produced in sites at the southern tip
of South America by 9000 BC. Life was more advanced during this so-called

Setting the Ceramic Clock

Pottery is the main diagnostic that defines coastal civilization in Peru. Ceramics developed around 2000 BC in ancient Peru. How do we know this? To establish an objective framework for the epochs of civilization, archaeologists devise ceramic sequences. They begin by recognizing an evolution of styles and technologies in an arrangement of ceramic remains recovered from archaeological sites, the more pristine and clearly stratified the better. Thus, when archaeologist John Rowe first set up the master sequence for all of Peruvian archaeology in the fifties, he chose for the prototype the Ica Valley, which, fortunately for us, lies just north of Nasca. Rowe defined the Early Intermediate Period as the time when Nasca polychrome slip painting (using ground flint or clay mixed with water to a creamy consistency) replaced Paracas resin painting in his samples. Then he and his students subdivided his polychromes into recognizable phases based largely on the kinds of shapes and decorative elements employed by the artisans. Pegging this relative chronology to specific dates requires that ceramic remains be found in the company of materials that can be dated on an absolute basis, such as by the radiocarbon method.

Lithic Period (which lasted until 4000 BC) than most of us would imagine. For example, archaeologist Tom Dillehay of the University of Kentucky and his colleagues have probed the turf of Monteverde, a lithic site in the Andean foothills of central Chile inhabited by some 100 people. These people gathered wild potatoes, fruits, nuts, tubers, and medicinal plants. They hunted mastodons with egg-sized sling stones and projectile points, using grinding and hammer stones to fashion them. Monteverde people lived in multiroom peat-covered log huts and conducted communal activities at a large centrally located wood-framed structure—all of this at least as early as 11,000 BC, according to the radiocarbon-dated material Dillehay collected.

Adaptive dispersal, the archaeologists call it: economic specialization that results from the human invention of improved technologies to master different environments. It happened as early as 7000 BC in the diverse ecologies of South America: the tropical lowlands, coastal desert, high sierra, and altiplano. But diversity divides; it promotes segregation. If a group lives apart from another, it tends to develop a separate dialect and different customs. How would this technodiversification ultimately lead to that high state of development we call

How Radiocarbon Dating Works

A tree grows in a reservoir of air the way a fish grows in an ocean, exchanging gases and nutrients with the environment for as long as it lives and breathes. Carbon dioxide (CO_2) is among the gases that all living vegetation absorbs, and carbon 14, a radioactive form of carbon, makes up about one ten-billionth of 1 percent of all the carbon in CO_2 (the rest consists of the stable form of carbon known as carbon 12). Carbon 14 decays to normal carbon with a half-life of 5,730 years; that is, the percentage of carbon 14 in a lump of carbon is cut in half in 5,730 years, in half again in 5,730 more years, and so on. Once a tree is cut down (i.e., disconnected from exchanging gases with the environment) and, say, made into a sarcophagus lid for the tomb of King Tutankhamen, its formerly fixed percentage of radioactive carbon begins to drop; therefore, the lower the ratio of carbon 14 to carbon 12 the archaeologist measures in the wood compared to that in the atmosphere today, the older the age of the sample and consequently the older the tree, the coffin, and its contents. The wonder of it all is that such minuscule amounts of radioactive carbon can yield ancient dates accurate to 50 years or so.

civilization, with its advances and specializations in technology, art, architecture, ceramics, and sedentary living that generally go hand in hand with improved social conditions? We would need social fusion to balance these divisive forces, and that happens, archaeologist Michael Moseley explains, only when social inequality becomes rationalized, which allows a minority to direct the activities of a majority of people.[3] But this is the stuff of archaeological debate.

It was in this environment that the dispersal of people and the accompanying diversity of behavior began to take place. Some 11,000 years ago hunter-gathering communities veered west, toward the sea, where the Humboldt current upwelling offshore offered an incredibly rich source of nourishment. Archaeologists have unearthed refuse deposits of shellfish and fish and seal bones dating to 9000 BC. One settlement from 5000 BC included a depressed plaza within a ring of shell piles six feet high. When the season changed, these people usually packed up their leaf-shaped projectile points and headed eastward onto the Andean foothills in search of deer and guanaco (a relative of the llama); however, remains of gourds, tomatillo, and a relative of the manioc root found at coastal sites as early as 6000 BC prove that late lithic people in the Nasca environment already had commenced to farm. They adapted their skills to take advantage of the diverse ecologies bordering the thin strip of level coast they roamed (Figure 16). Later, coastal fishermen improved their catch by devising harpoons, complicated fish-hooks made from cactus thorns, fishing nets made from bottle gourds and cotton, and finally watercraft to get beyond the surf line, where angling was difficult.

Figure 16. These early pictographs from the desert coast showing men hunting cameloids predate the Nasca lines by 1,000 years. L. Lumbreras, *The People and Cultures of Ancient Peru,* trans. B. J. Meggers (Washington, D.C.: Smithsonian Institution Press, 1974). Courtesy of Betty J. Meggers.

As people prosper, they proliferate. The Chinchorros culture on the north coast of Chile developed one of the first known cults of the dead. They mummified bodies by disassembling them, removing and preserving the organs. Putting Humpty Dumpty back together again, they fitted the arms, legs, and spine with wooden structures and padded the body with packing before coating the treated corpse in clay and painting details on the face—this a thousand years before the Egyptians.

Pyramids, too. By the middle of the second millennium BC, more large mounds would be erected in Peru's narrow coastal valleys than at any other time in Andean history. One of the most impressive ceremonial centers, Sechin Alto, boasts a stone-faced platform 40 yards high and 300 meters square surrounding aligned plazas and sunken courts. Undeciphered carved pictograms on the megaliths that line the wall depict armed warriors interspersed with dismembered body parts, the signs of conflict that come with expansion. The first true earthen pyramid appears in 1850 BC at Las Haldas (also on the north coast). Perhaps because most of them are made of adobe and lack the elaborate stone facing of pyramids of European antiquity, we tend not to hear much about them. This one was particularly impressive: seven layers high and 480 yards wide at the base (compare Egypt's Great Pyramid at 250 yards). It lies at the center of a walled town that housed several thousand people. Here was a true residential complex replete with a community center.

Moving closer to Nasca, at Chilca on the central coast of Peru, archaeologist Frederic Engel, who worked there in the sixties, discovered a cluster of Archaic Period houses constructed of willow and acacia posts, a village settlement with a population of about a hundred families. Probing burials in the adjacent dunes at the edge of the pampa, he turned up clothed and desiccated human remains accompanied by household articles. Basket fabrics (including bags and skirts) told of an early textile industry that would eventually evolve into a defining emblem of the high cultures of the south coast.

The Chilca occupations informed the archaeologists of an ever growing community. Fecal and skeletal remains suggest that as fishing and farming technology improved, the people grew larger and lived longer. Anemia decreased in the child population as some families enjoyed a better diet than others. By 5000 BC they had already domesticated animals, the llama, alpaca, guinea pig, dog, and duck among them. As the community enlarged it adopted one of the earliest forms of birth control. Female infanticide is one sign of the maintenance of social inequality suggested by archaeologist Moseley.

Once coastal horticulturists began to farm cotton (about 2500 BC), the art of making textiles began to proliferate. Artisans prepared fibers with spindle and whorl, and they wove fish nets, mantles, blankets, and skirts with needle and shuttle. Artists decorated the cloth with geometric motifs of birds, snakes, fish, and cats—figures and forms that begin to bear a vague resemblance to those that would appear on the pampa more than a millennium later (Figure 11).

The first canals in the Nasca drainage basin were constructed around AD 500, perhaps by independent farmers. These were simple affairs, not much more elaborate than channels a gardener might peck out with a hoe to allow water access to remote corners of a plot. Corporate groups soon expanded the system with large-scale building projects. These farm collectives probably started out as blood-related groups consisting of one or more families. Sometimes a single individual would gain dominance over the others by cunning and superior skills (as suggested by a building facade at the site of Huaca Moxeke, where friezes depict a pair of human faces along with two richly adorned individuals alongside a bound captive[4]). By reclaiming sizable areas of accessible land, larger and larger workforces could be marshaled to open up even vaster areas of the desert until water and land limitations outran the organization and engineering capacity of the group.

By 1900 BC, south coast people were making simple pottery. A thousand years later they had developed fine ceramic art. Pottery reached its zenith with the people who made the Nasca lines. As you live in life so shall you live in death. At least continuity in the world of experience is a reasonable supposition. Like no other culture in the Americas, the preoccupation with preserving the deceased reached extraordinary lengths in Peru, even rivaling Egypt in the Old World. Shortly before the ancient Nasca began developing their own style of ceramics, the people of the peninsula of Paracas 120 miles to the north created their celebrated necropolis, an underground cluster of burial crypts containing hundreds of mummy bundles and decorated polychrome ceramic wares featuring stirrup-shaped spouts often mimicking the heads of animals. (The corpses interred there show evidence of cranial surgery, even the removal of tumors.)

Paracas pottery was very fine, and Paracas textiles were highly admired, too. Weavers used alpaca wool imported from the Andes along with locally grown cotton thread. The highly colored embroidered mantles, hats, and tunics display humans with cat whiskers. To symbolize high office, figures are shown carrying staffs and trophy heads. Many exhibit a penchant for flying, for we see winged action figures with demonic faces floating about, their colorful decorated capes streaming behind them.

Figure 17. Lizard, monkey (?), and hummingbird—these brightly colored animals outlined in black, just as on the pampa, appear on Nasca ceramics. They also have been dated to the same period when the pampa drawings were made. The winged deity *(right)* frequently decorates Nasca ceramics. One anthropologist has identified him with the god Con. Were the Nasca drawings part of a rite portending his return to the pampa? Photos courtesy of Donald Proulx.

Just before the beginning of our Christian era, fortified villages and residential communities began to outnumber large pyramids and ceremonial plazas. The artistic imagery of this late Paracas period focuses more heavily on practical concerns like war and conflict. Some archaeologists think this is because governance was in the hands of a powerful elite class that distinguished its superiority via personal wealth derived through conquest. It was during the Early Intermediate Period (AD 1–600), a time of economic and political transformation, that the ancient Nasca people, a loosely organized group of extended families, first began to emerge. They were expert artists capable of creating stunningly colorful pottery, the predominant remnant of the past that would speak to us of their culture across the ages. On many of their pots we find birds, plants, and animals—unmistakably the same creatures they would also sketch on the gigantic drawing board of the pampa—all outlined in black (Figure 17).

So, there certainly was plenty of life in the general environment around the pampa before Nasca, and many of the cultural elements I've talked about can be identified with the true Nasca style that would develop down the coast from Paracas during the period AD 100–800. For example, archaeologist Katharina Schreiber's survey of the Nasca valley revealed ten habitation sites from Paracas times alone. We don't need to look far from the western coast of South America (to the classical world much less to worlds outside our solar system) for the roots of the Nasca enigma. There is a long history of human occupation in the region, and tradition was already in place waiting to be exploited and developed. Why that tradition took such an odd turn, why it yielded an unexpected wonder of the world, still remains to be explained.

What Remains of the Nasca Culture

People have asked me: How could terrestrials have created the Nasca lines when the pampa is barren? The Nasca desert may *look* desolate to the traveler who goes there today, but it was once surrounded by river valleys teeming with life, including vibrant human societies. Furthermore, there are many ancient cemeteries from which archaeologists have recovered useful information on the past. Not only were there hundreds of farming villages in the Nasca drainage, but Nasca graves also abound, and they have yielded up the colorful polychrome pots archaeologists label "in the Nasca style." Archaeologists have been able to arrange representative vessels in a smooth eight-phase sequence that covers the millennial span 100 BC to AD 800, exactly the sequence that spans the time frame of the Nasca geoglyphs.

If you look at the earliest ceramic phases, you'll see the influence of Paracas art in the polychrome motifs rendered in resin-base paints applied after firing. These often include double-spouted vessels that were probably used for libation, decorated with fanciful winged and fanged creatures. In about the middle of the sequence, the recognizable Nasca style begins to emerge. The decoration shifts to realistic objects—fruits, along with animals and plants—among them the same ones we find etched on the pampa. Look, for example, at the gentle imagery in the flock of hummingbirds in Figure 17, rendered in vivid prefire slip paints. In this so-called monumental or Early Nasca phase, the renditions are bolder yet simpler. In the later phases of the sequence, the pendulum swings back toward the fantastic; for example, masks of demons begin to appear on human bodies. New shapes develop, and the background becomes cluttered during this "proliferous" or Late Nasca period. Then military matters become a favorite topic, as the Nasca figures become still more disjointed by the very end of the sequence. A possible influence at this stage seems to come from the warlike Moche culture then developing on the north coast. One scene depicted on a geometrically shaped, double-spouted vessel from late Nasca times shows warriors disguised as condors decapitating their foe. A fish-caped soldier below them commits a similar act. Since our pampa sharks are often accompanied by trophy heads, these military men may have been part of a war cult. Archaeologist Alan Sawyer goes as far as suggesting that they collected heads because they believed the power of fertility, life's force, resided in the head.[5]

These ancient pots are windows through which to view the people who made them. The colorful ceramics of Nasca clearly reveal changing civic, social, and religious interests. Michael Moseley reads an interesting history of the Nasca culture in these changing artistic patterns. There was, he believes, a gradual secular trend away from the powerful-looking demonic terrors of Paracas art toward the simpler, undetailed bold figures of animals laid against a plain white or dark red background (that's the monumental phase). The proliferous period, when the background space gets filled in, was a time of outside influence, with many of the themes turning to war. Finally, at the end of the sequence both the designs and the figures themselves seem to break up; they literally become disjointed. From one end of the sequence to the other, there is a gradual loosening of religious imagery, before the interruption at the beginning of the Middle Horizon Period (around AD 600) by a highland culture 250 miles to the north known as Huari (Wari). Sites exhibiting the same distinctive imperial architectural style found at their capital of Wari Wilka (circular stone buildings and trapezoidal compounds divided into irregular sectors made of massive walls) continue to

The Moche: One of Many Peoples Who Influenced Nasca

About the time the people of Nasca first started making their lines, the Moche people of the north coast were building their great capital. At the site of Cerro Blanco (not the same one that flanks the Nasca pampa), they erected Huaca del Sol, the biggest solid adobe structure ever created in the Andes. It measures 350 by 165 yards at its base and towers over 120 feet high. Along with its slightly smaller companion, the Huaca de la Luna, it framed grand courtyards, adobe residences, and mausoleums for the aristocracy as well as workshops for the famous ceramics that no self-respecting museum of antiquity would dare be without. Moche ceramics are important historically because they tell tales of war and nobility. In one scene a Moche warrior subdues an opponent, knocks his hat off, and holds him by the hair. In another, two pallbearers lower a sarcophagus into the ground via long ropes, while vultures peck apart the body of the doctor (who committed malpractice?) that caused the death of the lord. In the hunting scene shown here, an overdressed noble does in a deer. Some of the characters in these scenes surely must have been real people, for they reappear in different settings. During the phase of Moche territorial expansion in the early fifth century AD, there was some limited contact with the people of the Nasca valley, to judge by the action themes that intrude into Nasca ceramics. Significant influence usually meant conquest and coercion of local lords followed by the erection of a ceremonial center according to the canons of their architectural designs and needs. It is doubtful whether the Moche went this far at Nasca, for the motifs on the colorful Nasca pots are never as graphically explicit as the ones on the cream-colored, dark-lined Moche vessels. Nonetheless, the ambitious Moche came as close as any culture before the Inca to uniting the entire coast of Peru, if for only a short time, into a single nation.

From J. Bird, "Preceramic Art from Huaca Prieta, Chicama Valley," *Ñawpa Pacha* 1 (1963): 29–34, courtesy Institute of Andean Studies.

turn up at strategic locations in valleys of the Nasca drainage basin. Evidently colonists from the mountains had interests extending beyond the peaceful exploitation of coastal lands. In the opinion of archaeologists Bill Isbell and Katharina Schreiber, steps were already being taken toward empire building by this highly urbanized culture. Though ceramic styles suggest close Middle Horizon ties between Nasca and Huari, there is little evidence to support direct control; perhaps Huari "influence" would be a better term.[6]

Considerably rarer than Nasca pots, Nasca textiles are nonetheless just as colorful as the ceramics, and they too seem to have served as a medium for artistic innovation. Despite their scarcity, more textiles have been preserved from this area than from anywhere else in Peru. Executed in alpaca wool obtained from trade with southern highland people, they are elaborately and colorfully decorated with fantastic animal motifs, the same ones that later turn up on ceramics.

The Nasca lines were not an outside job. Once I point out that archaeologists have discovered the remains of many inhabitants on and near the pampa, those who query me regarding Nasca's emptiness ask, "But where did they live?" In addition to ceramics and textiles, there is actually quite a bit of standing architecture at Nasca. When archaeologist William Duncan Strong surveyed the Río Grande drainage area in the mid-fifties, he discovered more than 47 habitation sites, 22 in the Nasca valley proper. Later, David Robinson cataloged 111 more, 60 in the Nasca valley, practically all of them at the edges of the valleys that flank the pampa. More recently Katharina Schreiber and Josué Lancho have reported on 300 sites. Adjacent to those sites lay tens of thousands of burials, most of them, like Egypt's tombs, plundered for their valuables from antiquity to the present (Figure 18).

Figure 18. Contrary to popular belief, there were plenty of people in Nasca 2,000 years ago to make the lines. Sadly, their skulls, still strewn about the pampa's edge, are quite easy to spot. Here Gary Urton and Lorraine Aveni look over a burial site looted in ancient times. Photo by author.

Strong's work first revealed the vast amount of looting that still goes on around the pampa today. One archaeologist wryly remarked that the intensity of local *huaquero* (one who seeks out *huacas,* or sacred treasures) activity was inversely proportional to the success of the local cotton crop. On several occasions, while driving up one of the valley back roads to gain closer access to the pampa on foot, I'd pass a peasant shanty with a rickety table piled high with offerings positioned squarely in the front yard. Think of a local farm market with its stand of

Figure 19. The countless pockmarks in this aerial photo, taken over habitation sites near the ceremonial and pilgrimage center of Cahuachi, reveal the damage done by the looter's spade since antiquity. Photo Servicio Aerofotográfico Nacional, Peru. *Inset:* A local farmer sells his wares, all dug from his own property. Until recently, digging up national treasures on one's own land was perfectly legal. Not much could be done to halt sales of mummy bundles to eager tourists. Photo by author

daily goods from the fields, and you get the picture, except that these vendors were peddling freshly dug ceramics, bits of textile, slings, even human skulls and mummies on special. Casual pot hunting for profit is accompanied by destruction on a larger scale out of agricultural necessity. We encountered many bulldozed sites where local farmers said they needed to make more land available for cotton cultivation (Figure 19). There is also a thriving market for such grave goods, with peasants and farmers being paid token sums for artifacts that eventually go on sale at auction houses abroad for large sums of money.

In addition to small clusters of houses, there are at least two very large complexes of architecture in Nasca. Archaeologist Helaine Silverman, who has mapped and surveyed a host of sites in southern coastal Peru, is among the most recent excavators of the monumental religious center of Cahuachi. She has cataloged more than 40 mounds, the principal ones dating to the first century AD. To the untrained eye, Cahuachi's eroding adobe walls today are scarcely discernible from the natural landscape. Only the looted remains of thousands of burials (scattered human skulls, teeth, hair, and bones covered by leathery skin) mark the spot along the side of a meandering desert track.

In the midst of these once elite burials, now turned into a veritable bone yard, lies the Great Temple, a stepped pyramid 75 feet high, fronted by a 50-by-80-yard plaza and surrounded by courts and large rooms. Don't look for stone facing and painted stucco, the sort of finish expected on a Maya or Mexican pyramid. The Great Temple is distinguishable from the surrounding low rises only to the discerning eye, its undermined adobe blocks seeming to melt away like ice cream on a hot day. Many visitors still pass it by unknowingly in a cloud of dust. (I've done it myself, more than once.) There would have been no such topographic confusion between 100 BC and AD 400, when the 70-acre site was neatly organized with its array of temples, enclosures, plazas, and adobe pyramids.

When Strong dug there in 1952, he originally thought the site was a state capital, an area built up by conquest to include the adjacent valleys 50 miles or so up and down the coast, but the facts that 70 percent of Helaine Silverman's ceramic finds are decorated and that she found little evidence of permanent domestic occupation mean Cahuachi more likely was a place for special activities. Just how special we would learn once Silverman's interests and our own began to merge. Because Cahuachi is perched on the south bank of the Nasca River just opposite the heaviest concentration of lines, Silverman proposed the hypothesis that Cahuachi once might have been a pilgrimage center, where groups of farmers from the Nasca, Ingenio, and other valleys congregated to perform religious ceremonies. The Ingenio Valley's biggest Nasca site, now named Ventilla, was surveyed by Silverman in 1988. An essentially urban settlement, it is positioned on the other side of the pampa and connects with Cahuachi via a 7-mile road that crosses the pampa.

What lies out there in the middle of the pampa in addition to those gigantic figures? Plenty of potsherds for one thing. To our surprise, the first survey of the pampa was conducted not by an archaeologist but by an astronomer. In 1969 Gerald Hawkins was investigating the possibility that the straight Nasca lines pointed to astronomical bodies at the horizon. (We'll meet him later and learn why.) Hawkins conducted his survey on one of the densest concentrations of geoglyphs, just south of the Ingenio River valley. Covering less than 10,000 square yards, his team arrived at the astoundingly high estimate of a density of 1,500 unbroken vessels per square kilometer (about 9 or 10 pots per football field of pampa). Some of these ceramics consisted of pieces of large jars (likely used to transport water), along with other undecorated domestic ware, but the bulk of the fragments were from highly decorated ceramics painted with exotic figures. Hawkins commented with eye-catching aplomb, "I see no way of avoiding the conclusion that the present evidence indicates many thousands of pottery vessels distributed in that small area. At the present price of such items in the antique stores in New York, the current valuation of this field of vases, before fragmentation, would be $15,000,000."[7]

Hawkins reported vessels lying on or very close to the lines. They seem to have been on the desert in situ, and there they could have remained for ages. Were they offerings? Warned archaeologist John Rowe, who advised Hawkins, sherds that you collect on the pampa prove only that people were crossing the desert at a particular time. If you find them on top of a figure, that indicates only that the marking is older than the sherds, nothing more. Fragments could have been scattered by the Nasca culture long after some revered ancestor made them. For example, in Mexico I have found Aztec sherds on mountaintop shrines surrounding Mexico City that came from the ruins of nearby Teotihuacan, which dates back to AD 100, but there is no evidence to support the idea that Aztec people inhabited that great site at that time (more likely they went there centuries later on pilgrimages).

Then there is the tourist factor. The edge of the pampa, particularly near the Pan-American Highway, has been one of the most heavily visited sites, especially since books by Maria Reiche and others brought worldwide attention to the pampa after World War II. How many backpacks full of brightly decorated sherds casual visitors carted off the desert we can only imagine (Figure 20). Persis Clarkson's surveys on the pampa at points very remote from the access roads show relatively few sherds. These ceramic remains weave a tantalizing tale about who went to the pampa and when. Though various histories conflict, there is still other evidence to look at that might help corroborate one theory in favor of another.

Figure 20. On a short, ten-minute walk on the pampa adjacent to the Pan-American Highway, I photographed this array of brightly colored Nasca fragments. Can you spot the modern intruder? Photo by author.

Exactly what became of the Nasca culture is another unresolved question. The Mochica in the north as well as the Nasca and other valley cultures in the south eventually were superseded, but by whom? As we learned earlier, the best candidate for immediate conquest of the Nasca area (about AD 750) was the Huari empire. Huari sites dating to that period include military garrisons, political administrative centers, and roads that stretch 700 miles from Cajamarca to Arequipa. Still later, control of the coast passed into the hands of the civilization of Tiahuanaco on the shores of Lake Titicaca in what is today the altiplano of Bolivia. This famous site, with its monolithic Gateway of the Sun, monumental stone platforms, and decorated stelae, first began to expand about AD 700, establishing a hierarchy of ceremonial and administrative centers in colonies extending over the highlands and down the river valleys to the coast. The Tiahuanacans would hold forth for nearly 300 years, longer than any empire in history, before gradually dispersing. So legendary was their capital that it would play a seminal role in the origin myth the Inca told to the first Spanish chroniclers who came to Peru in the wake of the conquistadores. Finally, in the last half-century leading up to European contact, the Inca would dominate the coast and highlands from Ecuador to Chile.

Where Written History Begins

It has been said that the stories of the Spanish conquest of Mexico by Hernán Cortés and of Peru by Francisco Pizarro are so remarkably alike that the student who has read one need not bother to read the other. Imagine a small contingent of cavalry and fearless firearmed foot soldiers (about 500 for Cortés and a mere 168 for Pizarro) confronting a massive empire at its peak of influence and in a relatively short period of time subduing it. Underrated by a ruler already preoccupied with other military matters, the invaders succeed in capturing the emperor; they hold him hostage, then betray and murder him. With help from rival neighboring factions, each conqueror manages to manipulate the leaderless people, who quickly capitulate. The Spaniards then demolish what's left of the besieged capital.

Actually, these stories of both Cortés and Pizarro, spiced up with pro-Spanish overtones, are far more detailed and complicated than the foregoing *TV Guide–*style résumé.[8] Today native resistance in Chiapas, Mexico, and parts of highland Peru and Bolivia attest to the sobering reality of a conquest period that still endures. True, Cortés's timing was particularly fortunate. He managed to manipulate an omen that predicted the return of one of the Aztec ancestors' major figures, the legendary Quetzalcoatl, who was bearded like Cortés and vowed he would return from the east.

Francisco Pizarro came at the right time too. When he set out on his inland march to the legendary gold-laden capital of Cuzco in 1532, the Inca empire already spanned the Andes and the coast from today's Ecuador to central Chile (the Inca settled there in 1476), but the country was in the midst of civil war. The Inca ruler Huayna Capac had died suddenly, probably from the smallpox that sped up the mountains far more quickly than the conquistadores who had delivered it to American shores. The struggle between his sons Huáscar (the legitimate ruler installed in the capital city of Cuzco in southern Peru) and Atahualpa (the younger of the two, who operated from the northern capital of Quito) had split the empire in two. All attempts at accommodation had failed, and Atahualpa, with the bulk of the military forces at his command, defeated and captured his brother just outside Cuzco and had him executed.

One of many brave and sagacious military men, Pizarro was thoroughly seasoned from years of experience in wars in Italy and Africa that had helped eliminate the Moors after five centuries of occupation of the Iberian peninsula. Never one to overlook an advantage on the field, Pizarro had heard of the uncertain state of the Inca empire. He began a march toward Cuzco to claim the city. Before arriving at the gates, he exchanged gifts with an envoy of the Inca king and offered all assistance in defeating any enemy he would name. But Atahualpa was no fool. When a second formal meeting in the highland city of Cajamarca broke down, Pizarro succeeded in ensnaring the young king in the ensuing battle initiated by Spanish cannon, musket, sword, and dagger. Two thousand natives were slaughtered in a mere two hours. "They were so filled with fear [of the power of the cannon]," wrote one observer, "that they climbed on top of one another to such an extent that they formed mounds and suffocated one another."[9] The horsemen rode out on top of them, wounding and killing them as they pressed home the attack.

Desperate to escape, yet quick to realize the Spaniards' intent in coming to Peru in the first place, Atahualpa offered to fill a room in Cajamarca's Temple of the Sun with gold to a height of 8 feet, provided the invaders secured his release.[10] Pizarro immediately accepted the proposed ransom. He even promised to restore Atahualpa to power in his northern kingdom, thus gaining access to the king's authority as divine ruler and proclaimed descendant of the sun over his considerable allied forces outside the city.

After holding him captive for nine months, the Spaniards sacrificed Atahualpa, even though he kept his promise. Already formally accused of treason for secretly mobilizing his generals on the outside to launch a counterattack, he was simply too dangerous to be kept alive. Accepting Christian baptism averted a more painful death by fire; instead, he was garroted (quickly strangled with a rope about the neck). Ultimately, the Spaniards would feed more than eleven tons of Inca gold objects (vases, jewelry, figurines, and ornaments) into furnaces at Cajamarca. Each soldier having been given his quota, the remaining 20 percent (the so-called royal fifth) was shuttled down to the galleons bound for Europe and King Charles I (Holy Roman Emperor Charles V) of Spain.

The conquest would continue. Manco Inca, the next in line of Inca descent, and those who came after him were still waging war 40 years later. Members of the Spanish clergy who came to the New World in the wake of Pizarro and Cortés would chronicle the developments from oral accounts of events (witnessed and interpreted through Spanish eyes) even as they "civilized" the people of the Indies (the Indians, as they called them) to the ways of Christianity.

So goes the first written history of Peru, and it comes almost a millennium after the Nasca lines ceased to be built. Some of these chroniclers, Garcilaso de la Vega, Felipe Guaman Poma de Ayala, and Juan de Betanzos among them, would mix blood with the natives, having Inca wives or mothers. Garcilaso, who wrote his account years after he left Peru, often exaggerates and romanticizes; nonetheless, his two-volume *Royal Commentaries* is a work of considerable literary merit. Guaman Poma's two-part letter to the king, entitled *New Crown and Good Government,* runs to 1,179 pages, with 397 elaborate drawings. Scholars regard it as one of the more authentic descriptions of Inca history. Some ethnohistorians, like Martín de Murúa, who wrote the *General History of Peru,* were unusually sympathetic toward the natives. Others, like the infamous Jesuit Francisco de Avila of Cuzco, who collected and preserved materials that make up the Huarochirí manuscript, the most valuable resource on the precontact Andean myth of origin, were accused of sexual abuses of native women, burning sacred objects including mummified remains, beating up villagers, and persuading the Indians to give silver to their venerated dead ancestors, much of which they kept for themselves. Entranced by the elaborate architecture of Cuzco, chroniclers Pedro Cieza de León and Bernabe Cobo wrote at length about it. Cristóbal de Molina paid particular attention to the calendar of ritual activities and ceremonies, making his work a resource fountain for the study of native religion before Spanish contact (he even took the trouble to learn the native Quechua language). Some government officials were chroniclers as well; for example, Juan Polo de Ondegardo, corregidor of Cuzco in the 1550's, became so insatiably curious about the Incas that he produced the very reliable *Information on the Religion and Government of the Incas.* Still others, like Pedro Sarmiento de Gamboa, who officially served Viceroy Francisco of Toledo, were commissioned professional historians.

The earlier these chroniclers appeared on the scene, generally, the more reliable is the record they have left us. Though their account begins late in the first half of the fifteenth century, it nonetheless helps us reconstruct a story of what native life was like. Their written descriptions can be pieced together with information the archaeologists glean from the material record of an even more distantly ancient Peru—from the architecture, ceramics, textiles, and other works of art they have managed to excavate.

Ways of comprehending and expressing a knowledge of the world can often transcend centuries of time and miles of space. Witness our knowledge of geometry and the ideal of scientific theorizing, both developed from ideas spawned in ancient Greece 2,500 years ago. Before we look at what written history tells us about the Nasca lines on the coast, where Spanish contact, unfortunately, happens to have been particularly sparse, we need to pay attention to what the chroniclers have to say about the people in power at the time of European contact, the people of the Inca empire far up the high Andes first confronted by Pizarro. Our attention will be rewarded, for we will discover that ideas, ways of thinking and expressing a knowledge of the world, resonate from the more recent mountain kingdom down to the coast and reverberate hundreds of years backward in time. To unravel the mystery of the Nasca lines, we must acquire a pan-Andean perspective.

The Inca Connection

By a long shot they are the most famous of all of South America's ancient civilizations. Who were the Inca and where did they come from? The stories of their informants and the styles of their works of ceramics and architecture make it clear that the legacy bequeathed the Incas rested upon the foundation of Huari and Tiahuanaco, the empires that preceded them. By the twelfth century, these once mighty states to the south had been reduced by drought and ecological mismanagement to less tightly controlled competing communities. Legend has it that out of their shambles emerged a skilled organizer and military leader named Pachacuti Inca Yupanqui ("Pachacuti" means cataclysm; the rest is a family name). This was barely a century before Spanish contact. A capable ruler, by the mid-fifteenth century Pachacuti managed to beat off all his competitors. Based in the valley of Cuzco, which he established as the southern capital, Pachacuti and his kin undertook a campaign that would lead in just a few generations to an empire that stretched from the northern capital of Quito (Ecuador) to Santiago (Chile), a region 3,400 miles long encompassing 385,000 square miles and 12 million people.

Aren't we all the chosen people? Just as Aztec legend claims descent from the remains of a once great culture, so too Inca legend boasts of its ancestors, born of the sun god Inti, said to have reigned at the city of Tiahuanaco. Impressive for its stately stone sculpture and a famous semisubterranean temple, Tiahuanaco was the capital and ceremonial center of an empire that once stretched around the southern reaches of Lake Titicaca, 300 miles southeast of Cuzco.

Pachacuti was the ninth in a line of rulers, the earliest of whom, like Moses and Odysseus of Western antiquity, may well have been quasi-mythical characters. Legend has it that the first Inca, four sets of brother and sister pairs, traveled underground from Lake Titicaca, finally emerging at Pacariqtambo, a mythical cave overlooking the place where the gods had instructed them to drive their staffs into fertile ground and make their home, in the valley of Cuzco. (As we shall see later, modern Pacariqtambo figures prominently in the story of the ancient lines of Nasca.) The ancestors would not be able to claim the turf on which to extend the rule of their god until they beat off the Chancas, unfriendly intruders on the northwest, and so it was that a ragtag band of settlers who had eked out a living on the slopes of the valley of Cuzco built legend into the history of one of the great empires of the world.

Of all the reasons we can imagine for the success of the Inca empire, the one I find most convincing is the strict order, the high degree of organization that was built into every component of it. Said an early Spanish visitor to the highland Inca capital, "Nowhere in the kingdom of Peru was there a city with the air of nobility that Cuzco possessed. . . . compared with it, the other provinces of the Indies are mere settlements. Such towns lack design, order, or polity to command them, but *Cuzco* has distinction to a degree that those who founded it must have been people of great wealth."[11] Thanks to the writings of Cieza de León and the other chroniclers, Cuzco is one of the few places in the Americas where, even though only a small portion of its once stereotypical walls of exquisitely carved polygonal andesite (granite) blocks remain, we nonetheless have some reliable information on how pre-Columbian cities were planned and organized. History and archaeology tell us that Andean ideas about time and space were inextricably tied to religious, social, and political principles, and all of these were embedded in the organizational plan of the city. The system that bound these elements together is one of the most unusual in the history of city planning, for Cuzco's basic layout is radial, a form of expression that looms as special and important in Andean society.

Central to the Inca urban plan was the Coricancha, literally golden (*qori*) enclosure (*cancha*), which they called the Temple of the Ancestors (the Spanish named it the Temple of the Sun). It must have been a marvelous structure, to judge from the Spaniards' descriptions of it when they got there in 1533. It was decorated in gold with a huge golden sun disk facing the great luminary as he rose. Historian John Hemming recounts one chronicler's description of this magnificent complex and how the Spaniards looted it: "These buildings were sheathed with gold, in large plates, on the side where the sun rises, but on the side that was more shaded from the sun the gold in them was more debased. The Christians went to the buildings and with no aid from the Indians—who refused to help, saying that it was a building of the sun and they would die—the Christians decided to remove the ornament . . . with some copper crowbars. And so they did, as they themselves related." The Spaniards pried off 700 plates, which the chronicler reported as averaging some 4.5 pounds of gold each when melted down: "The greater part of this consisted of plates like the boards of a chest, three or four palmos [2–2.5 feet] in length. They had removed these from the walls of the buildings, and they had holes in them as if they had been nailed"[12]—shades of Atahualpa's ransom.

The king was said to have sat upon a throne built into the east-facing wall, a magnificent facade pierced with holes inlaid with many precious stones and emeralds. Other accounts tell of tubs of gold, silver, and emeralds. Today, like so many important pre-Columbian buildings, the Coricancha is topped by a Spanish church, the Church of Santo Domingo. Enough of the temple has been excavated by archaeologists to reveal that it consisted of a rectangular enclosure fronted by four buildings of cut stone with thatched roofs. With its golden adornments, it must have been a truly important edifice, on a par with the church of the Holy Sepulchre at Jerusalem.

The Incas dedicated their Temple of the Ancestors to the most important heavenly bodies they worshiped: the sun, the moon, Venus, and the Pleiades. Venus, for example, was the attendant to the sun. He was thought to have been ordered by the sun to go sometimes before him (as the morning star) and sometimes behind (as the evening star) but always to remain close by.

A page from a manuscript produced shortly after the conquest by the chronicler Joan de Santa Cruz Pachacuti (no relation) Yamqui shows just how important the sky was to these people (Figure 21). It also dramatizes two basic principles of the Andean way of thought that still persist today: a dualistic cosmology and a vertically structured hierarchy. That all things should come in twos is not an idea unique to the Inca worldview. They say one can experience pleasure only by knowing pain. Day and night, winter and summer, male and female— these too are examples of common concepts that give rise to the notion that order in the world consists of paired opposites that complement one another. Cosmologies ranging from Maya to Mesopotamian attribute the origin of the world to complementary creators, like the Mesoamerican hero twins or the Chaldean personified deities who represent land and sky, as well as fresh and salt water. Even our modern model of the microcosmic world rests on the principles of positively charged protons and negatively charged electrons, and our Big Bang macrocosm is thought to have begun with the differentiation of the universe into matter on the one hand and radiation on the other.

The second paragon of Inca order, vertical hierarchy, is more peculiar to cultures that thrive in a mountain environment. In the Andean world all things are classified by their place in an up and down world. Take a car trip from the coast to the Andean highlands, and you'll experience the extraordinary variation in Andean ecology in a single day. Within a few hours you rise from the foggy maritime environment of Lima, Peru's capital city, to frigid tundralike passes bordered by snow-topped mountains 18,000 feet high. Each climate zone along the ascent exhibits its own microclimate and productivity: cotton fields, cactus, tree fruit, squash, and fisheries on the coast, to maize in mid-altitude, to ever hardier varieties of potato and related tubers in the highlands. Finally, you level out on the forbidding elevated plateaus, the puna, where herders graze their llamas and alpacas. Anthropologist John Murra's studies reveal that in Inca times, control of these vertically arranged economic zones was maintained by systematically relocating people and enacting strict laws dictating who should have access to farmland within each region, even where they should live within that

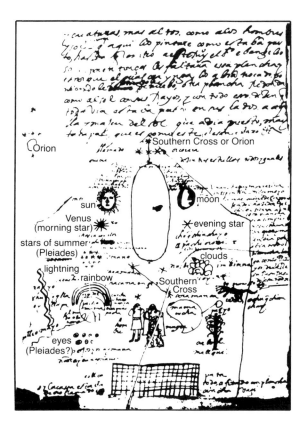

Figure 21. A drawing by the Spanish chronicler Joan de Santa Cruz Pachacuti Yamqui illustrates the symbolic meaning of the Coricancha, Cuzco's Temple of the Ancestors and center of the radial ceque system that organized the Inca capital. Clearly astronomy was part of the picture. From *Skywatchers of Ancient Mexico* (Austin: University of Texas Press, 1980).

region, a clear indication of the extraordinary degree of organization that existed within the empire.[13]

Pachacuti's picture of the Coricancha aptly captures the essence of the dual and vertical foundation principles. If the diagram is cleaved vertically, the left side of the ledger represents things masculine, while the right side pertains to the feminine. For example, notice the sun and the Pleiades (a closely gathered group of stars) on one side and the cosmic cat (it symbolizes Pacha Mama, or earth mother) on the other (extreme right). The vertically arranged dualism turns out to be the key that unlocks the doorway of cosmological expression in the architectural plan of the whole of ancient Cuzco. Divide Pachacuti's diagram horizontally, and discover at least three layers: the heavens (note the sun and moon) lie at the top, the real world of people and trees at the center, and the underworld at the bottom.

The city of Cuzco is situated 13.5 degrees south of the equator at the junction of two rivers in a mountain valley 11,000 feet high in the central Andes. It is said to have been expressly planned and laid out by the Inca Pachacuti himself in the shape of a mighty puma. Cuzco is protected on the north by the huge fortress of Sacsahuaman with its zigzag walls made of colossal worked granite blocks; this represents the puma's head. The feline hindquarters and tail are styled out of canalized rivers made to join in a *tinkuy*, a Quechua term that stands for the harmonious balancing and blending of opposites where things come together. The area is still called by locals Pumac Chupan, or the puma's tail.

The Inca called their empire Tahuantinsuyu, which means Four Quarters in Quechua, because of its basic quadripartite plan. Though the capital, Cuzco, boasted a population of more than 100,000 at its height and contained more than 4,000 buildings, records tell us that except on festal occasions, only the nobility and high-ranking visitors ever penetrated the inner sanctum of the city center. Only they could gaze upon the exquisite masonry buildings that surmounted wide plazas, many of them displaying gold sheathing and housing carved stone effigies of the deities. Ringed by mighty snow-capped mountains, the view from the *ushnu*, a ceremonial platform in the middle of the plaza, must have made a lasting impression on dignitaries who came from afar and entered this navel of the world laden with precious gifts for the emperor.

Cuzco was segmented into halves called Hanan (upper, in the northwest) and Hurin (lower, in the southeast), and each half was sliced into two sectors, or *suyus*. The reason for dividing the city this way may have had as much to do with the watershed environment as with principles of kinship and hierarchy. Lines between suyus roughly demarcate the flow of underground water in the Cuzco valley, which naturally follows a radial plan (Figure 22). Suyus served as an organizing principle that defined water rights to the kin-related groups or *ayllus* who farmed the wedge-shaped plots of land between the river valleys. The people believed they received their underground water by right of birth directly from their ancestors, who were believed to reside in the body of Pacha Mama. Differ-

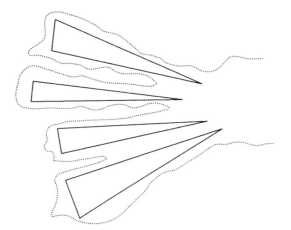

Figure 22. The radial way of organizing space is actually quite logical in a land carved by rivers and streams and their ever branching tributaries, as this drawing of neatly arranged (hypothetical) triangular geoglyphs, with their tips pointing to a common center, shows. Drawing by Julia Meyerson.

ent segments of the populace were required to honor and nurture her by making sacrifices to feed her mountain body at certain places and times.

Four major roads radiated outward from Cuzco, one from each corner of the central square. Just as our astronomers map out an infinite universe, the Inca envisioned these lines to extend to the remotest domains of the Inca empire, as far as Quito to the north and central Chile to the south and beyond. Suyus were ranked, as were the hierarchically organized ayllus who lived within them. The organizing principle of the moiety division, or halving, was based on whether citizens were located upriver (in the higher-ranking Hanan district) or downriver (in lower-ranking Hurin). So, the structuring characteristics of verticality and dualism pictured in Pachacuti's diagram of the Coricancha emerge clearly in the city plan.

The hallmark of urban social organization in Cuzco was the ceque system, a kind of mnemonic device built into Cuzco's natural and human-made topography that served to unify Inca ideas about religion, social organization, calendar, hydrology, and astronomy. *History of the New World,* written by the Spanish Jesuit chronicler Bernabe Cobo in 1653, has left us the most thorough and detailed description of the system, a scheme that also may have been adopted as an organizing principle in other cities of the empire. He wrote, "From the temple of the Sun as from the center there went out certain lines which the Indians call ceques; they formed four parts corresponding to the four royal roads which went out from Cuzco. On each one of those ceques were arranged in order the *guacas* and shrines which there were in Cuzco and its district, like stations of holy places, the veneration of which was common to all."[14] Cobo's chronicle testifies to the extraordinary power of the organization of the Inca state, for he goes on to describe in detail and locate precisely each of these imaginary radial lines called ceques that make up the giant map of the city and indeed the entire universe. He tells us that in the immediate vicinity of Cuzco, ceques were grouped zonally according to their location within each of the four suyus. Cobo describes each ceque and traces it out in the landscape by its line of huacas (guacas). By "huaca" he means a sacred place in the landscape, an opening in the body of Pacha Mama where the living mother earth can be fed sacrifices to the ancestors who live inside her.

Little did I realize in 1976, when University of Illinois anthropologist Tom Zuidema and I first began to work together to map out the ceque system, that our fieldwork in Cuzco would have a huge impact on our findings down on the pampa of Nasca a short while later. Zuidema had been working on an interpretation of the chronicler's record of the system for 20 years before we met. As he saw it, Cobo listed 9 ceques associated with each of three suyus—the northeast (centered around the district named Chinchaysuyu), the southeast (Antisuyu),

---

Quipus and Ceques

The description of the ceques and their linear radial hierarchical structure is suggestive of Andean quipus, the knotted string devices on which the Inca kept records. The Spaniard Garcilaso de la Vega relates that the Incas "used to follow my reading holding on to their quipus to be certain of my exactness. They knew a great deal of arithmetic and had an admirable method of counting everything . . . which they did with knots in strings of different colors. They added, subtracted, and multiplied with these knots" (*Royal Commentaries of the Inca* [1609], trans. H. Livermore, Austin: University of Texas Press, 1966, vol. 1, p. 124). Quipus found among grave goods may have given the total of the deceased's possessions, perhaps the number of head of llama he or she owned. The code of the quipu is yet unbroken, but recently Gary Urton (in *The Social Life of Numbers*, University of Texas Press, 1997), who has been analyzing a large sample of quipus, has suggested that there may be more information in them than simple numerical tallies.

The quipu constituted a tactile form of language, rather like Braille. A typical quipu consisted of a thick cotton cord (the primary cord) from which were suspended thinner subsidiary cords, each containing clusters of knots according to a decimal system. Thinking hierarchically, we may liken the cords to ceques and the knots to huacas. Often, additional cords dangled from the subsidiaries and still others from them, sometimes reaching the fifth order. Yet the quipu was capable of carrying more information than Braille writing, for it also included a visual element. In many cases, the cords exhibited different colors and color combinations, and the component fibers were twisted in alternating directions. In fact, the original plan of the ceque system was handed down to the chroniclers on a quipu. Why write with a cotton cord? For the same reason the Egyptians chose papyrus and the Babylonians tablets of clay: cotton was the most readily available material, the staple crop of the coastal region conquered by the Inca.

Photo © Persis Clarkson, Museo Ica.

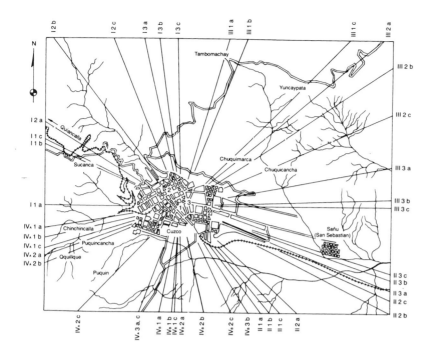

Figure 23. A crooked ceque system? *Top:* Tom Zuidema's idealized map of the radial ceque system first appeared in *Native American Astronomy,* ed. A. Aveni (Austin: University of Texas Press, 1977). *Bottom:* Brian Bauer's more recent map, a part of which is shown here, reveals that ceques are not quite so straight. Question is, how was the system conceived in the mind of the builders? Map © Brian S. Bauer. From *The Sacred Landscape of the Inca: The Cusco Ceque System* (Austin: University of Texas Press, 1998).

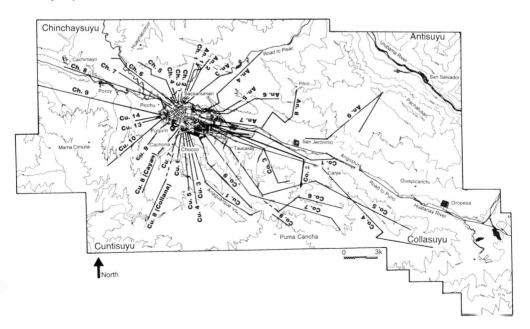

and the southwest (Collasuyu)—while 14 were associated with the northwest (Cuntisuyu) quadrant, for a total of 41 radial lines. I have adopted a simplified version of his idealized map in Figure 23.

Huacas consisted of natural or human-made temples, intricately carved rock formations, bends in rivers, fields, springs or other natural wells (called *puquios*), hills, even impermanent objects such as trees. In most cases, the water theme and its association with the agricultural calendar are given heavy emphasis in Cobo's description. The situation of these huacas must have been rather important, for Cobo goes through the trouble of locating and describing all 328 of them in the ceque system. Cobo's descriptions are loaded with concrete information connecting agriculture and the flow of water with what happens in the sky. Inca knowledge about the environment is directly tied to aspects of everyday life, particularly to the specific assignment of rites of worship and sacrifice.

Where do people fit into the ceque system? Cobo also tells us that each ceque was assigned one of a set of three hierarchical groups that represented the three social classes (extended families, or "partialities," as he calls them) and were required to tend to their huacas. There were, in descending hierarchical order, the ceques that were maintained and worshiped by the primary kin of the Inca ruler, those that were worshiped by his subsidiary kin, and finally those tended to by that segment of the population not related by blood to the ruler. The attendants of these ceques came to their huacas offering the appropriate sacrifices at the proper times, says Cobo. The assignments on the hierarchy of worship rotated sequentially (from primary to subsidiary to unrelated and back to primary again), proceeding from one ceque to the next, all the way around the horizon in a clockwise direction in the northern suyus and counterclockwise in the south.

The organization of communal work activity, particularly having to do with agriculture and irrigation, was yet another facet of life in the old Inca capital prescribed by the ceque map; for example, representatives of each of 40 families drawn from the suyus participated in a mock or ritual plowing that took place every year just before planting time in the plaza of Hurin Cuzco, with each delegate plowing a designated portion. Even rules for the servicing and maintenance of the irrigation canals were specified by the order of the ceques. This idea of physically dividing up a central ceremonial place as a field for negotiating social relationships remains alive in contemporary Andean communities, as we will learn shortly when we deal with anthropologist Gary Urton's findings in communities near Cuzco as well as adjacent to the Nasca pampa. These would play a direct role in our work on the pampa.

Historical Nasca

For all the mountain-based attractions that captivated the Spaniards (gold and the rich spoils of the Cuzco-based Inca empire), there was little on either the south or north coast to arouse the interest of the materialistically oriented, "civilizing" invaders. Still, in the middle of the fifteenth century, a fairly wealthy enclave of farmers and fishermen flourished along the south coast. Their articles of trade have been found as far north as Ecuador, and textiles and spondylus shells from that area made their way back south to Nasca. But everything would be transformed in 1475 with the first shot of a double-barreled conquest that would spell disaster in the next century.

Evidently attracted by this wealth, around 1475 the Inca king Pachacuti, Bernabe Cobo tells us, sent his brother to lead 30,000 soldiers down to the sultry coast. The people of the Ica, Nasca, and Pisco valleys quickly sued for peace, though the tribes to the north, the Chincha, fought fiercely and held out for months. Having set up the worship of their sun god, the Incas repudiated the gods of the local tribes. Garcilaso says that they moved these natives from one valley to another or wherever they needed to share in the duties of communal labor. We don't know where the centers of authority lay or from whom the mighty Incas took over, although Garcilaso, if he can be trusted, tells us that a brave lord named Chuquimarcu, who dominated a wide area around the Cañete River valley just north of Nasca, held out for four years against Inca Tupac Yupanqui's invading armies.[15]

Pedro Cieza de León, the Spanish soldier and chronicler, claims to have seen the bones from Inca massacres still lying in the fields 30 years after the Inca conquest, and Huarco, one of the conquered towns, derives its very name from what happened to the locals who opposed the mighty Inca—it means gallows. Another chronicler, José de Acosta, says Tupac launched a surprise attack during a ritual fishing ceremony. Clearly, coastal people, then mostly fragmented into tiny communities, were no more a match for the well-organized Inca than they would be half a century later for the conquistadores. In short order Tupac set up the Inca garrison at a strategic watershed point 25 miles up the Cañete River on one of the trunks leading to the major north-south Inca road. The conquerors were there to stay.

Writing in 1551, Cieza de León paints a picture of utter desolation on the coast:

> From the Valley of Ica one walks [some 70 miles] until one sees the beautiful valleys and rivers of Nasca. These valleys were in times past heavily populated

and the rivers irrigated the fields of the valleys in an orderly and prescribed manner. The past wars consumed with their cruelty (as is well known) all of these poor [Indians]. . . . In the principal valleys of these of Nasca . . . there were buildings . . . which were ordered to be built by the Inka. And of the natives I have nothing more to say than that they say that their ancestors were very brave compared to themselves and were esteemed by the kings of Cuzco.[16]

The battles tied to the Spanish conquest all arose out of the inevitable greed among the Spaniards as they divided up the spoils of war, and Cieza does refer to a series of skirmishes between Pizarro and the Spanish commander Diego de Almagro, who had been awarded the southern part of the Inca empire by the king. The Indians who died were members of the native contingents that accompanied various expeditions fighting up and down the Andes. Then he goes on to give the only specific reference I know of in all of the chronicles to any remains out on the desolate pampa of Nasca: "Through all these valleys and through those which I had been, there passed the beautiful and grand road of the Inkas, and through some parts of the sand dunes can be seen marks by which one finds the road which passes through there. From these valleys of Nasca one goes until arriving at Hacari [the modern town of Acari south of Nasca]."[17] These roads (*capac ñan,* or royal roads, they called them) were a hallmark of the Inca empire. As at Cuzco, one of them led out of each quarter of the capital, ultimately passing to the corners of the empire. In his fascinating landmark study of Inca roads, archaeologist John Hyslop, who walked segments of most of them, describes some as highways in the modern sense, that is, main arteries consisting of well-built roads, with markers, prepared surfaces, raised elements, even steps.[18] These served travelers on state business, yet other roads are no more than narrow paths with little formal construction. Hyslop's composite road map documents a network 25,000 miles long. My contact with him would help reveal some extraordinary parallels between Inca roads and Nasca lines.

The road Cieza refers to is almost certainly part of the great coastal highway, closely paralleled today by the Pan-American Highway, which runs from Tumbes near today's Ecuadorean border to Santiago, Chile. It cuts through agricultural terrain as it passes perpendicular to hundreds of river valleys, alternately ascending to the pampas that lie between (Figure 24). Archaeologist Katharina Schreiber has reason to be convinced that this line is the Inca royal road. Tracing Inca artifacts on more than 800 sites, she got a very neat linear alignment from the ruins of Cahuachi on the south bank of the Nasca River across to the Ingenio. Moreover, she found that an Inca administrative center was positioned exactly where this line drops off the pampa and enters the Ingenio Valley.

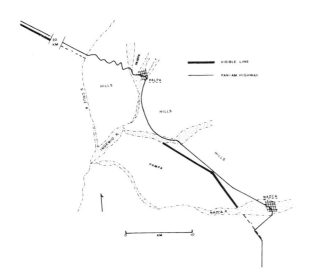

Figure 24. The transpampa line (in heavy black) is one of the few Nasca lines that does not connect to a line center. This ten-mile feature is almost certainly the coastal branch of the Incas' pan-American highway. Note that the line becomes the modern version of the highway at either end. I think it might be an extension of the road Cieza de León wrote about five centuries ago. Map by author. From *The Lines of Nazca*, ed. A. Aveni, 1990, courtesy of American Philosophical Society, Memoirs, vol. 183.

The Inca knew what they were doing when they placed their garrison at Inkawasi. It lay at a strategic intercoastal spot to control the single most important commodity shared by inhabitants then and now—water. The creation myth told in the Huarochirí manuscript is rife with stories linking water with native cosmologies in both the uplands and the lowlands. The earth itself was believed to be a living creature that rose up out of the ocean. Anthropologist Frank Salomon's introduction to a translation of the only genuine native document that speaks of the culture's origin vividly describes the combination of low and high land in terms of the complementary dual poles I talked about earlier: all of Peru is imagined as "a single world mountain made of all the Andean ranges, rising from femalelike valleys to malelike snowcapped heights."[19] Water is the active part of this world. It rises out of the ocean up into the sky as the Milky Way, carried there by the dark cloud llama constellation, who takes a long drink from the sea every night before he ascends, then crashes down from the (male) mountains in storms that fecundate the welcoming earth. The Huarochirí myth's upland-lowland relationship is loaded with what Salomon calls "hydraulic sex": "voluptuous earth women offer their parched bodies to the virile water *huacas* who rush down from the heights."[20] In one seamy episode the (male) lake, Collquiri, his dam broken, clumsily gushes down to his sweetheart, Capayama, and uncontrollably releases himself over her body:

> Capayama's elders shouted at Collquiri from their . . . (spring) village: "Son-in-law, everybody's mad at us! Don't send us so much water!"
> "Shut it off!"

"Hey, Collquiri! Hold back on the water!" they yelled.

With them shouting like that, Collquiri plugged the hole with a blanket and other stuff. But the more he plugged it the more the barrier crumbled and the more the water kept bursting through over and over again.

Meanwhile the people from down below kept yelling at him nonstop: "PLUG IT UP!!"[21]

We do know that once the Spaniards gained control of the Nasca area, the caciques, or chiefs, later sold all the land. One Pedro Suárez allegedly bought the entire Ingenio Valley in the middle of the seventeenth century, though we don't know what he paid for it. One of the early caciques was the *curaca,* or principal chief, Don García Nasca or Ñanasca, a member of the family from which both the modern town and the ancient culture acquire their name. In a nifty bit of archival detective work Gary Urton managed to uncover a copy of Ñanasca's last will and testament tucked away in an archive in Lima. It was filed November 4, 1569, and as we shall see, it tells all about the initial subdivision of the boss's lands and the all-important apportionment of water based in large part on indigenous ideas having to do with principles of irrigation.

The Visita de Acari, dated to 1593, is one of the earliest documentary "visits" to the *encomiendas* (royal grants of trust over the natives) to the coast after the Conquest. It, too, would prove to be a seminal source in providing Urton with clues about the social organization of people living in the towns that bordered the pampa in pre-Columbian times, an organization very like that found in ancient Cuzco, and this in turn would offer us an understanding of their motives for constructing the lines in those particular locations.

Oddly enough, as time marches closer to the present, we begin to acquire less and less information about ancient Peru, at least up to the beginning of the twentieth century. By the middle of the sixteenth century, a generation after Pizarro's entry into Cuzco, the native population all over Peru suffered a drastic depletion, especially on the warm open coast, where European-borne disease hit hardest. For example, after the Conquest, the population of Chincha, a town of 40,000 north of Nasca, fell to 4,000 by 1550 and dropped as low as 1,000 by 1560. Of the empty Nasca valley Cieza wrote, "I believe there are no Indians at all to profit from its fertility."[22]

Smallpox combined with epidemics of plague and typhus in the 1580's and 1590's took a share of the toll, but historian John Hemming believes that the decline resulted more from the chaotic administrations that overtaxed and overworked the natives. Culture shock and civil wars added further to their misery. All of this was coupled with the evil deeds of bands of Spanish marauders who, after the death of Diego de Almagro, roamed over the coast wantonly looting and pillaging native villages, killing llamas for candle tallow and taking corn without paying the Indians. Eventually the conquistadores and their descendants would use the spoils of war to establish sprawling haciendas. What remained of the native population was accorded few rights in exchange for hard labor, and consequently the Indians precipitated to the bottom of the social strata, where they remain today. One frustrated chronicler admitted that the government in the past was decidedly better and more valuable.

In the fog that descended upon the historical record in the late sixteenth and seventeenth centuries, elaborate descriptions of gleaming cities (like Cobo's account of the glorious capital of Tahuantinsuyu) faded from the scene. The architecture was dismantled, and the enormous andesite blocks were used to build churches, in whose walls we can sporadically rediscover them. The clergy and their successors, many of whom wrote the chronicles, became the natives' best friends, but the protection the downtrodden might seek from them was purely paternalistic. The Spanish usurpers unsympathetically continued with the process of conversion. They did it single-mindedly and with an air of superiority, for most of them were convinced that all native religion was the work of the devil. As a noted Mexican chronicler said of the Aztecs, who concurrently underwent a similarly painful decimation:

> Thus we terminate our brief and condensed version of the calendar. I understand, I realize, that I could have enlarged the book and described more things in a detailed way, but my sole intention has been to give advice to my fellow men and to our priests regarding the necessity of destroying the heathen customs which they will encounter constantly, once they have received my warning. My desire is that no heathen way be concealed, hidden, because the wound would grow, rot and fester, with our feigned ignorance. Paganism must be torn up by the roots from the hearts of these frail people![23]

With their great treasures all melted down or lying buried beneath crumbled walls, the very existence of one of the great New World cultures slowly receded from memory. It would take more than two centuries before outsiders would return, this time with a quest of a different kind to motivate them.

4 SEEING IS BELIEVING

REDISCOVERING THE PAMPA

> Then what did the lines point to? Indeed what was their
> purpose? "That," and he twisted the stem of his glass
> with a Holmesian air, "is what I intend to find out."
>
> **Astronomer Gerald Hawkins to writer-explorer**
> **Tony Morrison**[1]

It was 1565, just 32 years after Pizarro had garroted Atahualpa. A festival in Bordeaux, France, featured an unusual display of "savages" from twelve foreign nations including Greece, Turkey, Arabia, and America. Imagine recreating an entire village of South American captives replete with native people in their natural habitat, a colonial Disney World. The conquerors' desire to plunder and destroy native remnants may seem at odds with our contemporary wish to preserve them, but then there were different forces at work in late Renaissance Europe. A revival of learning countermanded the religious fervor that fueled the drive to stamp out the ways of the devil.

Margaret Hodgen,[2] a British historian of anthropology, thinks there are at least three developments at work that underlie this preservation instinct. First, there is commercialism, the need for information about New World peoples as potential customers for European trade. Second is a deep-seated religious uncertainty and discomfort about "savage" morals (maybe before we engage in conversion we ought to learn more about who these people really are). Finally, there is a basic interest in people as individuals, a curiosity about how human beings behave. Why do the natives worship idols? Why do they pray to the sun? And even more fundamental questions: Are these South American inhabitants beasts or people, or had God made creatures somewhere in between? What, then, divides man from beast? If they are people, then what is the source of this human diversity they seem to exhibit? Why is there a division of races? Did all humanity come from the same strain, now dispersed from the ruins of the Holy Land as the Old Testament explains? The story goes that after Solomon's death, the twelve tribes of the Hebrews of Palestine were split in two: Israel in the north, Judah in the south. Eventually the Assyrians defeated the Israelites and carried them off into bondage, God's punishment for worshiping idols. They were never heard from again.

The idea that the New World was the ultimate refuge of the first Israelite tribes was written down as early as the 1550's by Friar Diego de Landa, a Spanish chronicler of Yucatan. He reports that one of his informants told him that his Maya ancestors came from the east via twelve paths that God had opened up across the sea. The discovery of pyramids and high mounds all over the New World from the Great Plains to the Yucatan Peninsula to the rocky coast of Peru—structures resembling the pyramids of the Old World—would assure the Lost Tribes theory a position in the forefront of orthodox explanations about the origin of all Native American people for the next three and a half centuries. Wrote the historian Caleb Atwater in 1820, "Examine the loftiest [Ohio] mounds, and compare them with those described as being in Palestine. Through the wide world, such places seem to have been preferred by the men of ancient times who erected them."[3]

Throughout the eighteenth and nineteenth centuries, artists, poets, and fiction writers, even some historians, continued to champion one of the most popular and enduring theories of the origin of Native American civilizations. This was the age of the great Romantic movement that rejected reason as a way toward acquiring truth. Emotion ruled. You could feel it in the emotional strains of Schubert's symphonies. You could see the exotic in violent or passionate scenes in Delacroix's and Turner's paintings and in the romantic novels of Hugo and the poems of Coleridge. Rousseau wrote of the Indian who freely roamed this wild land, untouched by the misery and pollution of industrial Europe, the noble savage who represented a greater distant past from which world culture had declined. Americans became particularly enthralled with spiritualism, exotica such as communication with the dead, theosophy, and Rosicrucianism. Swedenborg's out-of-body visits to alien worlds, precursors of the New Age movement, all rode the tide.

Lost continents were logical components of a worldview that looked backward to an imagined greater past, a Garden of Eden that had perfected superior morals, greater gods, and a higher technology—all lost in a tragic replay of the Old Testament tale of the fall of man. This imaginary vision portrayed the Inca, the Maya, and the Aztecs (not to mention the Pawnee and Arapaho) as descendants of survivors of a cataclysmic disaster that had submerged a great landmass far to the west of the Greco-Roman world beyond the Pillars of Hercules (the Straits of Gibraltar). No less authoritative a source than Plato himself had spoken of a continent bigger than Asia Minor and Libya combined whose people had ruled parts of Asia as far east as the Caspian Sea. These so-called Atlanteans were beaten back by the Greeks shortly before most of the nation's 12 million inhabitants perished in either an earthquake or a volcanic eruption that caused a great tidal wave. Believers in lost lands would later point to the tips of the Azores and Antilles as remnants of bygone glory. Even as late as 1880, Ignatius Donnelly's *Atlantis: The Antediluvian World* (then in its eighteenth printing) and still later Lewis Spence's *Atlantis in America* (1925) made the best-seller lists.

In 1875, a meeting of the prestigious International Congress of Americanists in France was ruptured by a heated debate over the alleged ancient Chinese discovery of yet another landmass far out in the Pacific Ocean, much closer to Nasca. This place was called Lemuria (Mu for short), the southern hemisphere antipode to Plato's mid-Atlantic continent (Figure 25). According to James Churchward, who claimed he possessed 2,500-year-old original tablets from its Asia-bound colonizers, Lemuria was larger than all of South America. Its name can be traced to a popular work from the mid-nineteenth century by German naturalist Ernst Haeckel on the origin of the human race. Haeckel theorized that there was only one way to explain the peculiar distribution of exotic plants and animals naturalists were finding all over the world; the lemur, for example—how

Figure 25. Lost continents counterbalance the globe, Atlantis in the Atlantic and Mu in the Pacific. In the late nineteenth and early twentieth centuries, these two imagined lands were believed by many to have been the places of origin of the ancient ancestors of all Native Americans. This diagram is from a popular work by James Churchward, *The Lost Continent of Mu* (New York: Ives Washburn, 1932).

else could lemur remains get to both Asia and America? So he proposed the existence of an in-between continent on which they evolved and from which they migrated. Lemuria fit perfectly into the Pacific basin ringed by Australia, Japan, Alaska, and the west coast of the two Americas. Hawaii, the Marquesas, Samoa, the Carolines, and Easter Island form a link to the South American mainland, the summits of the once mighty mountains that crowned the land of Mu.

The history of Pacific Mu differs little from that of the hypothetical continent that counterbalances it in the Atlantic. It is a story of religious creationism and cultural retrogression, of the grandeur of times past and the downward shift from civilizations that did not evolve progressively but rather were created in pristine perfection out of whole cloth. Here was a tale that offered an antidote to the gloom and doom of Darwin's evolution by natural selection. Mu became the tragic place where man first came into being. From there noble colonizers civilized all the rest of the world only to see their homeland destroyed. Savagery came from civilization and not the other way around, wrote Churchward. The native races of these exotic lands are the decrepit survivors of true high culture. The great eruption of Krakatoa heard round the world in 1881 fueled such ideas, even though there was not a shred of evidence in the archaeological record to support them. Today Atlantis and Mu appear as fantastic creations of a too-rapidly progressing, industrial civilized world dissatisfied with itself, its people in search of enlightenment from civilizations long past.

Now that the sea floor has been thoroughly mapped, geologists find only a mid-Atlantic ridge that zippers the zone between the continents and a series of subcontinental plates ringing the Pacific, and still there is zero archaeological evidence to support the once popular theories. Strangely, the idea of lost knowledge buried in vanished continents persists in the popular literature, but then, many disbelieve DNA evidence in criminal courts and that a wheeled probe has roamed over the surface of Mars. The true romantic has neither appetite nor trust for scientific argument or evidence.

The inquiring spirit of the Enlightenment also gave birth to the collector, the assembler of the Noah's Ark of the Americas, a treasure trove of all its natural and man-made objects. *Cabinets de curiosités*—compartmented boxes in which were arranged objects unlike any of those that adorned civilized Europe—teased the roving eye, gave us the delightful antiquarian word "curio," and led ultimately to our concept of the museum.

In early colonial times such cultural curiosities (a shrunken head from the Amazon, a tomahawk from the St. Lawrence Valley) were generally regarded as forces of evil. To understand why this idea prevailed throughout the sixteenth and seventeenth centuries, one need only look at the divisions that arose all over Europe as a result of differences acquired by straying from the accepted canon. The Protestant Reformation had assaulted the custom of Roman Catholic rites, and there were enormous difficulties in the rapidly expanding market economy in Europe, not helped along by communicating with colonial people who spoke a multitude of tongues. The tale of the Tower of Babel in Genesis had already told how people defied God by trying to build a tower to reach to the heavens. God punished them by confusing their tongues and scattering them about the world. These people, along with their rites, customs, and curios, served as a reminder of the deviation from God's original plan. (The counterargument, decidedly a minority view in the sixteenth century, alleged that the creative act happened at different times and places and under different conditions; therefore, human diversity only manifests things as one might expect them to be.) Regardless of the theories of human origin, almost everybody agreed that knowledge of our past should be collected, preserved, and studied with a view toward unifying the races, thus correcting the errors of the past.

In 1799, eight years into the start of the Republic, the French established the first anthropological institution, the Société des Observateurs de l'Homme. It billed itself as a scientific organization dedicated to bringing happiness and perfection to man resulting from "the study of himself and from the contemplation of nature."[4] Its motto was "Connais-toi toi-même" (Know thyself). Its *observateurs* in the empirical spirit of the Enlightenment would collect and study everything from rocks and fossils, arms and tools, clothes and religious objects, to words and customs, the whole of it housed in a great museum. Its interests would span every field of human inquiry from psychology and religion to geology and technology. Affiliated scholars, like Joseph-Marie Dégerando, would begin to set up for the first time a systematic study of social phenomena—what would become the discipline of anthropology.[5]

And collect they did: London established its first zoo or menagerie (literally a household of animals) in 1599. It lodged six lions, one wolf, one tiger, and a porcupine. Italy alone founded five botanical gardens in a single decade of the sixteenth century. Specialists gobbled up collections of coins, medals, stamps, globes, gems, fossils, shells, Roman statues, and Egyptian idols. Seeing is believing. "Chambers of rarities" became "halls of curiosities," with large artifacts, some of dubious authenticity, like a dragon's head and a mermaid's tail, adorning both walls and ceilings. Smaller objects such as minerals, spoons, watches, arrowheads, even human skin samples from around the world, were all neatly classified into compartmented cases. Here were wonders of the world in which spectators could become immersed, tangibly reaffirming their faith in things marvelous while at the same time seeing the true picture of ancient history revealed before their own eyes.

By the seventeenth century human handicrafts were separated out from natural objects and given museum locales of their own. Such exotics only whetted the appetite for additional helpings of unusual treasures from faraway lands. Many of the artifacts of the Andes were obtained through gold and silver mining and grave robbing. Serious collectors like Martínez de Compañon, bishop of Trujillo, a city on Peru's north coast, commissioned mapping and collecting expeditions to the nearby ruins of Chan Chan and Huaca del Sol. Other expeditions were mounted that combined the quest for collectibles with the spirit of the adventure traveler.

In 1814 the German naturalist Baron Friedrich Heinrich Alexander von Humboldt published his multivolume *Vues de Cordillères,* which offered the first collection of descriptions of the monuments of New World civilizations. While Napoleon was launching his famous expedition to Egypt to explore and collect antiquities from the ancient civilizations of the Nile, Humboldt was climbing South America's highest peaks and marveling at the similarities between the cultures of America and the classical world: "A people who regulated its festivals according to the motion of the stars, and who engraved its *fasti* [days of ritual celebration] on a public monument, had no doubt reached a degree of civilization superior to that which has been allowed by . . . the most judicious of the historians of America."[6]

The battle lines were drawn. For many the archaeological artifacts—the crude tools, savage arms, and grotesque idols assembled by the collectors of antiquity—only reinforced the theory that all these cultures, unlike that of the conqueror, never raised themselves up into that higher echelon we call civilization. On the other hand, if people were found living in savagery, maybe it was only "because they had degenerated from an originally higher culture which had been conferred upon man by 'divine intervention,'" as Richard Whately, archbishop of Dublin, lectured in 1854.[7] How else could one account for the barbarous condition of the people of Peru and Mexico the conquistadores had confronted? Left to itself the world does not progress; it remains stagnant or degenerates. As the nineteenth-century anthropologist Edward Tylor would put it, in defiance of any concept of pluralism all cultures progress (or fail to progress) up a stepwise hierarchy of values through savagery and barbarism to civilization. Race and culture were linked by the rungs of the ladder of achievement.

Can we really blame our predecessors for looking to the Middle East for the origins of the native North and South American tribes? After all, Hebrew ethnology as revealed in the Old Testament was the only primitive way of life known to early nineteenth-century readers. What travelers and collectors saw in South America was only a natural, undeveloped version of ourselves, the way we were. Tylor's influential works *Researches into the Early History of Mankind* and *Primitive Culture* appeared within the same decade as Darwin's *The Origin of Species* and *The Descent of Man*. These books were weapons in the great debate about how both biological and social life developed. Tylor's natural law of progress became the social analog of Darwin's natural selection by human adaptation. For Tylor, the history of man was simply a chapter in the history of nature.

For others, Humboldt's findings seemed at odds with this depiction of native peoples as savage or barbarian. How to explain the spectacular architecture we find at Tiahuanaco—surely not by invoking inferior, uncivilized Andean people to build it? According to one version of the myth of Con-Titsi (Kon-Tiki) Viracocha told to the Spanish chroniclers, the world was created at the great ruin near Lake Titicaca's shore by a bearded white god of that name. There a master race developed and used its superior skills to subdue all other peoples, thus spreading its culture throughout the Americas.

In 1841 the travel narrative *Incidents of Travel in Central America,* by diplomat-explorer John Lloyd Stephens, topped America's best-seller charts. E. G. Squier's *Peru: Incidents of Travel and Exploration in the Land of the Incas* (1877) would be its belated South American equal, both in picture (see Figure 26) and narrative. Ephraim George Squier was a tireless traveler and a prolific writer. He started as a newspaper editor in Ohio in the early 1840's. Fascinated by the Indian earthworks at Newark and Chillicothe in his own back yard, he began to take up archaeology as a serious avocation. By the end of the decade he had produced an impressive volume, *Ancient Monuments of the Mississippi Valley,* the first publication of the newly founded Smithsonian Institution. Squier followed that in 1852 with *Nicaragua: Its People, Scenery, Monuments,* also based on firsthand contact.[8] W. H. Prescott, author of the then most celebrated work on the history of Peru, urged Squier to visit and chart the many unexplored sites of Latin America, something the proper Bostonian armchair historian had never been able to do himself.

Like the Stephens work, Squier's Peru volume followed from his appointment as a U.S. government official, purchasing agent to Peru. He began his work at coastal Pachacamac shortly after arrival in nearby Callao, the port of Lima. Though he did map part of the enormous walled city of Chan Chan (then called Chimú) on the north coast, most of the rest of his account focuses on the great highland

Figure 26. Hiram Bingham, discoverer of Machu Picchu, was first attracted to Peru's lost cities by romantic views such as this rope bridge over the Apurímac River. For nearly three centuries after the conquest and colonization of South America, few outsiders visited the ancient sites or wrote about the cultures, until the early archaeological explorations of E. G. Squier and others in the 1870's. From E. G. Squier, *Peru: Incidents of Travel and Exploration in the Land of the Incas* (New York: Harper, 1877).

sites. Making his way by boat from port to port down the south coast to Arequipa, prior to ascending the high cordilleras on the way to Tiahuanaco and Cuzco, he glided by the Nasca region (which lies several miles from the coast) with nary a mention of an archaeological feature, much less any geoglyphs. Squier does speak of the lush Pisco and Cañete valleys to the north and Tacna, now near the Chilean border, to the south; he writes only of the endless crescent-shaped, ever-shifting *medanos* (sand hills) and the "skeletons of men, horses, and mules that had perished on the way."[9]

You can tell a lot about what is on people's minds by what they read. A century and a half ago, pop culture was tuned in to travel and adventure narrative. The Louisiana Purchase had more than doubled the area of the continental United States, the Lewis and Clark expedition mapped out the Oregon Trail, and the California gold rush was imminent. The Erie Canal, which had opened wide in 1825, provided the major west-to-east conduit for all marketable goods emanating from the heart of the continent. (It would help make New York City the financial capital of the world.) Navigated the other way, the canal would also

Seeing Is Believing

serve as the great route out of persecution for New England's religious dissidents, general seekers of fortune, and that handful of oddball collectors, adventurers, and searchers of an exalted past. Beyond Ohio and Illinois lay the crumbled adobe remains of the Anasazi of southern Colorado, Utah, Arizona, and northern New Mexico. The ruins of Mexico's Teotihuacan, with its great pyramids of the Sun and Moon, resided farther south in the sunny Sierra Madres. Just about as far as one could get from staid and settled New England lay the remains of one of the rare high civilizations of the world, the hidden cities of the Inca of Peru.

Lost tribes and lost cities—ideas about how they originated and why they vanished would continue to mesmerize not only the adventure reader but also the miller who would provide them their literary grist, the full-fledged archaeological expedition leader. One of the world's great treasure hunts took place in Peru at the turn of the twentieth century. Maybe I'm just a biased Americanist, but I believe the story of Peru's most famous lost city and the career of the daring expedition leader who found it ranks with Howard Carter's unearthing of King Tut's tomb in 1922. The discovery of spectacular Machu Picchu begins with a story told by the chroniclers about the last descendants of Inca royalty who hid

Figure 27. Connected to Cuzco by the Inca trail (a remnant of an old Inca road), Machu Picchu, with its famous sun pillar, is today's number-one tourist attraction in the Andes. Photo by Lorraine Aveni.

out in the wilds of the Andes three decades after the fall of Cuzco, the conquistadores in hot pursuit. Early Spanish visitors had told of a secret location named Vilcabamba, where King Titu Cusi built a sanctuary and pleasure dome. There he remained in seclusion for several years before the Spaniards finally subdued and executed him. Vilcabamba was never visited or destroyed by the Spaniards, but it was condemned by the chroniclers as the "University of Idolatry," where professors of sorcery and masters of abomination yet preached (Figure 27).

The story of the lost city attracted the attention of Yale professor of history Hiram Bingham. Born in 1875, he had learned mountaineering at an early age. His interest in Latin American history took him to Colombia, where he traveled the route of Simon Bolívar. Then it was on to Lima, where the Inca captivated his attention. He had read every word of Squier, particularly his fascinating descriptions of the rope bridges that spanned the intermontane chasms. His appointment at Yale gave Bingham ready access to funding for expeditions to a number of Inca sites, but it was the mystery of this particular lost city that would occupy almost all of his attention for the better part of the three years that led up to its dramatic discovery in 1911.[10]

Bingham had also read of Antonio de Calancha's 1639 description of the lost city, of its magnificent Temple of the Sun, its sanctuary and cave burials, and the Inca road that led to it. Once the city had been built, the Inca fled Cuzco, taking the best of the golden sun images with them to their new capital in the province of Vilcabamba. "It is a hot country of the Andes . . . mountainous [and including] parts that are very cold, intemperate bleak uplands." The landscape's hills are of silver, "and it produces gold of which in those days much was found. . . . It is a land of moderate comfort, large rivers and almost ordinary rains," wrote one chronicler.[11] Piecing together such tantalizing clues from the old documents, Bingham was wise enough to ally himself with local treasure hunters who possessed a working knowledge of the landscape and good contact with the people. He successfully sought the assistance of the National Geographic Society to mount a series of expeditions to find the legendary royal highway.

In *Lost City of the Incas*, Bingham proves that nobody chronicles the excitement of discovery better than the discoverer himself. He climbs the craggy 9,000-foot mountain, today called Huayna Picchu, in an oxbow of the Urubamba River 30 miles northwest of Cuzco, peeks over the top, and marvels at the panorama before him: "Suddenly I found myself confronted with the walls of ruined houses built of the finest quality of Inca stone work. . . . they were partly covered with trees and moss, the growth of centuries, . . . hiding in bamboo thickets and tangled vines. . . . Hardly had we . . . rounded the promontory than we were confronted with an unexpected sight, a great flight of beautifully constructed stone-faced terraces, perhaps a hundred of them, each hundreds of feet long and ten feet high."[12] What could this place be? The opportunistic academic-turned-explorer unswervingly answers his own question. Machu Picchu was the original city of Vilcabamba, the last residence of the Inca emperors, and its architecture surpassed even that of Cuzco.

Today nobody questions that Bingham found a hidden city. Despite being walked over by thousands of tourists annually, Machu Picchu is still regarded as one of the most marvelously preserved ruins in all the Americas, even if its grand-scale architecture falls short of what once was Cuzco's (most of the latter has now been demolished), but whether it was *the* city of which the chroniclers spoke (and which later became lost to history) we cannot be sure, for others have since been uncovered.[13]

Later Bingham did manage to find a secret Inca road into Machu Picchu from the plundered capital of Cuzco. The Incas in fact had set up an elaborate system of stone-paved roads between the Urubamba and Apurímac river valleys where the city lay. Today the road between Cuzco and Machu Picchu has become the popular backpacker's Inca Trail (last year 40,000 tourists walked it). One can still visit its *tampu* (tambo), or masonry terraced resting places overlooking the scenic panorama.

Exploring the highways on the coast would come later. There were, after all, fewer obvious pyramids or temples. Nor were there many impressive mountains for an adventurer to climb, only a dry desert with scarcely a sign of habitation upon it. Archaeologist Max Uhle didn't put his spade into the turf of Pachacamac, the great coastal oracle, until 1896, but when he finally did, he was astonished to find signs of occupation beneath layers of Inca remains. Yes, there *were* people on the coast before the Inca, and Uhle's ceramic detective work would lead him along trails up and down the coast to the sites of the Moche Valley north of Lima as well as to the desert cemeteries of the Nasca and Ica valleys to the south. Uhle dug up quipus, textiles, mummies, ceramics, but even he failed to mention a single Nasca line or figure.

The corregidor of Rucanas, in Andamarca, 250 miles northeast of Nasca, had already written in 1586 that people living on the coast before the Incas had built roads that could still be seen as "narrow as a street and bordered by low walls,"[14] but the first modern description of an ancient coastal road crossing the pampa of Nasca that I could come across was produced about a generation after Uhle, in 1924, in the writings of Alfred Louis Kroeber, an archaeologist at the University of California. Kroeber first recognized what we would help establish definitively over half a century later at Nasca, that many of the modern-day roads are built upon their prehistoric ancestors:

> The road between the Jequetepeque and Saña valleys follows and in part runs over a prehistoric road. One hears much of Inca roads in Peru; but in the coast area their authentic remains are scarce. In the interior, according to all accounts, they are better preserved. The Pueblo Nuevo–Saña road is the only one I have myself observed which is indubitably pre-Spanish. *There is one which is probably prehistoric between Ocucaje and Huayurí, connecting the Ica and Río Grande drainage. This passes across a wide, nearly level, desert pampa, and is marked by a border of stones taken out of the broad roadbed.* It has been traversed by countless burro trains and more recently by automobiles, so that its ancient condition is difficult to judge.[15] [Emphasis added]

This is without a doubt the bright white streak visible in Figure 2, but it is not a Nasca line.

The Pampa Becomes a Blackboard

> Our plane vibrated threateningly, buffeted by winds churned by the early-morning air of the Andes. Jungle-covered slopes flanked the aircraft, as the pilot almost magically held the plane midway between the valley's sides—mindful that frequent down drafts could suck us into a mountain if we strayed too far off the median. . . . what I was seeing below me was so fantastic that I was instantly hooked on flying and aerial photography. I've been to Nasca so many times since then, always coming out of the sky, that the locals have nicknamed me E.T. They wonder why this smiling, tall, blue-eyed woman keeps returning. It's really very simple: I return there as if to an old friend.[16]

Marilyn Bridges, an award-winning landscape aerial photographer, uses images more than words to express what the Nasca experience is like when viewed from above (see the frontispiece for a sample of her beautiful artwork). Today any visitor to the pampa can acquire her perspective. Ante up $60 or so to one of the private local airlines, Aerocondor or Aeroica, in exchange for a harrowing half-hour ride in a Cessna piloted by a daredevil, macho individual unafraid to dive-bomb a condor or fake a trapezoid landing or two (for a tip). Warning: do not attempt this thrilling trip after a heavy lunch.

The popular conception is that the Nasca lines were meant to be seen from the air. In fact, their revelation to the outside world as lines originated in an airplane. I've been unable to trace that discovery to a particular individual, but when the first commercial companies, Faucett and Panagra, initiated service over

87

Seeing Is Believing

the mountains in the late twenties, a number of pilots remarked that they noticed lines on the desert floor. In 1931, nearly 60 years before Bridges, the geologist Robert Shippee and navy pilot and aerial photographer George Johnson made the first aerial survey of Peruvian archaeological sites. The materials they gathered inspired Paul Kosok, a Long Island University historian imbued with a passion both for Peru and for the lens that hovered over it. He wrote in the early fifties: "Aerial Photography! This new technique has become a wonderful tool in reconstructing the past. Indeed, it has raised archaeology to a new level. By a kind of preliminary 'armchair exploration,' many unknown ancient sites, whose discovery by conventional field methods would often take considerable time and tremendous physical effort, can now be located easily and rapidly. But more important, aerial photography makes it possible to obtain almost at a glance, a comprehensive and dramatic picture of the archaeological remains of a valley as a whole!"[17] These words open the section of a book that would become the defining document on the meaning of the Nasca lines for the second half of the twentieth century. But let's not get ahead of our story.

The lines had already been rediscovered at ground level a few years before they were sighted from above. As mentioned earlier, much of the credit goes to Toribio Mejía Xesspe, of the first school of native archaeologists reared on Peruvian soil. Mejía was a disciple of Julio C. Tello. Harvard trained in archaeology, Tello had followed Max Uhle's lead in tracking down the history of the pre-Inca people of the south coast. His ambition, energy, and charisma attracted a cadre of bright students to a dig he had been helping to coordinate with the young American archaeologist Alfred Kroeber in the fall of 1926 at one of the many burial sites, a place called Cantalloc, near Cahuachi on the Nasca drainage basin adjacent to the pampa. According to one story, Kroeber and Mejía ascended to a high dune for a better view. When they turned their gaze 180 degrees onto the pampa, they spotted the desert markings.

A walk on the pampa gives a very different impression from an aerial view. It inspires different ideas too. Being well read, young Toribio remembered the comment of the corregidor of Rucanas y Soras about prehistoric roads on the coast. In his spare time, he decided to return alone and do some surveying. Mejía's first inclination was to connect concentrations of lines with cemeteries at the pampa's edge. Evidently he was also familiar with chronicler Bernabe Cobo's description of the ceque system of Cuzco, for he referred to the Nasca lines as "seqes," and it wasn't long before he reached the conclusion that somebody once walked the lines. They were probably sacred pathways ("caminos religiosos," he called them) associated with worship and sacrifice to a cult of the dead. At least that is what he wrote in an obscure but important report in 1927.[18] His opinion didn't attain wide circulation until it was read at an international conference held at Lima more than a dozen years later and published in its proceedings a year after that. Mejía says nothing of animal figures in his report, only the straight lines.

Though he made no extensive study, it is young Kroeber who gets credit for the first written deposition on these curious features. In a 1926 report, Kroeber gives this remarkably insightful description of what are unmistakably Nasca lines:

> There are a half-dozen *caminos del Inca*, or "ray roads," in the quebrada, mostly running out from near the southmost point; several more between rocky points in the quebrada next northeast of La Calera . . . and about eleven radiating out from an islandlike rocky knoll 3–4 m high situated northeast of the northeast point of La Calera. . . . These roads stretch across the open pampa, at most running a little up the lowest slopes of the hills. One end regularly points to a knoll, hill, promontory, pass or other landmark . . . ; the other end may do the same or lose itself on the plain. The roads are 3–4 m wide and are made merely by removing all the larger stones from the surface. They make excellent motorways over the pampa, where not subsequently dissected by washes, but are generally not so used because they lead nowhere. Purpose: religious processions or games?[19]

Not only did the perspicacious Kroeber recognize the radial patterns we would later map, but he also produced two maps and two photos, labeling them "Ancient Paths," and made extensive observations of the underground aqueducts or filtration galleries.

By the late thirties, when aviators revealed that the pampas all the way up the coast harbored faint remnants of lines, the Nasca phenomenon began to attract wider attention. Geoffrey Bushnell, curator of archaeology at Cambridge University's museum and the author of a number of archaeology textbooks, said this about the Nasca curiosity in 1939: "Whatever the explanation, the setting out and execution of these perfectly straight lines and other figures must have required a great deal of skill and not a little disciplined labor."[20]

Hans Horkheimer, a Peruvian historian at the University of Trujillo, independently reached a similar conclusion in the mid-forties. He was first attracted to the lines when he sighted them from a plane in 1945 while returning home to the north coast from a meeting in Chile. The professor would spend more than two months on and about the pampa. He was particularly intrigued by the giant trapezoids; he called them "plazoletas," or "little plazas," concurring with Bushnell that they were constructed "con precisión estupenda" ("with amazing precision").[21] Tapered figures like the triangle, he reasoned, would have been the natural form that best fit a landscape contoured by stream systems with many tributaries. This was the ideal contour that would allow the geometry to converge at a single point, as illustrated in Figure 22 (after one of his drawings). The trapezoids he saw as places for people to walk along, to convene or assemble, for sacred re-unions with cults of the dead. (Persis Clarkson's pampa survey would later reveal that what Horkheimer considered to be tombs were actually cairns or rock piles devoid of any human remains.) Reaching farther, Horkheimer speculated that different groups met on different trapezoids depending on who their ancestors were. What about the narrow lines that feed into the geometrical figures? These, he theorized, were genealogical lines that provided information about the origin and kinship among the various cults that were united on the plazoletas.

Unlike Kroeber and Mejía, the doctor from Trujillo, who came to the pampa nearly 20 years later, does seem to have been well acquainted with the animal figures, and he offers a similar ground-level explanation for them too. They were made to be danced on, paraded over, he says. Ancient Nascas choreographed sacred dances on the figures in connection with the worship of the dead. Even if there was little evidence to support them, I think Horkheimer's imaginative ideas hold some substance. His combination of religious and social function together with practical considerations about the landscape would be further developed 40 years later by Gary Urton and others.

Were the Nasca lines meant to be viewed from the sky by the gods, or were they intended to be walked upon on the ground by the people? Aerial versus terrestrial theories, the former popular, the latter scarcely known outside academic circles in Peru: that is where things stood in the forties, but the aerial theory would balloon out of proportion, not to be deflated in the slightest until 50 years later. The celebrated Chapter 6 of Paul Kosok's magnificent oversized picturebook *Life, Land, and Water in Ancient Peru* would emerge as Air Nasca's bible.

Paul Kosok was a man with multiple interests. Trained as a historian, he had also educated himself in archaeology, even acquired skills as a musician and conductor. Kosok's major interest in Peru was water, systems of irrigation to be specific. He was on a year's leave of absence from Long Island University to pursue his study when he heard about the long straight lines. In June 1941, Kosok and his second wife, Rose, diverted and took a trip to Nasca. What Mejía viewed as religious roads, Kosok, with "water on the brain," took to be irrigation channels. Then a chance occurrence out in midpampa suddenly gave him reason to change his mind: "While investigating this region in 1941, I was suddenly struck with the thought that these remains could have had some connection with early calendrical and astronomical observations."[22] He documented this lightning flash of intuition with a photo allegedly taken by him showing a straight line leading directly to the setting sun (Figure 28). The date was June 21, winter's first day in the southern hemisphere. "What a great thrill—we realized at once that we had apparently found the key to the riddle."[23] I vividly recall quoting this famous statement and showing the picture in a lecture on our preliminary fieldwork at Nasca that I delivered at the American Museum of Natural History in New York in 1987. After the question-and-answer session, a well-attired, handsome, elderly

Figure 28. The largest astronomy book in the world? This "eureka" photo, made by the Kosoks in the early forties, shows the sun setting along one of the Nasca lines on the June solstice. "What a great thrill—we realized at once that we had apparently found the key to the riddle," wrote Paul Kosok.

woman approached the podium and commented, "That was an interesting talk, but you made one error." And what is that, I asked. "That picture," she replied, "Paul didn't take it; I did." And who are you, I inquired in surprise. "I'm Rose Kosok, his ex-wife."

Kosok aptly titled that seminal chapter in *Life, Land, and Water* "The Largest Astronomy Book in the World." It launched the celebrated astronomical theory for the origin of the lines. There he explains how the lines formed a giant calendar by pointing to important astronomical positions of the sun at the horizon. It is hard to know what previous considerations had led him to this perspective of the pampa as a gigantic slate replete with calendrical viewing instructions. (He does refer in his book to Sir Norman Lockyer's work at Stonehenge, which had been published in 1906. By positing astronomical alignments at Stonehenge, Lockyer was the first astronomer to cross the disciplinary dividing line into the realm of archaeology.) Kosok even goes as far as expressing an interest in the possibility of dating the lines by observing the long-term shift in the position of stars at the horizon until they line up with the geoglyphs, another idea pioneered by Lockyer, but not without harsh criticism from the archaeologists of his day.

Seek and ye shall find. Returning to the pampa, Kosok discovered more celestial alignments, though he isn't very systematic about telling his readers where: "A number of the lines and roads were found to have a solstitial direction: A few with equinoctial direction could also be identified. Moreover, various alignments were found to be repeated in many different places."[24]

Where would such an elaborate scheme about precise timekeeping fit into an ancient pre-Inca culture on the south coast? What ends would it serve? These are the archaeologists' questions, and Kosok gave cultural justification for the astronomical hypothesis by explaining, in the style of the times, the social developments he believed might have taken place during the earliest periods of Nasca occupation. These people had developed an advanced agricultural system that transformed their loosely organized tribal society into a highly efficient, complex civilization, he argues. To them, the heavens directed the seasons and controlled the earth. A sophisticated, precise science would have to be developed everywhere in the world where people recognized the correlation between the timing of objects that move in the heavens above and more tangible, seminal natural events here on earth below, like the stop and go of water flow in the agricultural environment surrounding the pampa. The specialty associated with determining the precise nature of this correlation fell to the astronomer-priest class. The seasonal dates that could be determined by the celestial directions set out by the lines were part of the storehouse of knowledge written in the great astronomy text on the pampa.

At this point Kosok's story includes a dark motive that provided the scientific elite with an advantage over the rest of society: "This combination of truth and ignorance, of scientific honesty and social deceit, gave the priest a tremendous control of the people,"[25] for only the priests were fully aware of the forces that controlled human destiny. Like the Maya, who devised a complex, esoteric calendar, the precocious astronomer-priests of Nasca went far beyond the needs of the people. This tale of a power-hungry elite who hoodwink an unthinking public is familiar in Hollywood portrayals of evil empires and their uses of science. I think it stems from a popular tendency, since the Industrial Revolution, to harbor a mistrust for science and technology. Unfortunately, there is nothing in the story told by Kosok that can be identified with any facts at hand about the cultures of coastal peoples. He was merely following a maxim Humboldt had written down a century earlier: "The power of a class of society is often founded in the ignorance of the other classes."[26] For Kosok, all people with the same cultural antecedents basically responded in like manner to similar natural and social environments. So an irrigation-based society in South America would behave no differently from one in the Middle East. Sounds simple, and it is.

To make matters worse, Kosok offers little systematic evidence specifically to support his astronomical-orientation hypothesis. Evidently he did take the trouble to list the most likely sun, moon, planet, and star alignments that might have been recorded, and in several instances he does tell us that he took compass readings of several line directions, but he never deals with the question of why people would bother to make odd geoglyphs hundreds of yards, even miles long. Why make avenues wider than a football field just to point out the sun, and why lay the whole project out on, of all places, a foggy desert where spectacular sunsets are the exception rather than the rule? These intriguing questions would be passed on to Kosok's enigmatic disciple and defender, an iron-willed person who had not a fiber of enthusiasm less than her mentor and who would catapult Kosok's astronomy book into the limelight of world-class ancient mysteries, and would do it on a shoestring.

Queen of the Pampa

If Paul Kosok's tome was the great canon of the Air Nasca theory—the idea that the lines have to do with things above—its missionary was an eccentric, charismatic German known to many as the ultimate authority on the pampa, Maria Reiche. Though Reiche wouldn't walk Nasca's deserts until years later, she already knew Peru quite well. An athletic and adventurous loner, she escaped Germany at the age of 29 on the eve of Hitler's Third Reich by answering an ad for a governess in the house of a German consul in Peru. There Reiche acquired jobs teaching and tutoring, then translating technical publications from German to Spanish in Lima's National Museum. Trained in mathematics and fairly knowledgeable about astronomy, she was distinctly familiar with a popular book by her countryman Rolf Müller that dealt with theories of building alignments around the world, including orientations to the sun in ancient Peru. Müller had theorized that the *intihuatanas,* carved miniatures in the shape of vertical pillars made of solid rock (like the one in Figure 27), functioned as sundials. Reiche comments:

> This article roused my interest in the astronomy of the ancient Peruvians and I began to examine some of the ruins and stone structures of the Incas, and their predecessors, many of which were probably built for observation of the heavenly bodies and the fixing of important dates throughout the year. When later I came to the coast, I abandoned this study. I did not imagine then, that it would be near the coast that the most important astronomical monument of Peru and perhaps the world would be found.[27]

Part-time work cataloging Paracas mummies under Julio Tello's supervision soon attracted the venturesome foreigner to the south coast. In 1939 Toribio Mejía took Reiche along on one of his field trips to the pampa. The effect was magical: "The Peruvian earth has put its spell on me," she wrote.[28] "There is nothing but sand, nothing alive, no plants, no birds, no sound—nothing but an immense silence and solitude."[29] The solitary demeanor Reiche would maintain throughout most of her long life was a perfect fit to such an environment. When the wiry tutor-turned-explorer encountered Paul Kosok in 1941 and learned of his discovery of a Nasca line that pointed to the winter solstice sunset, she realized the possibility of packing all her interests—antiquity, mathematics, and astronomy—into one basket.

With modest funds from Kosok she departed for Nasca late that fall. Barely 40 years old and marvelously fit, she looked forward to discovering many solstice pointers by roaming the rugged pampa. Except for sporadic sojourns into the outside world and a brief period of restricted travel during the war years, Reiche would spend practically all of her waking hours attempting to decipher the world's largest astronomy book. At first she lived a hermit's life in an outbuilding of a small hacienda at the side of the Pan-American Highway, spending her days hiking over the pampa, recording, measuring, and clearing every figure she saw. In the dimly lit evenings she would make notes and construct maps and charts. A year after instituting her rigorous regimen, she claimed to have run across at least eleven more solstitial lines.[30] Sun lines led to moon alignments and finally to geoglyphs aligned with the stars.

A shy and withdrawn person by nature, Reiche nevertheless always managed to turn a flirtatious eye toward the media. Biographer Tony Morrison attributes the popular appeal of the idea of ancient mathematician astronomers launched over lining up pampa sunsets to Reiche's frequent newspaper articles and letters to the editor in *El Comercio* and *Noticias,* Lima's biggest and Nasca's only newspapers, respectively. "Interesting archaeological revelation discovered by Miss Reiche," reads one; "One day we expect to decipher the puzzle—if God so wishes," quotes another; "This building was one of the finest testimonies of the ancient astronomers," says a third.[31] Reiche seems to have been cultivating herself as an archetype, the indefatigable woman of science rediscovering herself by unveiling the existence of bygone practitioners of her very own skill. You find yourself in the minds of those you conjure, then you dissect and examine them. In effect, you discover yourself through their accomplishments. This is a theme that resonates throughout the history of the study of ancient culture, and it is particularly prevalent at Nasca.

Kosok's articles in popular magazines of the late forties, among them *Life, Natural History,* and *Archaeology,* fueled public interest in the mystery on the desert, which in turn helped to raise funds for more survey work. Reiche acquired the use of an old truck and, now becoming a person of influence, she persuaded the government to take aerial photos of the pampa.

Reiche didn't have the pampa all to herself. Alberto Rossel Castro, a local Nasca priest who had done some surveying of his own en route to advancing Horkheimer's kinship theory, was critical of Reiche's field methods; she was changing many of the indigenous names of places and thereby altering local history. On why the lines were built, Padre Alberto ended up taking a position midway between Maria Reiche and Hans Horkheimer. Even if some of the lines were astronomically oriented, he regarded the Nasca lines as an archaeological more than an astronomical monument. He also contended that some of the lines were remnants of cultivated fields, an idea that has never been borne out by the archaeological evidence.

Josué Lancho, headmaster of a local school, also had long expressed a quiet skepticism concerning Reiche's theories about ancient astronomers on the pampa. His polite, gentlemanly nature, coupled with little interest in the limelight, had prompted him not to speak out, especially when his famous ideological competitor resided but a few doors away. "Why look for anything complicated," he once confided to Tony Morrison.[32] Unlike Reiche, Lancho had always thought every construction out on the pampa was technologically uncomplicated. Everything could have been eyeballed and executed with poles and ropes. He even proved it with a group of his students, who constructed their own lines using only the simplest equipment.[33] Lancho also claims to have found a number of lines that terminated in water sources. Could the lines have been made to walk upon to induce the water god, to persuade him to allow their canals to run with the precious liquid of life, he wondered. Our own studies would later support many of Lancho's findings about the watery connection.

Given the time Reiche spent out on the pampa, the amount of material available in print under her authorship is remarkably scant. Her best-known work dwells mostly on the description, care, and preservation of the figures (particularly on the plant and animal etchings). Critics have been quick to point out that her attack on the problem of the origin and meaning of the lines is undisciplined and speculative when taken in the context of what we actually know about Andean culture, both then and now.[34]

Picking up ideologically where Kosok left off, Reiche pushed the idea that any agrarian people living in an arid climate would surely need a precise calendar. Anxious anticipation of the rainy season in the mountains that would result in the flow of water in the rivers that led to the coast "must have reached to almost a state of fear," she wrote. "To overcome this uncertainty, no effort would be too great . . . and those who were able to calculate the time, must have attained power and respect among their fellow citizens."[35] Curiously, Reiche didn't bolster this hypothesis by pointing out that local economies surely must have been delicately tuned to the contrasting ecologies of the coast and the high Andes, which border on one another in the relatively narrow zone of the south coastal desert in the Nasca area. Maria never focused much on the remains left by ordinary people, and I think her thoughts never really de-escalated from the high-minded world of the archaic Einsteins she fabricated to build the observatory on the pampa.

Reiche's biggest contribution concerned not the lines but the figural drawings. Ever since Paul and Rose Kosok traced out the first one (a pattern of complex, fingerlike projections protruding from the corner of a trapezoid just off the edge of the pampa near the town of Llipata, north of the Ingenio Valley), nobody really had an explanation for them. What they portrayed she did not know, Reiche admitted when she first wrote about the astronomical significance of the animal figures in 1958. She speculated that the monkey figure resembled the arrangement of stars in the constellations of Leo, Leo Minor, and Ursa Major. For Reiche, the spiral-tailed creature is part of a star map on the pampa connected to the ancient seasonal calendar. Furthermore, an accompanying drawing suggests that both lines that leave and enter the monkey terminate at the base of a thin trapezoid 180 yards long, which is intersected by sixteen parallel zigzags. These zigzags and the trapezoid cross at an angle that Reiche claims is perfectly symmetric about the local north-south meridian. That means these two directions could have been employed to mark the rising and setting points of the same stars. Now, since the north star, the northern pivot of celestial motion, isn't marked by any lines, these directions also could have been used by locals to fix true north. Maybe it was this coincidence that led Reiche to compare the figure of the monkey with a prominent configuration of stars in the northern sky, the Big Dipper. The stars of the handle form the monkey's arms while those of the minor constellation of Canes Venatici represent the head, and Leo and Leo Minor make up the tail. Following this sinuous logic, I made an honest effort to superpose the relative positions of these stars from a sky map upon the monkey figure. I found that although the stars (many of them extremely faint) do fall in the general locations she indicates, any resemblance to the actual monkey figure seemed fanciful.

More constellation identifications: the bird with the long neck pointed "in the solstice direction," according to Reiche;[36] the hummingbird aligned with the December solstice sunrise; and the spider, she believed, was ancient Nasca's analog of our celestial hunter, Orion. Reiche also tied one of the whale figures to the December solstice sunset, because the sun on that date set over it as viewed from a starlike center that she said was connected directly to the figure by a line.

Today the influence of the Kosok-Reiche astronomical blackboard theory of the Nasca lines remains both deep and widespread. Virtually every work dealing with Nasca since Kosok's day has at least alluded to a possible astronomical function for the lines, and many authors uncritically accept the hypothesis as proven.[37] Reiche's astronomical theories continue to receive little detailed critical assessment. Maybe there is simply something convincing about scientific quantitative arguments cast in print. I have found that even though her astronomical calculations are generally correct, it is difficult to view Reiche's solution to the Nasca puzzle in a positive light. She never clearly states a set of criteria either for selecting the features she measured or for choosing the astronomical phenomena she tries to align with them. Reiche almost totally excludes from her work any evidence that emanates from study of the Nasca culture. She leaves out people and makes no reference to whether the chroniclers or indigenous Peruvians ever mention the existence of such constellations. Indeed there is no study of peasant astronomy I know of that corroborates the existence of any of these constellations. Without appealing to the data of ethnohistory, ethnography, iconography, and archaeology, how can one ever hope to arrive at an explanation that can be tested by reference to observable evidence? How can one say one has completely studied the pampa?

You can't have astronomy without higher mathematics, so say the experts. Maybe this is because we think of geometry and astronomy in the Western scientific sense as purely esoteric pursuits that go together. When Alexander Thom, a professor of engineering at the University of Cardiff in Wales, first began to

Astral Earthworks in North America?

The astronomy-geometry explanation of ancient ruins has enjoyed a reign of popularity in twentieth-century studies of upper North American earthworks, but the evidence usually given to support the astronomical theory can be circumstantial: the images engraved in the earth are large, best viewed from a skyward position, and there are many Indian legends that deal with constellations. Besides, these people frequently turned to the stars for religious inspiration. The Ohio earthworks and the effigy mounds in Wisconsin and elsewhere made in the shapes of snakes, birds, and bears date from the Early to Middle Woodland Period of the Hopewell culture (about the first millennium AD). Some believe they represent constellation patterns in the form of templates over which the actual stars in the sky position themselves at the right time. Thus, the 400-yard counterclockwise bend in the Serpent Mound in Adams County, Ohio, becomes the curve in Ursa Minor's tail, with fixed Polaris representing the egg in the snake's mouth. The same for the Marching Bear Group of effigy mounds on the outskirts of McGregor, Iowa, near the Wisconsin border. The curved line of march of the ten 100-foot-long "animal cracker" figures is basically directed east-west, imitating the flow of star patterns over the top of the pole (especially the constellation of the Great Bear's motion during the summer months). The nearby bird effigies line up with the Cygnus position when Ursa Major is over the pole. (For an elaboration of this idea, see T. Cowan in *Archaeoastronomy in Pre-Columbian America,* ed. A. Aveni, University of Texas Press, 1975, p. 217.)

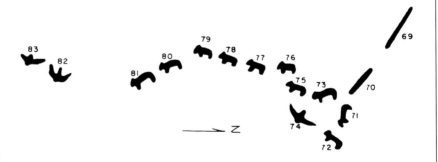

The Marching Bear Group from the Effigy Mounds National Monument in McGregor, Iowa. From *Archaeoastronomy in Pre-Columbian America,* ed. A. Aveni (Austin: University of Texas Press, 1975), p. 217.

study the astronomical alignments of the megaliths in Great Britain in the early fifties, he strongly suspected that the Bronze Age people who built Stonehenge constructed the hundreds of rings of stones on the British Isles and the adjacent continent according to precise geometrical principles. Seeing vestiges of his own engineering skills in his ancient ancestors, he wrote, "They were intensely interested in measurement and attained a proficiency . . . only equalled today by a trained surveyor. They concentrated on geometrical figures which had as many dimensions as possible arranged to be integral multiples of their units of length . . . [and] the basic figure of their geometry, as of ours, was the triangle."[38] Likewise, the geometrical hypothesis for the origin of the Nasca geoglyphs explains that the lines, at least in part, were produced as a cerebral exercise. In both the precise execution of their contours and the exact units of measurement encapsulated within their proportions, the drawings were disguised to reflect a hidden knowledge of geometry.

While engineer Thom rooted out a megalithic yard (about 2.7 of our feet) from his measurements, mathematician Reiche sought a South American unit based on proportions that make up the human body. Leonardo da Vinci would have been pleased, and the idea sounds sensible enough. Our foot, digit, and cubit all originate in the human body. Reiche settled on a standard length of 32.5 cm (about 12.8 inches). She says it was derived by placing a string between the thumb and index finger and extending it to the inner part of the elbow.[39] (I get 34.3 cm for my frame, but then I'm 5 feet 9 inches tall, considerably longer than the typical mummy residing in a circumpampa grave.) Reiche believed that most of the biomorphic figures were reproduced as precise scale models based on multiples (the tenth, twentieth, even thirtieth) of this standard meter stick. How did the ancient Nasca line makers trace the curvy contours? By connecting circular segments of radii that are multiples of the basic unit, laying out each portion by cords tied to stakes at different centers of curvature, but not before the figures were first drawn to scale in chalk on pieces of starched cloth, she speculates.[40]

On our first visit to the pampa in 1977, Tom Zuidema and I were transported three miles from the town of Nasca to the Cantalloc fishing-rod figure (Figure 9). Reiche's brown Volkswagen van had its trunk stuffed with poles, ropes, cords, spools, and a backpack. After displaying her tattered hand-drawn sketch of the figure, a frail Reiche, then in her early seventies, walked us over to the spiral. She drew a ball of cord and a handful of odd-sized screwdrivers from her pack and proceeded to show us how they did it (Figure 13). First she measured a length of cord by holding one end between thumb and index finger and extending it to her elbow. Jabbing a screwdriver into the ground near the center of the figure,

Nasca Blueprints?

The largest figure adorning the miniature pampa Cantalloc is the needle and ball of wool, or fishing rod, as locals variously call it, a thin triangle 1,000 yards long from which a zigzag emanates (Figure 9). It winds its way across the triangle, slicing over it sixteen times before winding up into a double spiral at the broad end. Just how precise is a typical Nasca spiral? To answer our own question, we decided to measure and map this one out. At first glance, the Cantalloc spiral looks rather crude in its construction. It was difficult for me to imagine that the builders could have paid much attention to principles of symmetry or even to the use of precise units of measurement in executing it. But how might they have constructed it? In the first place, the whole arrangement and shape of the spiral seems to be dictated by the natural contour of the relatively flat pampa on which it is situated. If you follow with your eye the continuous line, just over two miles long, that departs from the apex of the thin triangle, you will discover that the zigzag pattern it makes penetrates just to the edge of the pampa where the land slopes steeply into the quebradas on either side. Second, the spiral seems to be made up of straight and circular segments linked together. It looks suspiciously squeezed into an oval shape, with its long axis following the direction of both the immediate landscape and the axis of the triangle. On the west side of the intersecting triangle, there is barely enough room to continue two arms of the spiral. Just twenty yards separate the western edge of the triangle from the precipitous drop-off into the quebrada. (The near ground level view in the photo shows the zigzag feature neatly framed by the quebrada.) All of these observations led me to

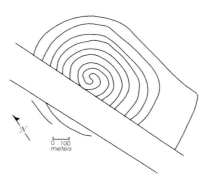

contradict the notion that the dimensions and proportions of the figure were conceived on some sort of blueprint prior to construction and then executed on the pampa. In fact, we can approximate the actual shape of the figure quite well by linking together straight lines and arcs of circles.

From *The Lines of Nazca,* ed. A. Aveni, 1990, courtesy of American Philosophical Society, Memoirs, vol. 183.

she let out a length of cord from its handle. With a second screwdriver attached to the other end of the cord, she scratched out a four- or five-foot arc in the midpath of the spiral until she got slightly off track. Then she pulled a third screwdriver out of the pack, chose another point also near the center, and reinitiated the whole process by plugging that screwdriver into the earth in like manner and tracing out a similarly curved segment beginning where the first arc ended, and so on.

The only problem with this technique is that in order to reproduce a figure, one needs not only to vary the length of the string but also to shift constantly the position from which the arc is swung. Worse still, the width of the arc being duplicated is sometimes wider than the basic measuring unit. To Tom and me, the whole process seemed to exhibit the same arbitrariness as the method elucidated by engineer Thom for constructing the egg-shaped megalithic circles of England and Scotland. As Josué Lancho says, "Why look for anything complicated?"

Later Reiche would devise an imaginative way of combining the astronomical and geometrical secret knowledge hypotheses: the geometry of the spider harbors secret astral information encoded within the numbers that underlie its units of construction![41] For example, she found that the spider's abdomen could be approximated by a dozen linked arc segments whose radii totaled 147.5 meters. This she recognized as a whole multiple of the cycle of phases of the moon (5 times 29.5 days equals 147.5 days). There is no explanation for why this relationship should exist in the first place, much less how this information might have been used by the people who drew the figure. Yet the precision she implies (I think mistakenly) carries with it that sense of awe associated with any mystery that raises such fundamental questions as: How did simple people construct such complex figures? How much work was involved? How was it all planned out? What knowledge of geometry and math did the builders possess? We would offer very different answers from Reiche's—answers that would make us unpopular on the pampa—but not before other equally unpopular outsiders began to poach on Reiche's now well-recognized turf.

The Stonehenge Controversy: Was It a Calendar and an Observatory?

Long before the Nasca lines were erected, Stonehenge was among the most extraordinary prehistoric structures in the world. For over five centuries it has posed a riddle that has yet to be solved. Stonehenge is a circular structure made up of huge standing stones weighing 25 tons or more called megaliths, with hanging stones, or lintels (*henges*), placed across the tops of certain pairs of them, all positioned within a ditch and bank earthwork. It has stood starkly isolated on the barren Salisbury Plain of southern England for 5,000 years. As at Nasca, of all the ideas that have been put forth to explain the purpose of this famous earth and stone work, the hypothesis that it was a calendar and an observatory is by far the most popular, not to mention the most disputed. The main axis of the structure is a dead giveaway. Built early on in the plan, the broad avenue that leads out of the horseshoe-shaped arrangement of the five inner henged stones, or trilithons, is aligned toward the rising sun on the first day of summer. This alignment could have signaled the start of an ancient tradition of marking the beginning of the seasonal cycle by registering the place of the sun at its greatest northerly extension on the horizon, a tradition preserved throughout history, for even today at Stonehenge the sun still keeps its ancient appointment. Astronomer Gerald Hawkins, who studied the ruins closely in the early sixties, claims to have unearthed at Stonehenge other cyclic celestial phenomena that he believed the builders deliberately encoded into the architecture. For example, according to Hawkins, alignments among the

Stonehenge across the Sea

Then what was their purpose? When Tony Morrison, an explorer and BBC photographer, asked Gerald Hawkins that question over lunch in a posh Lima hotel in 1968, the confident British-American had already achieved renown among astronomers (and scorn from archaeologists) for claiming to have deciphered the age-old mystery of Stonehenge in southern England using his high-speed Smithsonian computer. His brief scholarly reports in *Nature* magazine in 1963 were followed by a best-seller, *Stonehenge Decoded,* and a series of TV programs. CBS's *Mystery of Stonehenge* was as popular in America as the BBC's *Chronicle* episode was in the mother country. Here was another archetype of the discoverer: a trained skeptical scientist backed by an institutionally organized expedition (his work was supported by the National Geographic Society) comes to the remote hinterlands to apply the acid test that would be required to admit an

---

station stones (four large boulders that mark the corners of a perfect rectangle situated on the inner periphery of the ditch and bank) not only point to the sun's winter and summer standstills but also mark the extreme position of the full moon (reached every nineteen years). As interpreted by Hawkins, Stonehenge is both an observatory and a calendar for charting the movements of the sun and the moon, even for predicting eclipses: an observatory because someone standing in the correct place within the stone circle could witness time-marking events directly, and a calendar because, like notches on a bone or marks on parchment, the standing stones constitute an unwritten yet indelible record of the flow of natural events and society's activities that keep pace with them. Studies of this architectural wonder of ancient Britain would inspire Nasca decoders more than once.

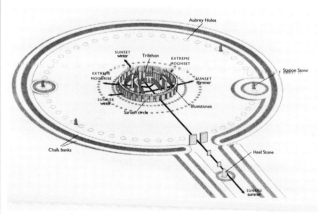

This is what Stonehenge probably looked like during the final stages of construction some 1,200 years after it was initiated, about 2750 BC. Drawing by Robert Paquet in A. Aveni, *Ancient Astronomers* (Montreal and Washington, D.C.: Publications St. Rémy and Smithsonian Institution Press, 1992), p. 28.

unorthodox hypothesis into the hallowed halls of academia. "Science demands proof, and speculation remains speculation until scientists as a whole accept the proof," Hawkins told Morrison.[42]

That Hawkins's path was destined to cross the Nasca lines seemed preordained. As he put it, the markings "offered an opportunity to apply the principles of astroarchaeology to an ancient preliterate construction."[43] Skeptical second-guessers suggested that he went there to bolster his theory that Stonehenge was both a precise astronomical sighting device and a computer for predicting eclipses, by demonstrating that his method, applied elsewhere, was also capable of giving negative results.

Above all, Hawkins needed to lay out a systematic approach to testing the astronomical orientation theory of the lines, something that Reiche had failed to do. He concentrated his efforts on three sample strips of pampa, each 5 yards by 1.2 miles, in the region where the Pan-American Highway approaches the south side of the Ingenio Valley. This is the zone of heaviest concentration of the figural drawings, the place where most of the animals are located. The astronomer undertook six expeditions to this site, for a total of nineteen days spread over twelve months. As I mentioned earlier, one of his expeditions incorporated the first systematic ground survey of pampa remains. Learning from his mistakes at Stonehenge, where he had used unreliable maps, Hawkins commissioned his own aerial survey, which he used to obtain the alignments of 21 trapezoids and 72 linear features centered in the area.[44]

What would Hawkins regard as satisfactory confirmation of the astronomical orientation of the Nasca lines? He tells us in his final report to the National Geographic Society, "We would expect all the lines to be satisfied by some unified postulate such as the rising and setting of the sun and/or moon at key dates in the calendar, or the rising and setting of the brighter stars. . . . no matter what hypothesis is finally adopted, we must expect an almost total explanation for the lines; otherwise, we have the unsatisfactory situation of explaining only part of the construction work and leaving the 'why?' for the remainder of the lines unanswered."[45]

I find it hard to imagine that such a reductive strategy—the single-cause hypothesis that explains everything—could ever yield decisive conclusions about the meaning of the Nasca lines. After all, there is plenty of evidence that astronomy is often a component (rarely the sole factor) in the design of Native American sacred structures. Case in point: the chroniclers are explicit that the ceque system of Cuzco binds together social, economic, and religious as well as calendrical and astronomical dictates in its design and layout. True, some ceque lines, like the ones directed to the December solstice or the antizenith sunset positions, may have served as astronomical sight lines, but others led not to the stars but to mountains, bends in rivers, water sources, and other sacred places in the environment.

The astronomical targets Hawkins chose to test his Nasca alignments included the four sun stations (rising and setting at the summer and winter solstices) and the matching moon standstills (eight as it turns out) used in his original study of Stonehenge.[46] In addition, he also chose the rising and setting points of the 45 brightest stars, and for good measure he threw in the brightest star of the Pleiades, or Seven Sisters, which, though much fainter than the dimmest object in his sample, had an "acknowledged importance in pre-Columbian culture."[47] Clever scientist that he was, Hawkins tried to define his problem so that he could arrive at a yes or no answer to each astronomical question. Were there more hits on the chosen astronomical targets by the alignments than one would expect if the matter were left to pure chance? Answer: No, neither for any time period nor for any combination of targets he selected. Because he found no significant coincidences, Hawkins concluded that the lines "as a whole cannot be explained as astronomical nor are they calendric."[48]

When I first started reading about Nasca, around the time I got involved in our study of the astronomy of Cuzco's ceque lines in the mid-seventies, I realized that there were flaws in Hawkins's study. First, he chose astronomical targets that were significant largely from the perspective of an observer in the high northern latitudes, the same ones he used in the study of Stonehenge, but a skywatcher in the southern hemisphere (especially a tropical one) sees a very different sky. For example, Hawkins didn't include in his selection the rising and setting position of the sun on the day of its passage through zenith and antizenith, a phenomenon that occurs only in the tropics, and he didn't test out the points of intersection of the horizon with the southern Milky Way, along which Andean people named and located an array of dark-cloud and star-to-star constellations to trace what they regard as the celestial continuation of all terrestrial rivers.

To his credit, Hawkins was more systematic than Reiche, but he seemed to be making the same mistake she had made—he was leaving out the people. For example, although he used the solstice dates as possible targets, he never looked at where the sun rose or set on other dates in the seasonal year that might have been of local, say, agricultural importance—like where the sun sets on the dates when water begins to run in the streams. In my opinion, the negative results of this precise statistical survey still couldn't be regarded as the final word on the astronomical significance of the Nasca lines.

How widely news is broadcast has a lot to do with the size of the market it ends up reaching. Hawkins's pampa survey appeared in a relatively obscure scientific report published by the Smithsonian Institution. (Later, when pioneering the new interdiscipline of archaeoastronomy, I invited him to write a short version of his Nasca work for a scholarly book I edited on that subject in 1975.) But Hawkins acquired a champion in journalist and explorer Tony Morrison, who seems to have been the one who initially attracted the celebrated, if controversial, Hawkins to the pampa. Morrison produced a popular book that achieved much wider circulation. His *Pathways to the Gods,* an adventure-filled look at some of the curious characters who came to Nasca, gives us a heavy dose of Hawkins's thinking.

While I have always found Morrison's book a reliable source for general information and references, I felt that it overglamorized the scientific detective work, focusing as much on the sleuth as on his subject. Won over by Hawkins's methods as well as his results, Morrison oddly tags some of the geoglyphs as astronomically oriented by giving them suggestive names, erroneously implying that an astronomically positive solution to the Nasca puzzle has already been reached. For example, he uses bizarre interpretive labels, such as "The Great Rectangle-Plaza of the Pleiades" for a very large trapezoid on the northern edge of the pampa. Evidently Morrison labeled it as such on a copy of Hawkins's map because Hawkins found that the Pleiades aligned with two rock cairns at opposite ends of the figure in AD 600–700. It happens that this date closely matched the radiocarbon date (AD 610) assigned to the remains of a wooden post found nearby. On the same map, adjacent to a triangular extension of another long trapezoid, appear the words "Rising of the Pleiades (610 AD ± 30 years)." Another feature, a series of parallel lines, acquires the sticker "Grid of the Pleiades," and a similar "Grid of the Sun" lies to the east. One edge of the long trapezoid called "Plaza of the Sun" is shown pointing to the rising sun on the June solstice. All of these labels, applied to the chosen few among a number of randomly oriented lines, appear in his popular text without discussion. Anyone but the most cautious reader who looks at these figures would clearly gain the false impression that the case for astronomically oriented Nasca lines has been proven unequivocally. True, Morrison qualifies his opinion in the text by stating, "A few [alignments] were good candidates for sun calendar markers [but] . . . the entire maze was not a vast sun-moon-star calendar," and "Gerald Hawkins had confirmed that the computer results would not support a time-clock-calendar theory."[49] So why the contradiction? Why are we being told two different stories? I don't know, but the outcome has been that for those who fail to read between the lines, astronomy remains firmly entrenched on the pampa, at least in the public eye, and popular works continue to fuel that questionable belief.[50]

The first task I undertook when I began contemplating research at Nasca in the mid-seventies was a thorough review of the literature. As I probed, I was struck by the common characteristic shared by all the astronomical explanations for the Nasca lines. Each investigation seemed to ask the same question: Do the lines point to astronomical phenomena on the horizon? Answer yes or no. Each investigator appeared driven by a method of research that assumed the astronomical problem could be solved in a straightforward manner: choose some astronomical targets (the same list gets trotted out worldwide—solstices, equinoxes, lunar limits, etc.), see whether Nasca lines match these targets, and forget about looking at any other kind of evidence. It was difficult for me to imagine that tackling what seemed a very complex problem in this manner could ever offer anything of lasting substance. One needs to ask, what's the context? Largely culture blind, most investigators consistently avoided any mention of affairs that must have mattered to the ancient Nasca populace, like planting, rainfall, irrigation, and other seasonal or periodic activities that surely would have played major roles in the lives of those born, reared, and deceased generation after generation in the valleys adjacent to the Nasca pampa. But then, maybe these approaches only reflect the highly specialized times in which *we* live. Disconnect the lines from their cultural setting, and they will always remain a mystery, Helaine Silverman once told me. Maybe that's what we want.

The Vulnerable Pampa in the Age of Aquarius

Remember Atlantis? Ups and downs together with a distaste for and distrust of the official historical record formed the base of the Atlantis theory: civilizations come and go on our planet, rising and falling like a ride on a historical roller coaster. In the past we raised ourselves to far loftier heights than we experience in the present. Such was the view toward Atlantis. Just look at Egypt, where art, architecture, and hieroglyphic writing appear unified and full blown, without a hint of development out of a single primitive state, not to mention the Maya, Aztec, and Greek myths all telling of repeated cataclysmic destructions of past worlds.

The real Atlantis (and there may have been many of them around the world) had all the trappings of modern civilization, including electricity and internal-combustion engines. Discontent arose, just as in the modern world, out of factional differences in an economic system run by unregulated big business interests. No wonder lost continents were popular in the days of Rockefeller and Morgan!

At least since the classical age, say Atlantists, we have been riding the downslope, the evil powers in our society destroying and suppressing past knowledge. History is rife with book burning, from ancient China to Greek Alexandria to the destruction of the Maya codices by Spanish conquistadores. Having fallen out of harmony with nature, we are headed for another Armageddon. Learn the lesson of Atlantis, so say the prophets and proponents.

Figure 29. In the late sixties and seventies the pampa became a hot new medium for a host of avant-garde interpretations of what the mysterious Nasca lines were really all about: a New Age Nasca. Photo by Lorraine R. Aveni.

"All the great examples of antiquity . . . served to locate man in the cosmos, both in space and time, bringing knowledge of the heavens to the earth."[51] The ziggurats of Babylon, Egypt's pyramids, Mexico's temples—the measures of each of them, their ratios and their square roots, encapsulated the diameter of the earth, the distance to the moon, the spacing of the planets from the sun, even the basic dimensions of the tiniest atoms. Universal constants like pi and the golden mean, fundamental time units like the length of the month, the year, and the 26,000-year period of the precession of the equinoxes, all the magic numbers that underlie the blueprint of our universe are secretly locked away in the spacings between pyramids. If all of this sounds like a protest emanating from the restless industrialized world of the late eighteenth and early nineteenth centuries—a society dissatisfied with the course of civilization that was led to search for enlightenment by looking backward—guess again. It was the 1960's, the dawning of the Age of Aquarius. This gaze toward the future was wrought from a different set of dissatisfactions; still, the eye had taken on that same decidedly backward cast toward a presumed repository of superior knowledge, and there were plenty of elaborately illustrated, convincing-looking coffee-table books to tempt the public by providing conduits to the fountain of lost knowledge (Figure 29). Ancient remains became the legacy of previous races that once possessed all the knowledge of modern physics, mathematics, and astronomy and were wise enough to encode it into their mammoth architecture for posterity—just for us. Peter Tompkins, who wrote the words that head this paragraph, is among a cadre of popular writers who believe in such lost knowledge.

Where there are leaders there will always be followers. In the wake of Paul Kosok's and Maria Reiche's theories about the great scientific achievement of the Nasca timekeepers, coupled with Tompkins's secret knowledge texts, high-tech fantasizers befitting the age would come to the pampa. Arch diffusionist Maria Scholten d'Ebneth carried the directions and proportions she found in Nasca geometry all the way over the globe to the Andean highlands and beyond, as far as the land of the Maya. The patterns on the Nasca textiles prove that "anthropogeometry" lay at the basis of the Nasca figures, she said, for the proportions of both place the relative locations of Cuzco, Tiahuanaco, and Pachacamac at key points of the design. She even included a map of the Americas to prove it. The Internet has yielded up a wondrous array of Nasca hypotheses that probably tell us more about us than them. For example, there is the story about the group of black slaves who rebelled against Tiahuanaco. Originally Olmecs from Mexico, they stole Viracocha's aircraft (presumed to be a real person, Viracocha is dubbed the original architect of the Nasca lines), flew to Nasca, and became the first vandals on the pampa when they attempted to obliterate his aircraft runways.

The New Age also spawned ingenious high-tech explanations for the Nasca lines. "I know damned well someone flew at Nasca. You simply can't see anything from ground level. You can't appreciate any of it from anywhere but from above," wrote the adventurer Jim Woodman.[52] Remember the Nasca flying creature whose painted image adorns so many late polychrome pots (Figure 17)? Could he be engaged in the very posture necessary to appreciate the Nasca lines?

Might he even be supervising their construction? What convinced Woodman that the Nasca drawings were meant to be seen from the air was a short flight over the pampa in a Cessna in 1973. Like so many before him in this age of customized discovery, Woodman discovered the Nasca lines for himself. All it took for him to conjure up an explanation that suited his own perspective was a strong conviction that all people solve practical problems by developing technological solutions. One way to appreciate a seeming maze of lines that antedated the era of flight, he reasoned, would be to devise a way to float above them in a lighter-than-air craft. His story continues: "I bought a balloon—a sport balloon . . . and got my pilot's license."

Just how did the ancient people of Nasca manage to construct such a device? They used lightweight, tightly woven fabrics, the kind we find in textiles used as body bags at Nasca grave sites, Woodman proposed. Using Thor Heyerdahl's Kon-Tiki method, Woodman set out to prove that if he could do it, then they must have done it too. *Condor One* became the first balloon equal to the task at hand. Woodman and his sponsors, the International Explorers Society of Miami, Florida, crafted it from indigenous materials. The gondola was made of reeds, the balloon's 80-foot-high walls were woven with 185-by-95 threads to the square inch, and it was all laced together by reed cordage.

Woodman was fascinated by what he called burn pits, circular "scorched areas" at the ends of some of the trapezoids. He thought they were remnants of huge fires whose ascending heat columns were once used to power the balloons. That was how Woodman would power his *Condor One*—by holding its 52-foot opening for over four hours above a conduit connected to a roaring fire.

Believe it or not! The expedition was ingenious and the experiment a total success. One would hardly think it possible to inflate 80,000 cubic feet of bag with a smoke fire and then lift a 360-pound load to a height of 400 feet over the pampa and hold it there for two full minutes. Woodman's feat awed even the imperturbable Maria Reiche, who made a rare public appearance for the flight, as the desert aviator triumphantly concluded, "Nasca was not an ancient landing field, it was just the opposite. The lines were takeoff sites for a religion that worshipped the sun. My flight was a modern demonstration of an ancient religious ceremony."[53]

Another practical explanation for the Nasca lines arrived just in time for the 1980 winter Olympics. This bizarre hypothesis was conjured up by the German engineer George von Breunig, and it suited his interests perfectly. Breunig's intuitive flash took shape after he was led by Reiche to the place where she takes all her inquisitors, the zigzag fishing-rod figure on the remote pampa of Cantalloc.

The small stone piles that seemed to mark the places where the zigzags turned immediately grabbed Breunig's eye. This was his impression:

> Looking at the arrangement, people familiar with downhill skiing will immediately think of a slalom race, because the tracks look very similar, with the sole exception that in down-hill skiing wooden poles are used to show the course of the track instead of piles of stones. Thus the piles of stones, when linked with the zigzag configuration, provide reason to think that the configuration might have been used for running events, in which case the piles of stones mark the turning points in the curves. And the use of stones instead of wooden poles is logical, because in this area stones are the only readily available material.[54]

When one needs written support to back up an explanation for a pre-Columbian enigma, one goes to the historical chronicles. Breunig rooted out a host of passages on Inca runners: Cieza de León told of Inca messengers who ran the roads of Peru, and Francisco de Avila remarked on the people of Huarochirí who ran llamas to sacred Pariacaca Mountain to pray. Breunig also cites Garcilaso's description of young Inca nobles who ran from place to place to conduct mountain rituals. The bawdiest of all ancient tales he acquired from an early-twentieth-century bishop of Lima: at the time of the festival of avocado ripening, men and women would strip naked, and when the signal was given the men would chase the women (who were given a head start). Whenever a man caught up with a woman, or so the prelate relates, they would have sex. (I have been unable to corroborate this account.)

The archaeological record does confirm Breunig's general hypothesis about running. Staff-bearing gods that decorate Nasca ceramics and textiles often exhibit running postures. But Breunig converts the different costumes they wore into ancient Olympic T-shirts, each representing a competing team. One amusing pot shows the figure of a man with his tongue hanging out. Your tongue would hang out too if you ran all those figures in the hot tropical sun, retorts Breunig. For this modern Nasca theorist, these scenes were not about religious dancing; they had a more earthly (and earthy) purpose.

Good engineer that he was, Breunig studied the depth profile of the curves along the fishing rod's path. He claimed they were asymmetrical, with a higher bank at the outer edge, particularly at the turns. This is exactly what one would expect on a well-used track, he argued, where dirt gets kicked outward when a runner pivots his foot as he rounds a bend at the sharp angle of a zigzag. (Never mind that hundreds have walked this track since Reiche used it to demonstrate her research techniques.) Just how does one run the Grand Prix of Cantalloc?

Everybody starts at the broad base of the triangle. By the time the first of the runners arrives at the point 800 yards away, the field is spread out into a single line; runners then wind their way through the mazelike zigzag, the entire field ending up at the spiral. The physical and documentary evidence taken together left no doubt, at least in engineer Breunig's mind: the Nasca people were running competitively on the pampa.

Of all that has been written about the pampa, there is one author above all others who eclipses even the revered Santa Maria when it comes to popular recognition. It may come as a surprise that this particular individual spent no more than a few days on the pampa, yet his ideas still resonate throughout pop culture. Erich von Daniken is the archetype of the con man in an age of gullibility, especially when it comes to the interpretation of antiquity. What I find so ingenious about the way the Swiss hotelier turned antiquarian decoder captured the public's fancy is that he offered them an ideal contemporary parallel to the lost-world theories of the nineteenth and early twentieth centuries. What is different is that he seeks the source of higher knowledge in superior aliens far away in space rather than advanced terrestrial civilizations far backward in time—the ancient mysteries monomyth with a clever space-age twist. In his 1968 best-seller, *Chariots of the Gods,* he basically tells us that if it *looks* like an airfield, then it *was* an airfield.[55] Space aliens gave rise to our culture by interbreeding with earthlings. At Nasca they laid out runways on which to taxi in, land, and take off. The natives copied them. They made the lines to induce the extraterrestrials to return, the way the Papuans after World War II created metal birds out of old aircraft parts, cleared and leveled the jungle, and lit it up brightly at night to entice the visitors (American pilots) to come down from the sky, those gods in their flying machines.

Where do the animal geoglyphs fit into Daniken's astronaut scenario? When the gods from space failed to return, the people created the zoomorphs as sacrificial symbols. As proof of the runway hypothesis, Daniken displays a photograph of a turn bay on one of the alien aircraft runways. It turns out to be a 2-yard-wide segment of the condor's legbone (Figure 8*b*).

Defenders of the extraterrestrial hypothesis cite plenty of evidence in literature from around the world to infer that we have been visited by aliens. Ezekiel's vision of the cherubim has been likened by many another writer to the first recorded appearance of a UFO:

> As I looked, behold, a stormy sign came out of the north, and a great cloud, with brightness round about it, and fire flashing forth continually, and in the midst of the fire, as it were gleaming bronze. And from the midst of it came the likeness of

four living creatures. And this was their appearance: they had the form of men, but each had four faces, and each of them had four wings. Their legs were straight, and the soles of their feet were like the sole of a calf's foot; and they sparkled like burnished bronze. Under their wings on their four sides they had human hands. And the four had their faces and their wings thus: the appearance of the wheels and their construction: their appearance was like the gleaming of chrysolite; and the four had the same likeness, their construction being as it were a wheel within a wheel. When they went, they went in any of their four directions without turning as they went. The four wheels had rims and they had spokes; and their rims were full of eyes round about. And when the living creatures went, the wheels went beside them; and when the living creatures rose from the earth, the wheels rose. Wherever the spirit would go, they went, and the wheels rose along.[56]

Daniken cites it too. For him a vision is a vision and the ancient scriptures literally say what they mean.

Archaeologist William Stiebing Jr. thinks Daniken may have pulled heavily on the immensely popular science-fiction film *2001: A Space Odyssey,* which also appeared in 1968.[57] It included technologically advanced aliens whose legacy is confronted by our apelike ancestors. Daniken also took a lead from the then-popular (and recently revived) theory of panspermia, the idea that all humanity arose from life-giving spores that drifted through space and landed on earth millions of years ago.

Without a doubt, Daniken hardened the views of the French adventurer Robert Charroux.[58] He saw the whole pampa as a monumental exercise in the collective unconscious directed upward and far away toward our "Initiators," adding with a twinge of mysticism: "It is logical to assume that those Pre-Incas either were in contact with the Initiators mentioned by tradition or had preserved a memory of them. Thousands of years ago, in obedience to direct orders from the Initiators or for the purpose of perpetuating the teachings they had received in the past, they . . . created the vast page of writing that is Nasca."[59] Because the planet Venus is the companion of the sun god Inti in Andean lore, Charroux deduces that the extraterrestrials are none other than veritable Venusians, and because all great ideas offer an explanation for just about everything, he adds, "On this hypothesis, the drawings of birds at Nasca represented the spacecraft of the gods; the spirals, lines and geometric figures represented their landing installations; the flowers represented an offering; and the animals represented the ritual blood sacrifice that primitive people have always felt they owed to the gods: A form of worship, but also an appeal to the ancient visitors, an invitation for them to return."[60] Like Daniken, Charroux has an explanation for just about every mystery on the face of the earth, from the Turkish Piri Réis map to the Egyptian pyramids. All are products of the great beyond.

What should we make of such grandiose ideas that would have us reach out to other galaxies in search of answers to the Nasca mystery? Historian Jacquetta Hawkes once wrote of Britain's great enigma, "Every age has the Stonehenge it desires—or deserves."[61] She was critical of high-tech scientists, rushing head-long into one of Britain's most ancient monuments, computers in tow, to decode the mystery of Stonehenge without even looking at the archaeological or other cultural evidence. Likewise, in an age of technological achievement and dependence, the public fascination with the more splendid artifacts of ancient man has teased out some rather narrow-minded, present-centered explanations for the Nasca lines. As Daniken put it, "Incredible technical achievements existed in the past. There is a mass of know-how which we have only partially re-discovered today."[62] Like many other popularizers, Daniken assumes that all that lies be-tween us and them is knowledge quite like our own. It has only become lost in time. In the end, I think this direct-pipeline approach to the past is too facile, too superficial, too ego- and ethnocentric to help us understand the meaning of the Nasca lines, for it relies solely on the sphere of experience of the modern world, a world Daniken and Breunig all too willingly project onto the past with-out justification. What compels us to deny the possibility that other civilizations can create ideas we ourselves had never contemplated? Are we so narcissistic that we can admire no motives for collective human action other than the ones that drive us?

Time magazine once declared the mid-seventies "boom times on the psychic frontier."[63] It was all part of the revolt against the materialist-rationalist explana-tion of how the world works, explained the social pundits. Proponents of rejuve-nated Jungian psychology spread about the notion of synchronized events that lay outside the realm of probability. The parasciences gained new respect, course offerings on parapsychology at college campuses around the nation rocketed. Israeli psychic Uri Geller demonstrated the bending of spoons and keys by the force of his own thoughts, psychic surgeons were healing tennis elbow by touch, and a book entitled *The Secret Life of Plants* urged frustrated gardeners to employ mind rather than thumb in order to carry on a meaningful dialogue with their greenery. According to a 1978 survey, the Devil was positioned at 37 percent, angels at 54 percent, on the "I believe" meter. (UFOs led the pack at 57 percent.) More than one in three Americans believed in precognition, and half of the sample polled said that they regarded astrologers as scholars. Contemporary pampa fantasies inject drug use into the story line. This is probably because the coca leaf, from which cocaine is derived, is grown in Peru. (Coca is actually a valuable nutrient in the native culture and is not consumed the way it is in our culture.) Helaine Silverman tells the story of being badgered by a group of documentary film makers to confirm that ancient Nasca shamans once envisioned themselves looking down upon the geoglyphs as they soared over the pampa in drug-induced trances.

By the close of the seventies' "age of gullibility," Reiche was pushing octogenarian status. Nearly crippled by Parkinson's disease, she confined herself to her room at the Hotel de Turistas, making occasional appearances in the lobby to utter her short standard lecture in whispered tones and to sign a few *Mystery on the Desert* books for admiring tourists. By now Reiche was also a superstar. Schools in Nasca closed on her birthday, and her adopted country even honored her with a place on a postage stamp. As a lasting memorial to her achievements, in 1988 some members of the Nasca city council sent a team of workers to lay out a corner of the pampa for a gigantic etching of Reiche's countenance. Under pressure from archaeologists who feared destruction of a national treasure, and after much controversy, the National Institute of Culture intervened, aborted the project, and erased the incomplete figure.[64]

The wizened symbol of authority on the Nasca pampa had weathered all attacks on her theory, from Hawkins's heavy blows on the scientific side to darts wildly cast by purveyors of sixties and seventies pop culture. The Kosok-Reiche explanation for the origin of the lines wore well, and it would continue to live on in print in all the standard textbooks. As late as 1981, the respected Peruvian archaeologist Luis Lumbreras wrote an only slightly more measured response to the astronomical theory in the revised edition of his book compared with what he had penned in the first edition in 1969: "This is not a farfetched hypothesis since astrology everywhere originated during the early stages of agriculture, when the correlation was noted between the motions of the stars and the times and intensities of the availability of water."[65]

The explanations of native Peruvian scholars from Mejía and Horkheimer of old to the young Lancho said more about religion and the social customs of the indigenous cultures of Peru than they did of putative mathematical, geometrical, or astronomical prowess, but their nativist ideas just didn't cut it in the sphere of pop culture.

By the late seventies and early eighties, the pampa was a mess. Motorcycles and dune buggies tracked across the vulnerable figures in the wake of all the TV programs and pop literature that fantasized about them. The handful of guards Reiche had hired to protect the pampa by patrolling the Pan-American Highway were no match for the sightseers who flooded the site, just the way they had poured into and desecrated Stonehenge a decade earlier. Unlike Stonehenge, you can't fence in the Nasca lines, but other events would oddly conspire to save the pampa. The terrorist activities of the Sendero Luminoso, or Shining Path, a left-wing Maoist guerrilla group operating in the high Andes, began to encroach upon the normally placid coastal area in the eighties, a sign of local dissatisfaction with the ruling government from the right. Any traveler to Peru in the early eighties would have had no trouble witnessing a declining economy. Galloping inflation had led to black-market monetary exchange on the street. Pocket-picking and muggings became the rule rather than the exception. When the bombings in Lima and attacks on tourists began to occur almost weekly, tourism plummeted. It was in this rapidly changing atmosphere, in the handful of years just before the crescendo of the government crisis in Peru, that our own Nasca research began to coalesce.

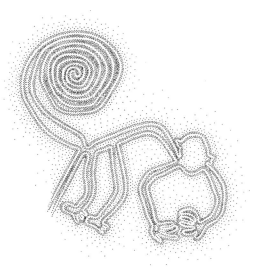

PART THREE. CEREMONY

5 SACRED LANDSCAPES

A NASCA FOR A NEW MILLENNIUM

> We still do not have any paradigm to account for the meaning of the Nasca geoglyphs which are among the largest archaeological features on the surface of the Globe. They remain a mystery wrapped in an enigma.
> **Astronomer Sidney van den Bergh**[1]

Astronomy is one of the most exciting frontiers of science. The Hubble space telescope takes our eyes to the edge of the universe while Venera, Pathfinder, and Galileo probes penetrate the surface of Venus, poke around Martian soil, and peer into the hearts of comets. Our generation has witnessed the birth of galaxies in the discovery of quasars and the death of stars in black holes. Finding possible solar systems around other stars advances us ever closer to answering the question: Is life universal? And it has all happened in my lifetime! With such a future to look toward, why would any astronomer care to look over his shoulder to the past, to focus in on fuzzy images of people who possessed neither telescopes to propel humanity outward into the cosmos nor high-speed computers to follow the stars in their courses, back to a time when people regarded space as a crystalline dome centered on terra firma, and the stuff of stars was directed inward toward predicting the course of one's soul?

> O Great ones, gods of the night,—
> O Pleiades, Orion and the dragon,
> O Ursa Major—
> Stand by, and then,
> In the divination which I am making,
> In the lamb which I am offering
> Put truth for me.[2]

So wrote a fifteenth-century BC Babylonian astrologer as he talked to the stars.

But there is a connection betwixt past and future, and with it comes a reason for caring. We do need to know, don't we, whether our ancestors really were like us, whether they appreciated the beauty of nature for its own sake, whether their scientists (whoever they were) spoke like our own in the language of mathematics, whether they developed the same sort of reasoned explanations of nature's phenomena linking cause to effect in the world around them? Did they see the world arranged the way we do? Did they divide its components into the same categories: animate and inanimate; solid, liquid, and gas; lead, zinc, and tin; electron, proton, and neutron; planet, star, and galaxy? We need to know just how far back the common scientific thread of understanding nature we all share really extends. Probing our past is much like the quest for extraterrestrial intelligence, except that the element of time is substituted for space. Are we all alone in the present, or does the record of our past set a stage that helps us see who we are, where we're headed?

These were my thoughts as I thumbed through a newly acquired volume in the college library back in the mid-sixties. It was all about the Maya pyramids' being oriented toward the places on the horizon where different celestial objects appeared and disappeared, the Stonehenge astronomy theory brought to America. It made sense. We know the Maya Indians of Yucatan developed a sophisticated system of hieroglyphic writing and a very accurate calendar. The handful of surviving native documents that escaped the plundering hands of the Spanish conquistadores contain elaborate tables that mathematically calculated the motions of Venus and Mars. Part of one tattered codex even told how Maya astronomers could predict eclipses of the sun and moon hundreds of years in advance.

The idea of encoding information about the sky in a work of architecture, a calendar without writing, fascinated me. We have houses with passive solar heating that chart the movement of the sun in a sense, but Stonehenge and the Maya pyramids were different. Their orientations more likely had something to do with worshiping sky deities, making offerings to pay back their gods. If works of mortals here on earth lined up with the gods' creations in the sky, the cosmic and the urban axes would be locked together in perfect harmony. What a marvelous way to discover order.

Then the skeptic in me rose up. How do you know when things really line up? There are plenty of pyramids and myriads of stars. Sounds like the old target game of Pitch Till You Win: given enough throws, you're sure to hit the mark. If you look hard enough, you're bound to find a celestial match. Some critics argued that even the innovative Gerald Hawkins was in a sense finding what he was looking for. It was all very interesting, but I was already involved asking the everyday questions most astronomers like to think about, like "How are stars born?" and "How do they evolve?"

The college campuses of the sixties may have been rife with social rebellion, but the tail end of that decade also was an extraordinary period of curricular innovation, a time when teachers and students were being encouraged to think about new ways to make learning exciting, to put our books aside for a while and experience the real world described in them. Like many small liberal-arts colleges, Colgate had recently inaugurated a January term. Students would take a single course with one professor for an entire month, the farther off campus the better. It offered the perfect opportunity to go to Mexico and study the pyramids for myself.

Alfred Percival Maudslay, the British traveler and photographer and the first outsider to photograph the Maya ruins, confessed in 1889 in one of his early works that he became interested in the Maya ruins of Central America as an escape from the vagaries of the London climate. Old AP's quote justified my other motive, the ulterior one. London weather can't hold an umbrella (or a snow plow) to winters in upstate New York. We (Colgate geologist Bob Linsley, seven adventurous students, and I) departed from campus in two student-parental station wagons on New Year's Day 1970. We drove to, around, and back from Mexico, a total of 11,000 miles (gas was only 35 cents a gallon!), taking in practically every major site that was accessible: the greatest pyramids of all at 2,000-year-old Teotihuacan, ancient Toltec Tula (then thought to be a forerunner of the Aztec empire in the highlands), El Tajin's Gulf Coast Pyramid of the Niches (with one niche for each day of the year), and stately Maya Chichén Itzá and Uxmal in Yucatan. We looked, we climbed, we photographed, and we measured lots of pyramids.

Of all the sites we explored that month, the one that captured my attention most of all was Monte Albán. On an artificially leveled hilltop just outside the charming colonial city of Oaxaca, a long day's drive from Mexico City, this site is famous for its celebrated Tomb 104, a cache of jade excavated by the charismatic Mexican archaeologist Alfonso Caso in the forties. *National Geographic* had made a splashy presentation of the treasure, as would the new National Museum of Anthropology and History in Mexico's capital city when it opened two decades after the find.

Around 300 BC one of the expansionist Zapotec tribes of the valley of Oaxaca reshaped the top of the several-acre plateau in the spine of the Sierra Madres and fashioned a dozen mammoth stone buildings around a large open rectangular plaza laid out along a north-south axis. These buildings ringed a pair of central structures, the southernmost of which looks starkly like home plate on a baseball diamond, at least when it is glimpsed from the air. Unromantically dubbed Monument J by Caso, its axis points roughly southwest, way out of line with the other structures. We had read about this curious building in the National Museum guidebook, and once we drove up the hill and pulled into the tiny parking lot, we eagerly inquired of the site guard about this misshapen, oddly skewed building. He told us that, like most weirdly shaped, misaligned buildings, it was an observatory. "What does it point to?" one of my Spanish-speaking students asked. "The place where the sun goes down on the first day of winter," the caretaker replied, authoritatively waving a hand over in the direction of the distant mountains. It was only a couple of weeks after winter solstice, and since the sunset position doesn't change all that much around the solar standstills, I thought, Why don't we stay and watch? "Can we?" "¿Como no?" ("Why not?"), came the consenting reply we would hear so often from a people who delight in sharing their heritage with any outsider. We toted in our sleeping bags and gear, preparing (with official permission) to spend a night on Monument J under the stars. As we watched the tropical sun plummet almost vertically down to meet the mountains, it was already clear by late afternoon that there would be no meeting between the descending yellow disk and the extended axis of home plate; it wouldn't even be close. When the sun finally perched like Humpty-Dumpty in a shallow saddle of the horizon about five o'clock that afternoon, it missed the mark by more than 20 degrees (about 40 sun disks) to the north. Next morning the guide responded to our "What happened?" with "That's what it says in the guidebook."

That was my first venture into New World archaeoastronomy. Our eyes remained fixed on J's point, and when I returned a year later with a fresh set of undergraduate troops eager to explore the ancient places they had spent the fall term reading about, I brought along not only a surveyor's transit but also equipment to map the building and charts and tables detailing the course of every celestial body that crossed the horizon in the thousand years straddling the beginning of our Christian era when the building was occupied. We were well prepared to find an answer to the question "What sky object, if any, really did align with the pointer of Monument J?" I was surprised to learn that no archaeologist had ever contemplated such an exercise. We immediately ruled out the sun. It never came within 20 degrees of J's axis. When we looked at the stars, about the best we could do was to note that the Southern Cross and the nearby bright stars Alpha and Beta Centauri dropped below the skyline in the general area indicated by the point of the arrow, but it was such a broad area—again the target problem. Besides, there were no known references in Zapotec folklore to the Southern Cross and the two bright stars in the constellation of Centaurus. Here was an answer, but it wasn't a very satisfying one.

John Paddock, dean of Oaxaca archaeology, thought the whole business was pretty much a waste of time. When we paid him a visit at his modest homestead just outside the city, he asked the obvious down-to-earth materialist archaeologist's question: Why would a militaristically oriented people who controlled the Oaxaca valley in the days when Monument J was erected care about the stars, much less about aligning their temples with the heavens? Despite his antiastronomy opinion, Paddock was always a helpful colleague, and he grumpily consented to trek up to the plaza and offer his assistance on the matter of the chronology of Monte Albán's edifices (important information for someone studying astronomical alignments, because the stars constantly change their positions through time).

Paddock walked us around the site and apprised us of the latest finds. Employing a found twig for a pointer, he lectured us on inscriptions carved on the stelae dating back to the third century BC that told of bygone wars, captures, and alliances, and he traced out the body contours of one of the famous Danzantes, life-size stone carvings of rubbery-configured nude males, their genitals mutilated, their eyes closed, and a pebble in each one's mouth. More likely dead than dancing (as their name incorrectly advertised), he opined. Over on the east side of the plaza, opposite the point of Monument J, we entered the temple Caso had labeled Monument P. Paddock took us through its innards via a chamber halfway up the stairway, likely one of Caso's archaeological sections. It led back to a small room 6 feet wide and 15 feet deep. At one end of it, along the east wall, lay a stone-lined vertical shaft about 8 inches wide and 7.5 feet long. I could see that a spot of bright sky was illuminating the dark floor at the base of the shaft. On the days when the sun passed the overhead point, or zenith, I imagined the effect would have been quite spectacular, a column of dazzling light penetrating the inner sanctum. The sun crosses the zenith in the region between the Tropics of Cancer and Capricorn twice a year (the dates, which vary with latitude, are May 8 and August 5 in Oaxaca). We know that this event was important in Mexico, for one chronicler tells us, "To this day the Indians commence [the year] on the 16th of July . . . having sought to make it begin from the precise day on which the sun returns to the zenith of this peninsula."[3]

Marking the place of the sun on New Year's Day and celebrating the rites of renewal sound like reasonable functions for a building with a sky-oriented chamber at a major ceremonial center. As we spent the rest of the month mapping J, we wondered further about the astronomical record that might be hidden in P just 100 yards away, across the plaza to the northeast. Once I got off my fixation with J as a pointer and started to pay attention to the rest of the building, I noticed an interesting coincidence: a line run perpendicular to the doorway of J off to the northeast passed directly through the vertical sight tube in Building P. I followed the point all the way to the distant horizon and marked the spot on a map, 47 degrees east of north. Did anything of cosmic significance happen there?

Returning to the States, I spent my next spring on sabbatical as visiting professor at Tampa's University of South Florida, home of a fairly large planetarium. When I wasn't working on normal astronomy, I got together with its director, Joe Carr. We'd crank the Zeiss projector back two and a half millennia and cast up our new slides of the Monte Albán horizon to make a 360-degree panorama round the dome. It was the next best thing to being there. With masking tape, we cordoned off the region that corresponded to the alignment 47 degrees east of north. As we rolled the stars around in their orbs circa 300 BC, one of the brightest, yellow Capella in the familiar winter constellation of Auriga, fell into place precisely in the middle of the band. Interesting, we thought, but there was no more record of Capella than of the Southern Cross in the scant Zapotec inscriptions. There was, however, something compelling about this star above all others when it came to the event of the sun's zenith passage. Most stars, except those close to the celestial poles, have their seasons. Bright red Betelgeuse and blue Rigel in Orion adorn our winter night sky. We associate Deneb of the Northern Cross and Antares of the Scorpion with summer, when the belt of Orion disappears from view. Regulus in Leo enters the sky in spring, and so does bright orange Arcturus, and the great square of Pegasus, lost in the glare of the sun most of the summer, returns to visibility in the fall. In ancient Monte Albán, Capella's season was the solar zenith. According to our planetarium experiment, it returned to the sky precisely on the day when the sun arrived in the overhead position on the date archaeologists assigned to the construction of both J and P, which aligned with it.

We will never know exactly what happened on New Year's Day about 300 BC in Monte Albán, but the archaeological and astronomical evidence tells me that the keepers of the calendar might have used Capella's annual first dawning (which they sighted at 47 degrees east of north along the alignment axis) as a signal that it was time to reset the seasonal clock to the New Year, to prepare for the brilliant sight of the sun in the zenith tube that lay along the alignment, to conduct all the attending ritual ceremonies involved with getting ready for the rainy season, the planting, and all of the civic and religious affairs that dot the annual calendar. The signs from the gods were all tucked away safely in the architecture, part of the unwritten record that detailed the decidedly different way my ancient predecessors, the astronomers, had once practiced their art. It had taken two years for us to advance what we thought was a reasonable explanation for Monte Albán's lopsided architecture, reasonable because it made sense of phenomena unique to tropical astronomies and it served a practical function. Sun and star time-marking devices would doubly reassure an expanding state in the valley of Oaxaca that it could indeed find a way to regulate Zapotec standard time.

Monte Albán opened new horizons. Other possibilities for studying astronomically aligned architecture lay strewn across a vast field of inquiry never before tapped in the Americas: Maya observatories in the round, like the Caracol of Chichén Itzá, the twisted Palace of the Governor at Uxmal, the skewed grid plan of ancient Teotihuacan (one archaeologist thought it had been astronomically aligned via architects' benchmarks in the form of quartered circles neatly pecked into the floors of its buildings). The windowed cliff dwellings of the Anasazi marked the fringes of our own border, and far to the south lay the Inca palaces of the Peruvian Andes. New World archaeoastronomy was born, and it would blossom in the seventies because it offered a new way to explore ancient native practices of skywatching. An interdisciplinary field rooted in a decade open to mental merging, it would bring together the skills of site surveyor and mapper, astronomer, archaeologist, architect, and historian. My German-Mexican colleague, Horst Hartung of the University of Guadalajara, a specialist in Mesoamerican architecture, and I would investigate more than 100 sites in Mexico alone.

As I became fully seasoned in these new ways of exploring unwritten prehistoric astronomy, I got involved in more joint ventures with archaeologists. I organized national and international conferences. At one of them I chanced to come across one of the brightest, most dedicated and imaginative minds in all of Andean studies. He himself had been caught up in the new wave of interest in ancient astronomy churned up by the Stonehenge controversy. He would redirect my focus.

Begin at the Top in Cuzco

By the time I met him in 1975, Tom Zuidema, a thickly accented Dutchman and professor of anthropology at the University of Illinois, had already devoted more than twenty years of his life to interpreting what the Spanish chroniclers had said about Peru's ancient Inca. Educated at the University of Leiden, Zuidema's principal interest was social structure, especially kinship, a field regarded by most students of introductory anthropology as arid but necessary. During World War II, Nazi invaders had confined him in his home in Haarlem for two years, but in the early fifties Zuidema shot out of isolation like a cannon, traveling to Indonesia, the United States, and then to South America in search of exotic lifeways different from his own. He was particularly intrigued by the work of Bernabe Cobo, that sixteenth-century chronicler who wrote the most elaborate and detailed description of the ceque system of Cuzco (see Chapter 3).

Zuidema would spend the next 40-plus years of his life intensely focused on trying to comprehend what the ceque system was about. Recall that the need to control the watershed environment was the principal reason the Inca had divided the city into its four suyus and 41 radial ceques. Boundaries between suyus demarcated the flow of water in the valley of Cuzco. The radial ceques were the organizing principle for the *ayllus,* or kin-related groups that lived there. Suyus, ceques, and the ayllus themselves were all hierarchically ranked, basically by whether they were situated up or down river. This is not a strange concept if you stop and think about it: the space we build and occupy does tell a lot about where we fit in the social hierarchy. The loges at the opera and those stratospheric air-conditioned boxes at the sports stadium go to the wealthy, while the rest sit in the rear at concerts and wait in crowded lounges for tourist-class flights. The Inca, however, were a bit more meticulous about reserving space. The 41 ceques with the 328 huacas that marked them in the landscape amounted to a mnemonic device (like memorizing the first letters of items to buy at the supermarket instead of taking a written list) that organized Inca ideas about social organization, hydrology, the seasonal calendar, and, as we would later discover, astronomy.

Zuidema was especially interested in where the sky fit into the picture. No anthropologist had ever looked at precisely how all these elements came together and what the ceque system could teach us about Andean culture. For Zuidema, the relationship between ceques and bloodlines would prove to be particularly rich, filled with alien concepts that have few parallels in our culture; for instance, the *panacas* are kin groups of families that derive from the royal bloodline around the Cuzco valley.[4] Each panaca was said to have originated from the primary descendants of an Inca ruler. This is what led Zuidema to the belief that the arrangement of the ceques held the key to the history of the mythical bloodline of the rulership in Cuzco up to the time of its founding by the flesh-and-blood leaders who claimed descent from them. The turf of our states and cities may be divided into ethnic neighborhoods, sectors based on economic wealth, political districts, and voting wards, but there was no city divided up in quite so remarkable a manner as the old Inca capital. One can sense it in many of Cobo's descriptions of the huacas and their ceques. Each one encapsulates information about irrigation, the calendar, and religious worship, all at the same time. Take, for example, what Cobo has to say about just one of them (the seventh huaca of the eighth ceque of the northwest quadrant of Chinchaysuyu): "The seventh (huaca) was called Sucanca. It was a hill by way of which the water channel from Chinchero comes. On it, there were two towers as an indication that when the sun arrived there, they had to begin to plant the maize. The sacrifice which was made there was directed to the sun, asking him to arrive there on that hill at the time which would be appropriate to planting, and they sacrificed to him sheep, clothing, and miniature lambs of gold and silver."[5] To hear Cobo tell it, a hierarchy of worship existed in Cuzco, and Zuidema would be the first to explain how each ceque had been assigned one of a set of three classes (aristocrats, mixed bloods, and commoners) representing the social classes that tended to them and that rotated alternately as one counted ceques around the horizon.[6]

The ceque system also was used to regulate the organization of labor as well as other activities, particularly those having to do with agriculture and irrigation. Representatives of each of 40 families drawn from the four suyus would participate in a ritual plowing once a year in the central plaza of Hurin Cuzco. A delegate from each ayllu would plow a designated portion of the segmented plaza. Rules for the shared servicing and maintenance of the irrigation canals also were specified by the order of the ceques. The concept of shared performance of civic duties arranged in this manner (locals call it the *mit'a* system) would later surface in Gary Urton's studies at Nasca.

Tom Zuidema's careful reading of Cobo's and the other chroniclers' descriptions of radial ceques and their huacas uprooted a vast amount of information about the interrelationships among Cuzco's social classes, all expressed in the gigantic ceque map that was the city itself (Figure 23). When he came to Colgate in the fall of 1975 to present some of his work to our anthropology classes, he sparked my interest in the possibility of actually tracing out huacas in the great capital city. These weren't just landmarks depicting the sites of heroic battles, not tourist sites, but seminal places that spoke of how the ancient Incas lived and worked, how they worshiped their gods, even how they were related to one another by blood. What impressed me most about the ceque system was the time element interwoven within it. There was a right time to engage in this or that activity, and all of it was gauged by charting the course of the sun's movement by sets of horizon pillars. As we talked late into the night, Zuidema leafed through his tattered copy of Cobo's chronicle, each huaca locale heavily annotated in penciled marginalia with multiple comments in his already indecipherable Dutch script. Here was one of Cobo's descriptions rife with astronomical meaning, there another. For example, Chinchaysuyu—ceque 6, huaca 9: "A hill called Quiangalla that is on the road to Yucay where there were two monuments or pillars that they had for signs and when the sun arrived there it was the beginning of summer," or Cuntisuyu—ceque 13, huaca 3: "Chinchincalla is a large hill where there were two monuments at which, when the sun arrived, it was time to sow."[7] By sighting sunrises and sunsets over particular huacas, the Inca, like the Zapotecs of Monte Albán, seemed to be preserving a record of the most important dates in the seasonal year, without the necessity of a system of writing as we know it. These astronomical sight lines clearly were related to huacas of particular ceques, and this meant that astronomy, if only a part of the ceque system, was nevertheless an integral part—grist for the mill of the archaeoastronomer.

How real is the ceque system? Are there still traces of it? Can it be mapped? Does it still appear as Cobo described it three and a half centuries ago? In the hours before dawn, Zuidema and I cut a deal. We would go to Cuzco together the next summer, I with the surveying equipment, he with the knowledge of where to look for the huacas gleaned from the old Spanish chronicles. We would investigate the locations of the most important huacas, map them, and focus on our shared interest: where did astronomy fit into the ceque system? All we needed were some modest research expenses.

Earthwatch is an organization based in Belmont, Massachusetts. It specializes in offering opportunities for volunteers to travel with scholars and assist them in their research. Brian Rosborough, then president of the organization, had been inviting me for some time to take a group to Mexico to work on building alignments. Earthwatch would fund all my expenses, and in exchange I would employ a dozen or so people who signed up for a succession of three-week stints in the field. Archaeoastronomy was ideally suited to the Earthwatch program. A person can learn to operate the surveyor's transit in pretty short order. The computer programs for reducing the alignment data were all packaged (back in the seventies that meant they were on magnetic cards inserted into a Texas Instruments 59 calculator). The idea of combing ancient ruins in the earth to seek out connections with the sun, moon, planets, and stars that roamed the sky echoed the old saw "As above, so below." It was the perfect combination for the motivated tourist who craved something more cerebral than just a few weeks away from the job in an exotic place.

I telephoned Rosborough and told him the plan. He invited us to submit a detailed proposal, and a few months later we were on our way to South America. The volunteers we chose ranged in age from 17 (a young woman uncertain about whether to enter her first year of college) to 72 (a schoolteacher forced into retirement but far from intellectual burnout). Our Earthwatchers came from all walks of life. We had an IBM executive, a Hughes Aircraft draftsman, a nurse from California, and a school librarian from Massachusetts. All were eager to spend part of their summer vacations helping to advance the frontiers of science. I took along one of my brightest Colgate seniors to help with the organizational details. My wife, Lorraine, was my expert photographer. Bill Conklin, an architect and expert on Andean textiles, and his wife, Barbara, who then curated the Andean collection at New York's American Museum of Natural History, also joined us. The summer of 1976 would be the first of four Earthwatch-sponsored trips spent walking over the four suyus of the landscape of Cuzco (and later Nasca) in search of clues to the identity of the huacas, names of towns, springs, hills, that yet resonated with elements buried in Cobo's description of the ceque system. Zuidema and I, along with our charges, immediately set to work tracing out the astronomically related ceque lines.

We looked first for verification of Cobo's statement about twin pillars on the mountain called Chinchincalla. Cobo hinted that they were likely fashioned to encapsulate the setting sun at the December solstice, the time to finish planting. The most likely observation point would have been the Coricancha, the Temple of the Sun and the acknowledged center of the ceque system. We followed the line out from the Coricancha to Chinchincalla, huaca by huaca, from Cobo's description of three closely spaced ceques in the region of the southwest quadrant (Cuntisuyu) of the city; the sight line indeed turned out to coincide closely with the direction of the setting sun at the December solstice. We managed to delimit Chinchincalla on the north via information from local informants who confirmed the location of Pantanayoc, a huaca on the adjacent ceque on that side. Cobo described it as "a large hill parted in the middle that divides the roads of Chincha and Conde [cunti] suyu."[8]

Armed with the surveyor's transit, we followed more or less straight lines from these outlying huacas back toward central Cuzco and the Temple of the Sun, narrowing the angle as we went. Our course passed immediately over a steep slope, to judge from what Cobo has to say, the northern flank of the Chinchincalla hill. We figured the pillars must have been located higher up on that same slope. When we got permission from the town prelate to climb the roof of the Church of Santo Domingo on top of the old Coricancha to make better measurements, we confirmed that the December solstice sun set precisely in this direction. A decade and a half later, Brian Bauer and David Dearborn would confirm our findings. In 1990 they identified a possible location for the pillars on the western slope of the hill named Killke. The area was riddled with looters' pits and Inca pottery fragments. Bauer and Dearborn's probing yielded a stone terrace five meters long and fragmentary burial remains. The exact position of these ruins corresponded to the place on the horizon where the sun goes down on the December solstice.[9]

What about Cobo's other reference to horizon pillars? We found what we thought was the hill called Quiangalla, which marked the June solstice sunset on Chinchaysuyu's sixth ceque. What puzzled us here was that neither the Coricancha nor any other monument near it could possibly have served as a June solstice observing station, simply because this part of the Quiangalla hill isn't visible from the center of the city. Based on the huacas we could identify, we meticulously traced the June solstice sunset direction at Quiangalla from peak to peak back toward Cuzco with the surveyor's transit. Our sight line passed a long slope about a mile and a half north of the center of the city. We figured that if Inca astronomers marked long-distance June solstice sunset observations by a pair of pillars on Quiangalla, the most likely observation point would have been three miles to the southwest in the area of the huaca named Chuquimarca. This huaca lies in the hills north of the city on an entirely different ceque, but Cobo called it a Temple of the Sun, possibly a place where the Inca ruler spent his time enacting the June solstice rituals. Cobo also wrote that Chuquimarca lay near or on a mountain named Manturcalla. Though neither name is used any longer, by once again pinpointing surrounding huacas and finding colonial documents that mention Manturcalla in the context of other place-names nearby, we concluded that the most logical candidate for Chuquimarca was a complex today called Lacco, an intricately sculptured rock outcrop penetrated by caves and topped with ruins of buildings, terraces, stairways, even a canalized stream (Figure 30). Supposing Lacco to be the place we were seeking, we then traced the June solstice sunset line more exactly from it. Though these towers, too, were destroyed long ago, later archaeological probing proved fruitful nearby. (Brian Bauer identified a slightly different possible location for this set of pillars on a ridge below

Figure 30. Quiangalla, where the Inca sunwatchers marked the June solstice sunset with a pair of pillars, lay somewhere along the ridge of Huaynacorcor hill in the background (arrow). Viewers likely stood on the hill of Manturcalla at a temple dedicated to the sun called Chuquimarca, which Tom Zuidema and I identified with the complex of rock carvings in the foreground. Photo by author.

the place we marked. He based his conclusion in part on having found the remains there of four rather large pits dug nearly six feet deep into the ground.)

Having established this hill-hopping technique with the transit and moving from site to site in search of local place-names that resembled those Cobo had written down centuries before us, we turned next to a more complex set of alignments. The Inca had devised a far more basic astronomical sight line, the one defining zenith sunrise and antizenith sunset, the fundamental time axis about which Cuzco's seasonal calendar pivots. This alignment cut all the way across the ceque system. It involved Cobo's famous quotation about the sucanca, and it tied in with an earlier (anonymous) chronicler's description of the four little pillars that served the same function and were located in the same general direction. The second chronicler tells us that the sighting pillars were visible at about two to three leagues (six to nine miles) from the city and that they were used to regulate the sun calendar. These pillars were situated high on a hill overlooking Cuzco from the west, and

> When the sun passed the first pillar they prepared themselves for planting in the higher altitudes, as ripening takes longer. . . . When the sun entered the space between the two pillars in the middle it became the general time to plant in Cuzco; this was always the month of August. And when the sun stood fitting in the middle between the two pillars they had another pillar in the middle of the plaza, a pillar of well worked stone about one estado [six feet] high, called the *Ushnu,* from which they viewed it. This was the general time to plant in the valleys of Cuzco and surrounding it.[10]

Evidently the time for planting in different elevations in the vertical environment of Cuzco was marked out by the day-to-day horizontal course of the sun across the row of horizon pillars. The northernmost pillar served as a warning device that the planting season in the Cuzco valley was approaching (Figure 31). Farmers who cultivated crops at higher, colder altitudes, where plants grow at a slower pace, would be allowed sufficient additional time to sow their seeds before planting commenced in the valley. Though the chroniclers provided no evidence, Zuidema and I speculated that the southernmost pillar might have been used as a similar warning device during the harvest season, when the setting sun passed it in April on course from the opposite direction.

With independent archival testimony from two reliable chroniclers, there was little doubt in our minds that these particular pillars resided on the slope of Cerro Picchu (it still retains its old name) above the Carmenga district in the western section of the modern city. A third chronicler establishes this location:

"On the hill of *Carmenga* (i.e., Cerro Picchu) they have at *definite intervals,* small towers, which serve to keep track of the movement of the sun, which they regard as important . . . and they had a plaza where they say a long time ago there was a swamp or lake at which the founders smoothed over the mortar and stone. . . . From this plaza the four royal roads go out."[11]

We set up the surveyor's transit on the ceque's final huaca and shot a straight line over the mountains toward the Coricancha in Cuzco.[12] We marked the spot where this line crossed Cerro Picchu. Since the sucanca lay on the ceque line we were tracing and since the anonymous chronicler says the sun was sighted from the ushnu, we could now fix the important sunset line that crossed this ceque and thereby calculate the corresponding date in the agricultural calendar. As a bonus, we could also locate the site of the ushnu, already known to have been somewhere in the Hanan Huacaypata, the plaza of Hanan (or upper) Cuzco or the present Plaza de Armas.

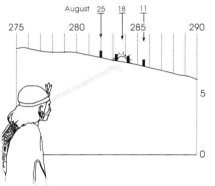

Figure 31. Sunset on the antizenith date over Cerro Picchu (marked by the intersection of the light pole with the horizon) gives away the location of the ancient Inca sun pillars (no longer standing). Inset map shows the rough layout of the pillars and the dates we assigned them based on the chroniclers' descriptions. Photo by author; drawing by Julia Meyerson.

After endlessly hiking up and down the 11,000-foot elevations around Cuzco, we managed to arrive at the crest of Cerro Picchu. The pillars are now long gone, fodder for a later era of builders. Even Garcilaso de la Vega, who mentions seeing them standing in 1560, says he knows they were destroyed by the time he was grown up.[13] So we erected our own sucanca on the spot by piling up stones; then we set up the transit and shot a series of lines down into the Plaza de Armas below. Here was our question: On what dates could sunset be viewed over the sucanca from various points in the plaza, all potential locations of the ushnu? One sight line we singled out was the one that corresponded to the August 18 sunset date (see the broad arrow in the inset of Figure 31). It was the very one that coincided with the sunset point on the day when the sun passed through the antizenith (the point directly opposite the overhead point).

Then a fortunate surprise offered us another telling clue. While visiting the cathedral of Cuzco, Zuidema noticed a 1653 painting by the Spanish expatriate artist Estrada Monroy. The panoramic scene (Figure 32), portrayed from the top of the cathedral looking toward the southwest, shows the city in the aftermath of the devastating earthquake of March 31, 1651, barely a century after the conquest. Near the center of the picture is a vertical column supporting a cross. Now, the chronicler Juan de Betanzos tells us that the conquistador Francisco Pizarro placed a "picota," or tall stone marker, on the site of the ushnu shortly after he conquered the city. If we join Cuzco's contemporary main square, the Plaza de Armas (the square in the foreground of Figure 32), with the smaller Plaza de Regocijo (the one in the background; today the two are separated by a row of houses) to form a single large plaza, the picota turns out to be positioned almost exactly in the center. The surprise was that Pizarro's substitute marker lay comfortably within the August 18 viewing band we had measured from the ceque line containing the sucanca on Cerro Picchu.[14]

Still more sight lines appeared at Cuzco. We later discovered a set of observations directed east toward the December solstice sunrise. Here the skyline of Cuzco was too distant to register a sunset over visible pillars, unless they were as high as a modest urban skyscraper. The mountain Omotoyanacauri (mentioned by Cobo and later contracted to Mutu by contemporary locals) probably served as the foresight. Mutu also made sense because of its pivotal connection with an Inca myth. It lies at the gateway out of the Cuzco valley that oriented people along the direction of a famous pilgrimage at the time of the solstice. The course took celebrants up the Vilcanota River to its point of origin. (A downriver pilgrimage also took place at the June solstice in the opposite season—more Andean dualism.) At the end of the line, about 60 miles from Cuzco, celebrants offered sacrifices to the place where the sun was born. We extended the upriver direction

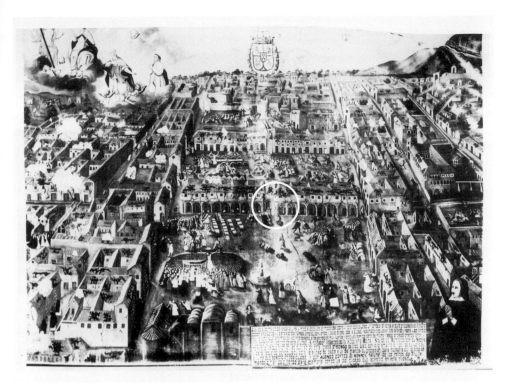

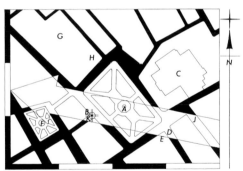

Figure 32. When the artist Estrada Monroy painted Cuzco in the aftermath of the earthquake of 1651, he provided us with a clue regarding the location of the ushnu (circled), "a pillar of well worked stone" at the center of the plaza, from which Inca calendar keepers reckoned sunsets over the Cerro Picchu pillars (see Figure 31). This helped them to determine the times to plant crops in the diverse altitudes of the Cuzco valley and environs. Inset shows the antizenith sunset line we traced from our field measurements. The position of the ushnu is marked by a target, which lies inside the broad arrow. Photo courtesy of R. T. Zuidema.

of the pilgrimage outward from Cuzco and found that it passed through the island of Copacabana in the center of Lake Titicaca. This direction follows the mythic course of the god Viracocha, who led the sun out of the underworld and who gave rise to the origin of the Incas as told in the old Huarochirí manuscript.

All over the world people make schedules; we call them calendars. Calendars are created when people find correspondences between activities essential to their lives and goings-on in the world around them. The ancient Greeks associated the first appearance of bright orange Arcturus in the predawn springtime sky with the ripeness of the grapes in their vineyards and their readiness for harvest. As the poet Hesiod wrote, "Then when . . . the rosy fingered dawn confronts Arcturus . . . cut off all your grapes (from the vine) and bring them home with you."[15] Some calendar makers fixed the appropriate cosmic direction in stone rather than in verse. The Mexican chronicler Toribio de Motolinía tells us that the Aztecs oriented their principal temple to mark the rising sun on the spring equinox, when they celebrated rites to honor the rain god, offering him sacrifices of children to pay their debt to him; but because it was slightly misaligned, they tore down and rebuilt the pyramid to get it right.

Ever the true environmental chronologists, the Inca recognized that important dates in the agricultural season coincided with visible signs in the natural environment, cosmic signals in this instance.[16] This led them to regard the two sets as going together, metaphors associating both humanity and sun penetrating the earth to the antizenith. Building the calendar into the structure of their city via visible sight lines only underlines the importance of keeping the right time in the efficient operation of the Inca empire. Viewed in this symbolic light, the sight line across the horizon to the sunset on its antizenith passage became a reflection in horizontal space of the all-important vertical-dual principle of organization that integrated society—a brilliant stroke of Inca genius.

Four seasons of fieldwork in the ancient Inca capital had netted us a host of astronomical huacas, and we thought we could pinpoint their original locations with reasonable accuracy. Though we knew for a long time that any sun pillars we might seek had long ago been dismantled, we could be sure that at least three sets of them had existed: a pair of towers to mark the June solstice sunset point as viewed from Lacco, a complex of rock carvings on a hill north of Cuzco; a second pair of towers to mark the December solstice as seen from the Coricancha, the center of the ceque system; and finally four towers situated on Cerro Picchu to mark the crucial time for the planting season, sighted from the ushnu and centered about the place where the sun set on its mid-August passage through the antizenith.

Three centers of observation with unequal numbers of towers was not what Zuidema and I had expected to find. Western astronomers would never have operated with such an asymmetry, and Garcilaso's and the other chroniclers' confused statements about the pillars (many early writers thought they were shadow-casting sundials, like those of Greece and Rome) reveal the shallowness of the penetration the Spanish Renaissance mind had actually made into the Inca way of thinking. To add to the unorthodox nature of the Inca sighting scheme, we had discovered a basic concept about Inca timekeeping and the sky in the passage of the sun along the vertical zenith-antizenith axis, a phenomenon that has no analog outside the Tropics. Our findings up in Cuzco would come home to roost down in Nasca.

Such was Cuzco's unique solar clockwork. The Inca had wisely divided up the responsibility for marking out the year among the clans who worshiped the huacas and ceques in different parts of their city. The eye has it. Above all, Cuzco emerged as a great urban center organized by a set of imaginary radial lines. Some of these lines incorporated a knowledge of astronomy (an astronomy quite different from our own, expressed very differently), and others did not. This came as a bit of a surprise to an astronomer trained in the sciences who tends to believe that there is one true universe and a singular, correct way to express how it works. But it isn't a surprise to the anthropologist, who, by virtue of engaging in the deep study of human culture, often uncovers unexpected ways of behaving and organizing knowledge that many scientists, all too unfortunately, might think a waste of time—but then anthropology is a profession whose gleanings have always seemed a bit unsettling.

From the Top Down to Nasca

It was the end of the 1977 field season in Cuzco, and Tom Zuidema and I thought it would be fun to forego the one-hour flight back to Lima. Instead, we would drive over the Andes and down to the Nasca valley to pay a visit to the famous lines. Four among the more adventurous residue of Earthwatch volunteers would accompany Tom, Lorraine, and me on a 300-mile trip that would take four days in a pair of rented Volkswagen Beetles, our luggage strapped to their tops.

The sojourn proved to be a fascinating climatological seesaw. Daily we would ascend to the near-freezing, rarefied atmosphere of the flat puna, passing llama herds driven against horizontally flying flurries of snow, only to plummet the unshouldered switchbacks and find ourselves, within a mere couple of hours, rolling downstream in a verdant 80-degree tropical valley. Then we would repeat the process, climbing back once again to the next barrier in the file of mountains separating Cuzco from the coast. Six flat tires and one landslide later we lifted ourselves up onto the last highland outpost overlooking the sleepy village of Puquio, about 50 miles above the pampa. By then, one of our Beetles had lost a muffler, but the other, far more seriously afflicted, was devoid of brake fluid. There we found ourselves perched at the head of a pass, futilely engaged in trying to siphon off part of the precious supply of antigravity liquid from the tank of one vehicle into the other with a short rubber hose, when a helpful truck driver (an institution on the Peruvian highway system) happened unheralded upon the scene. He obliged us by offering a substitute fluid, a supply of his own urine, which he gladly deposited directly into the brake-fluid tank of our crippled vehicle. "This should get you down to Puquio, where there's a mechanic." He smiled as he departed, leaving us agog, as well as evenly divided in the ensuing debate over whether we were being put on. Our western hang-up about human excreta isn't universally shared. Called human water in the Andes, urine plays a practical as well as a more esoteric role in binding the individual to the cosmos. Applying fermented urine as a tanning agent and to dye wool has a long tradition in the Andes, where it is also used in curing ills. For example, urine is supposed to be beneficial when applied in a compress over areas afflicted with internal pain.[17] As substitute brake fluid, it worked.

To say that Nasca's Hotel de Turistas is an oasis grossly underemphasizes the meaning of that term. With its spacious air-conditioned rooms, swimming pool, and a bar that serves icy Pisco sours, this welcome watering place seemed luxurious enough to render one guilt ridden, especially after all the suffering explorers like Hiram Bingham and our own Earthwatchers were required to endure in order to legitimate our discoveries. Having at long last arrived at noon, we cooled our heels with a sumptuous, lengthy lunch (a mistake, as it would later turn out), and then we drove out to the airfield at the edge of town. The low light of late afternoon (or early morning) turns out to be the best for viewing the Nasca line airshow. At first sight, we were a little disappointed with what $40 had netted for each of us. Taxiing out on the dusty runway, our Aerocondor Cessna lifted us out over the pampa at the southwest corner of the Nasca River valley and passed over a helter-skelter smattering of straight lines. As we crossed the washboard surface on a northwest-to-southeast course and leveled out at just under 1,000 feet, the concentration of lines began to thicken. Soon we spotted a small trapezoid jutting out of the side of a bigger one. A line from its clipped end zigzagged back and forth a dozen times over a distance of close to a mile. Then our first animal figure came into view. The 60-yard-long monkey with the doubly wound spiral tail looked as if it had been applied to the dark brown canvas in pink pencil. We spotted yet another trapezoid, this one almost a mile long and pointing south-southwest, then another half as long, its wide base bigger than a football field, directed east-northeast. Like a laser beam, a perfectly straight line shot out of its tapered end (Figure 15). At our request, the pilot followed it four or five miles straight up and over one of the hills that bordered the northeast corner of the pampa. Shutters snapped furiously as the ship's captain, responding to our obvious delight at what he could offer us, dive-bombed the condor, the hummingbird, and then the lizard, whose body was severed by the Pan-American Highway (unfortunately, it has now been damaged by tourism combined with the ravages of El Niño). Then it was on to the cluttered maze of figures on the south bank of the Ingenio, a labyrinthine spiral 89 yards wide that looked to have been ruled with a giant compass along with the complex of giant trapezoids, one of them overlying a bird figure (Figure 12).

Were the Nasca Lines a Stupendous Feat of Engineering?

Our analysis of the Cantalloc spiral (Chapter 4) proved one doesn't need a plan to make a Nasca figure, but it didn't answer the question of just how much investment of labor went into the construction of one of them. At the suggestion of British TV producer Peter Spry-Leverton, who had accompanied us to the pampa to film his *Mysteries of Peru* (ITV, 1984), we designed an experiment to get a handle on what sort of workforce would have been mounted to complete the task. Enlisting the help of a group of twelve of my Earthwatch volunteers, I drew my own Nasca figure on the spot, with no written plan and a minimum of technology. We selected a heavily rock-strewn segment of a remote region of the pampa, about a mile east of the Cantalloc fishing-rod figure.

Our Nasca line would be a rectangular strip about fifteen times as long as it was wide. We would attach to it a spiral composed of three interconnected, leftward-turning circular arcs of progressively decreasing radius. We measured out one pace as the base width, fixed this length on a piece of string, and then connected points on the ground perpendicular to the ends of the baseline with a second piece of string fifteen times as long as the first. Then we measured off the radii of the diminishing arcs and swung them from points in such a way that the resulting arcs connected together to make a reasonably continuous curve.

We used the method that I think was actually employed on the pampa to clear the figures (Figures 6 and 7). We divided our labor force into two groups. Members of the first group squatted an arm's length apart within the perimeter of the figure and proceeded to gather all the desert-varnished debris within their reach, stacking the pieces in neat piles. Workers in the second group collected the material from the piles in small boxes and constructed the border of the figure (shown in the pictures here). They were supervised by two individuals who placed themselves on either side of the main axis of the figure, offering corrective instructions whenever the border appeared to be uneven.

From *The Lines of Nazca,* ed. A. Aveni, 1990, courtesy of American Philosophical Society, Memoirs, vol. 183.

When the work was concluded, I sat down and made some simple calculations: We had cleared 32 square yards in 90 minutes, with everyone working at a leisurely pace. Therefore, a force of 100 persons working 10 hours per day could have cleared a little over 2,000 square yards of pampa in about two days. This is the equivalent of a good-sized trapezoid, say, 200 by 10 yards. Inspired by a sound work ethic, a contingent of 10,000 could have constructed all the features on the pampa in less than a decade. Indeed, the amount of labor required to etch the Nasca lines is surprisingly small.

This practical exercise proved that neither a complex technology nor a sophisticated knowledge of geometry detailed on a blueprint would have been required to make a Nasca geoglyph. Even if the Nasca lines are not stupendous feats of engineering requiring vast investments of energy, we are still saddled with the problem of explaining the origin of these unique and curious desert markings. (By the way, we later erased the figure and recovered the entire area so as not to baffle archaeologists of the future.)

The eyes really had it that afternoon, though the stomach didn't. A bit woozy and nauseated from the postprandial self-imposed turbulence, by the time we staggered out of the Cessna, no soul on earth could have convinced one of us that this imagery was anything other than a feast conjured up willfully and intentionally for the organ of vision.

Weary yet sufficiently overstimulated by what we saw, we applied for and received an audience with Maria Reiche early that evening. She had resided in the hotel since the late sixties, when fame via her little Nasca book had reclaimed her for society after 20 years spent in the dingy room in the old Hacienda San Pablo adjacent to the pampa. Assisted by a cane on one side and a young native woman carrying a bulging duffel bag on the other, Maria emerged from her quarters and shuffled across the patio to meet our group, along with three or four other eager tourists who had also flown the lines that day. A spindly 75, she propped herself up in a straight-back chair, knees locked together, and began to speak in a soft monotone a litany one could easily surmise had been heard before on many a night round the poolside lounge. She recited how she had traversed the pampa on foot all by herself, discovering and clearing one figure after another. Then she told how and why the ancient people of Nasca made the figures. Many of the animals were constellations, and the straight lines made up a calendar, she said. Beneath it all lay the secret of the Nasca, a precise mathematical unit of measurement. Next day Reiche would take us out to the fishing-rod figure to demonstrate her theory about how the lines were laid out using this single precise measuring unit (Figure 13). The planning and execution of all these figures out on the pampa mean that these people must have developed a kind of highly abstract thinking we would never have expected in a primitive culture, she reasoned. Some of this I found hard to believe.

But, she went on, sounding like a missionary, "my work will not be finished until I and those who follow me make painstaking and accurate investigations of the sizes and directions of every feature on the pampa. Only then will we penetrate the mathematical mind of prehistoric man." Following the fifteen-minute talk, Reiche's attendant unzipped the shamanic duffel bag and offered up its contents, a few dozen copies of the slim, hardcover trilingual pictorial book *Mystery on the Desert,* with subtext in German, English, and Spanish, for $10 apiece. I still treasure my copy, signed "Maria Reiche 25:8:77 Nazca," in understated scrawl.

Later, Tom and I introduced ourselves, and Madame Reiche was kind enough to invite us back to her room. There on her drafting table she had displayed a series of rough hand-drawn maps and pictures. Examining them, we were immediately struck by references to a multitude of lines that appeared connected to star or spoke patterns of the kind Kroeber had written about. We glimpsed large numbers of lines, some narrow, others very wide, often a dozen or more converging upon particular places. Using her magnifying glass, we were able to trace lines on the photographs that connected one point to another on the pampa.

In a simple way, these linear features conjured up a vivid reminder of the radial ceque system of Cuzco we had been tracing over the landscape. Could the same formal system that was used to organize space in a highland capital in the fifteenth century also have been used on the coast a thousand years earlier? Or were we just telescoping the thoughts of our immediate highland field experience onto a new vista? No matter, our business remained at the top. We had gathered a lot of data at Cuzco that needed to be analyzed and had tacked on a visit to one of the world's wonders to boot. Clearly, there was a lot more going on in Andean astronomy than met the eye in Cuzco, and we had barely scratched the surface.

Order on the Pampa?

Later that year I received a letter from one of Zuidema's graduate students who had been working in Cuzco. He sent me a draft of some notes he was assembling on a system of Andean constellations he had partially deciphered, and he needed an opinion on the astronomical implications of his findings. What he showed me, he contended, was a kind of sky calendar far more complex than anything he had anticipated, a chain of dark cloud constellations, each representing an animal and running the entire length of the southern Milky Way. Among the creatures that populated this curious zodiac were condor, toad, fox, llama, and partridge. What surprised him most of all was that the times when these celestial animals disappeared and reappeared over the skyline seemed to match up quite closely with the key points in the life cycles of their terrestrial counterparts; for example, in early October, when toads emerge from their subterranean winter hibernation and begin to mate, the dark cloud constellation of the toad rises just before the sun at dawn, climbing higher and higher into the morning sky with each succeeding day. That young student was Gary Urton, and it was my good fortune that when he finished his Ph.D. at Illinois he came to Colgate to teach.

The radial Nasca lines began to intrude into many of our discussions about ancient Peru. Having studied with Tom Zuidema, Urton knew all about the raylike ceque lines of Cuzco, so getting his attention was no problem. Together we looked up every Nasca source from book chapter to pamphlet we could get our hands on and kept coming back to the same handful of references: Paul Kosok's oversized picturebook *Life, Land, and Water in Ancient Peru,* Maria Reiche's *Mystery on the Desert* (we found a rare 1949 edition printed in Lima that was more informative than the popular 1968 book), and an assortment of *National Geographic* and *Natural History* articles. There were some valuable works in Spanish, too. Studying these materials, Gary and I were able to sharpen our recognition of the ray centers. We came away surprised that no one had ever made a survey or given a detailed description of them. Next we made an enlargement of Reiche's map, whiting out all the animals, spirals, and trapezoids, everything but the straight lines. Like recognizable elements of a photographic image emerging from darkroom developer, some rather profound interconnections began to appear from what remained on the page. Stretched over a 20-square-mile strip of desert floor bordering the south bank of the Ingenio River, four clearly defined spoked patterns stood out. We counted a total of 88 lines converging on them. Eyeballing the course of each of the lines, we noticed that they seemed to be directed toward other recognizable starlike centers, many of them situated on the north bank of the Río Nasca on the other side of the pampa. In fact, we could scarcely trace a single line on the altered map that did not connect to at least one of these focal points.

Excited by the possibility that a pattern underlay the organization of the Nasca lines, Urton and I could scarcely wait to go to Peru the next summer. The first thing we did when we got there was to pay a visit to the offices of the Servicio Aerofotográfico Nacional, then located on an airbase at the edge of suburban Lima. Back in the mid-fifties, this branch of the Peruvian military had completed a 1:50,000-scale survey of five or six square miles of the pampa that resulted in the spectacular overhead views of the Nasca animal figures often pictured in popular books. We wondered just how many more revealing photos lay salted away in their archives. What we saw when we accessed them for the region centered on latitude 14°42'S, longitude 75°08'W (the dead center of the pampa), truly astounded us. Countless numbers of straight lines crisscrossed every frame we inspected. Why had we found so little descriptive detail about these features in the literature? Evidently, while so much popular attention had been devoted to the vital statistics of the famous zoomorphs, the widths and lengths of lines had scarcely been described. In fact, nobody seemed to know where most of them began or ended. Yet it was clear to us from our little map-erasing exercise that these straight features constituted by far the majority of the features that had been etched out in ancient times.

We had visible evidence on the photographs that interconnecting patterns of lines existed, but what was the extent of this patterning? What order might lie behind it, and could we discover that order? If so, what principles of organization might have been involved in the construction of the lines and line centers? For example, could the patterns that were emerging be related to a social system like the one we had been studying in Cuzco, a system that also took the form of radial expression? To frame reasonable answers to these basic questions, we needed more information about the lines. We had seen enough from the air. Now we needed to walk the pampa. We needed to know precisely where the lines started and where they ended, where they led to once they left a center, where the centers of the spokelike networks of lines were located, what the immediate surroundings looked like, and how building them related to the host of other drawings found on and off the pampa. Armed with our maps and photos, we were ready to head for the desert and set out on foot. After a conversation with archaeologist Rogger Ravines, then director of the National Institute of Culture (INC) division in charge of Peru's ancient monuments, we secured permits to enter and explore the zone of the pampa on a preliminary basis. After a six-hour drive down the Pan-American Highway, we arrived in Nasca.

Nasca town (population 15,000) is a dusty farming center situated between the Andean foothills and the desert. Sand dunes frequently migrate like wind-driven amoebas across the Pan-American Highway, the only road in and out of town. Not many tourist dollars have trickled down to town improvement for a place that boasts one of Peru's major attractions. David Parker's delightful picturebook *Broken Images: The Figural Landscape of Nasca* (which includes an essay by archaeologist Helaine Silverman) vividly captures what daily life in this mestizo town is like, from kitschy touristic shops to graves of the dead amid a Third World people who struggle to make ends meet. The main street is a monotonous series of interconnected shabby white stucco buildings housing farm supply stores, cafes, and a few minimal hotels, stopovers for the heavy truck and bus traffic that moves up and down the coast between Lima to the north and Arequipa to the south, in the direction of Bolivia and Chile. Feeling quite like tourists, we happily stayed at the government-operated Hotel de Turistas. This was a wise decision as it turned out, for its shaded patio and pool would make for the ideal restorative after exploring the desert in the heat of the day.

Our first penetration of the pampa immediately gave us at least a partial answer to the question "Why do most investigators study the Nasca lines from the air?": Because working conditions on the ground are difficult. Gary and I discovered that the most efficient strategy was to rise at 4 AM, carry hot coffee in a thermos, and breakfast on the pampa. By sunup we were ready with a small surveyor's transit, like the ones used by road gangs. Cameras in place, we would spend the morning marking out features in the landscape, walking the major straight lines from start to finish, measuring their orientations with the transit, and taking notes on any remains discovered along the way.

We had scarcely set foot on the pampa when we discovered a fifth line center.

We might have anticipated it, for we could already notice an apparent convergence of lines off the southeastern edge of both Maria Reiche's and Gerald Hawkins's large-scale maps. Then, when we began walking some of the lines adjacent to the Pan-American Highway in order to approach one of the centers from the east, we discovered three more centers. On the last day of our first month in the field, we found another one. That brought the total to nine well-documented and mapped focal points spread over 20 square miles of desert floor.

Having had one shot at it, we were absolutely convinced the ground-based expedition was the way to go. Why? First of all, we need to remember that people on the ground made the lines. Second, for someone concerned with the directions of the lines, the most direct and accurate method of collecting information is to make ground-based measurements with surveying equipment. Third, for people who are really interested in the astronomical meaning of the lines, only on the ground can they view the visible horizon. Measuring it directly allows for elevation corrections that might affect possible astronomical orientations. Working on the ground also gave us a better sense of whether the local topography might have influenced the placement and orientation of certain features. Finally, ground-based work forced us to spend long periods of time in the vicinity of each feature studying remains and spotting subtle details we weren't necessarily looking for. Our minds were made up: we would follow the ground route.

With nine ray-center candidates in the bag, we returned home, our notebooks bulging, and began sorting through the observations. It didn't take long before Urton and I discovered a remarkable likeness among these centers of radiating lines. All of the ray patterns seemed to be positioned on natural hills or mounds, often topped by cairns, or piles of boulders. In fact, most centers seemed to be situated in that part of the pampa where the last hill, shaped by the Ingenio drainage, descends from the mountains and, like a finger, projects out onto the flat surface (Figures 33, 34, 35, 36). So, each center was situated on a prominent headland from which an observer could see a considerable distance. Adjacent to these cairns, we would often find deep holes. These huaquero pits made it clear that a previous visitor had thought that X (a cairn) marked the spot, but I doubt that our looting predecessors found anything of interest beyond the ubiquitous handful of ceramic fragments. Clearly nothing had been built here; there was no stucco, no adobe, no foundation. There wasn't even a sign that the natural shape of the hill had been altered. About 100 yards southwest of one of these ray centers (later numbered 30; see Figure 37), we found a square hole. I interpreted it to be a modern well, but my friends Ralph Cané and Duncan Masson later told me it was probably of ancient origin, maybe used by the line builders to obtain drinking water while working on the pampa (though Persis Clarkson tells me

Figure 33. Yes, there is order on the pampa. The lines seem to concentrate on hilltops, usually the last in a series (arrow) that descends out onto the flat desert. Photo by author. From *The Lines of Nazca,* ed. A. Aveni, 1990, courtesy of American Philosophical Society, Memoirs, vol. 183.

Figure 34. Closeup of the terminal hilltop shown in the preceding picture. Not a trace of architecture could be found at any of the ray centers, but there were plenty of potsherds. Photo by author.

Figure 35. A cairn marks the spot. This one has fallen, its remains strewn over the hillside. Photo by author.

Figure 36. From this hilltop ray center, two lines can be seen crossing a dry quebrada. Tom Zuidema is in the foreground. Photo by author.

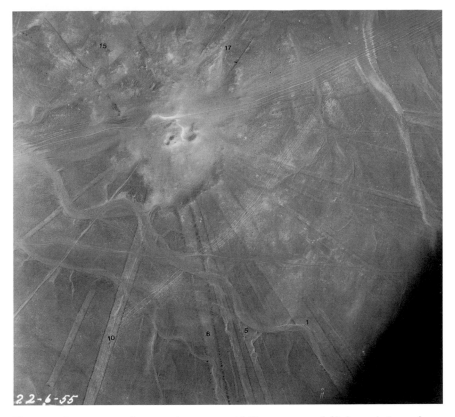

Figure 37. Ray center 30 features a huge trapezoid (Feature 15, top left), looters' pits, and more than a dozen converging lines ranging from the width of a shoe to half a football field. Photo Servicio Aerofotográfico Nacional; ground level photo by author.

the water table is more than 100 feet deep here). This would eliminate the need to trek all the way back to the Nasca River and climb back up onto the pampa again. "Pure intuition," as Cané put it.

By the end of the 1982 summer season, we would identify 62 ray centers and measure the orientations of 762 dead-straight Nasca lines attached to them. Some lines were eight miles long. We calculated that all the lines laid end to end would run nearly a thousand miles. Since we found line centers on the banks of the Ingenio River, we wondered whether the banks of the Nasca River on the other side of the pampa might yield up similar features. It became the starting point for our next field season (1983). Sure enough, line centers began turning up there as well, and so we proceeded with a systematic survey on foot that gradually took us northward out onto the pampa from the north bank of the Nasca River.

We proved there was order on the pampa. With the prominent exception of the transpampa line (which, you'll remember, surely must have been all that was

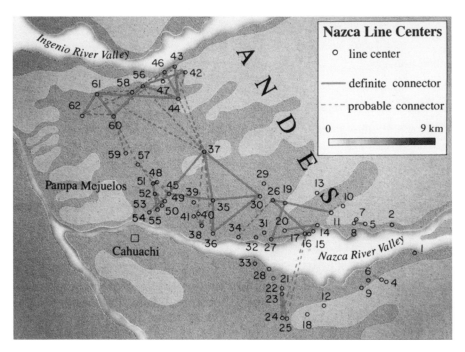

Figure 38. When we finally mapped the ray centers between the Nasca and Ingenio rivers, the lines connecting them revealed a multitude of zigzag pathways across the desert. Some lines even cross over the river (lower right). The heaviest concentration of centers is on the bank opposite the great pyramid of Cahuachi. Map by J. LeMonnier, *Archaeology* 39, no. 4 (1986): 37; courtesy of J. LeMonnier.

A Walk on the Pampa

What is it like to follow one of the 762 lines that crisscross the pampa? Take line center 35. It consists of a prominent oval hill about 100 yards long, 75 yards wide, and 50 feet high. Standing on the hill and scanning the horizon panorama, we immediately spotted 10 lines radiating outward, ranging in width from 8 inches to 50 yards. Seven of them opened out onto the pampa toward the Nasca drainage system in a southwesterly direction. The largest of the lot was a trapezoid 450 yards long and 50 yards wide at the base (bottom photo, p. 150). Some fragments the ancient Nascas cleared off its 16,000 square yards still lie neatly piled up in a dark hummock-shaped border a yard wide and half a yard high. Feature 6 is the longest line associated with this center, and it was the first to beckon us out there (top photo). All we could see of it from Hilltop 35 was its converging borders shimmering in the distance, looking like a pair of railroad tracks advancing toward the bumpy dune-lined horizon on the north bank of the Río Nasca. We weren't sure because of the haze, but it looked as if one of the dunes lay on line with the borders. Three hours later we knew for sure. We carefully followed No. 6's two-and-a-half-mile course southward across the pampa. (Notice the many well-worn footpaths that had run the course of these lines.) As we dropped down onto it from the top of the hill, we noted that its 17-yard base attached to two other features that merged with the line at the bottom of the hill; but once we hit the level of the pampa, the line narrowed to 12 yards, then abruptly to 6 at a range of 200 yards. Whoever fabricated this bizarre avenue made it far wider than necessary for one person to walk. From this point on it maintained approximately that width, so that Gary Urton and I could walk it side by side with outstretched arms and room to spare. Trailing our dusty footprints behind us, we noticed broken pieces of pottery here and there. Many were brightly painted with faces of exotic animals in that recognizable Nasca style. Others were of the common houseware variety perhaps used to carry water by workers who built the lines. Then, half a mile out, we caught sight of a line, the first of many, that would crisscross our path. Had we been looking the other way, we might have missed it, for we could see it only when it loomed within two or three steps of the intersection. What attracted us to it was a little stone pile about a foot high that marked the X-shaped crossing. A mile farther out, our line took us into a dry quebrada that had cut a 50-yard swath to a depth of 6 feet below the pampa. A rock cairn marked the entry and exit point at each bank so that we could see where we were headed when we fell below eye level. As we rose out of the dry quebrada, the line widened into a broad avenue that appeared to be taking us toward a distant dune (arrow) that fell short of the Nasca drainage basin by about three miles. The fallen remains of a stone cairn made up of fist-sized boulders marked the spot. As we ascended the shallow (15-foot-high) sandy promontory at the avenue's end and performed the obligatory dance of rotation, our eyes beheld no fewer than 40 lines of various dimensions darting off in every conceivable direction of the compass. We had discovered line center 36.

Photos from *The Lines of Nazca,* ed. A. Aveni, 1990, courtesy of American Philosophical Society, Memoirs, vol. 183.

left of the later Inca coastal highway the chroniclers talked about), scarcely was there a line that we could trace across the washboard surface between the Nasca and Ingenio river valleys that didn't emanate from one of the ray centers (Figure 38). If the Nasca lines were pointers that led out from the low mounds and hills that ringed the pampa, then what did they point to? Since astronomy was an essential part of the only other radial system of organization in ancient Peru known to us—the ceque system of Cuzco—might the sky also be tied into the structurally similar ray centers at Nasca? A reasonable question. It was time to run some astronomical tests.

What targets should we choose? When Gerald Hawkins did his Nasca line orientation study, he loaded the same standard sky targets that he had used at Stonehenge into the computer: the solar and lunar standstills, the 20 brightest stars, and so on. We had the advantage of some foreknowledge of Andean and coastal cultures that suggested more plausible objects to aim for. The zone along the horizon through which the rising and setting sun passed is the most obvious candidate. The sun's annual course would be a prime choice in setting up a seasonal orientation calendar (maybe the moon and planets, too, for correlations involving longer periods of time).

Rather than singling out only the usual solstices and equinoxes (the extremes and the midpoints along the 50-degree segment of the east and west skylines), we felt there were some special dates in the year that might have mattered in the cycle of subsistence on the coast; for example, what about the sun's position on the days of the year that mark the limits of the fishing season and the planting season? Because the sky at Stonehenge's latitude (51 degrees north) is noticeably different from that at Nasca's (15 degrees south), we figured we had better pay attention to sky phenomena that look different from Peru and perhaps don't even happen at Stonehenge, like the passage of the sun in the zenith and the antizenith, which was so important in Cuzco. Gary Urton's work in the high-lands pointed to the Milky Way as another possible candidate. We thought we should take a look at the extreme points of intersection of the horizon with the Milky Way, Mayu, or the celestial river, as Quechua people still call it, where water flows over the horizon into the underworld. Urton's research had shown that residents of contemporary Misminay, near Cuzco, still use this alignment to divide the sky into four suyus. We included other stellar targets: Alpha and Beta Centauri (the llama's eyes) and the Southern Cross, which we had learned about from both the Inca chroniclers and the contemporary anthropologists. We shouldn't forget the multitude of other indigenous sky crosses recognized by these people, especially the Cross of Calvary (from the middle star of Orion's Belt to Castor and from Beta Tauri to Procyon), along with the Celestial Plow

(Scorpio). Even more important were the Pleiades, so frequently mentioned as a sky timer and a navigation beacon by both coastal fishermen and highland farmers. Talking with north-coast anglers, Urton had discovered that good fishing off Moche began when the Pleiades first rose at dusk and ended when they disappeared (mid-November to mid-April). The dawn rise-set events for the same star group also marked the fishing season to the south of Moche (June to October). Furthermore, the chronicler Antonio de Calancha had written that the people of the Pacasmayo Valley on the north coast near the Moche Valley timed their year by the appearance and disappearance of the Pleiades. When the Pleiades appear very large, it means the fruit will ripen well, but the people will suffer if these stars appear small, says the Huarochirí manuscript.

To the computer we went, and the first plot it spewed out was a straightforward radial spray in azimuth of all 762 lines we had measured.[18] It showed a slight pile-up just west of north (the general direction to the next pampa adjacent on the north) and another clumping more or less to the southwest; this turned out to be the general direction of water flow into the Nasca drainage system, the simple lay of the land. Neither of these concentrations showed any obvious lunar, planetary, stellar, or other solar alignments. The Milky Way proved negative too. Our first plot pretty much confirmed the conclusion Hawkins arrived at based on a limited sample of alignments taken on the north end of the pampa: as a whole, the lines have nothing to do with astronomy.

Next, we decided to look more closely at the range of the horizon traversed by the rising and setting sun (roughly between 25 degrees north and south of east and west respectively). This time, rather than plotting the directions of lines, we would concentrate on the dates of the year that corresponded to the sun's position along the alignments. Of course every alignment in such a plot would necessarily correspond to a sunrise or sunset on some day of the year. Our question was whether the alignments were intentional.

The new plot showed nothing extraordinary about either solstice, but I did note a peak, about 50 percent above the anticipated number of target hits, in the range of azimuth 100–105 degrees. Filing through the calendar, we discovered that the sun reached this point between October 22 and November 2, when it was going south in spring, and between February 10 and February 20, when it headed back north in summer. A little calculation revealed that the noonday sun passes the zenith of Nasca precisely on November 2 and February 10 (arrow in Figure 39 inset). First I thought this was only a coincidence, but a look at a chart of the month-by-month measurements of the discharge of water through the Nasca drainage basin changed my mind. Early November was that very special time when sky and water came together, when water first began to discharge into the canals (Figure 39). It finally dawned on me that these were precisely the orientations that would fit the broader hypothesis that Nasca line building was connected with water and the mountains from which that precious liquid emanated. Ironically, this correlation between astronomy and hydrology had been hypothesized long ago by Paul Kosok in *Life, Land, and Water*. Why, I wondered, had he never bothered to test it?

Somebody once said that a scientist uses statistics the way a drunk uses a lamppost: it can give support, but it does little to illuminate the solution to the

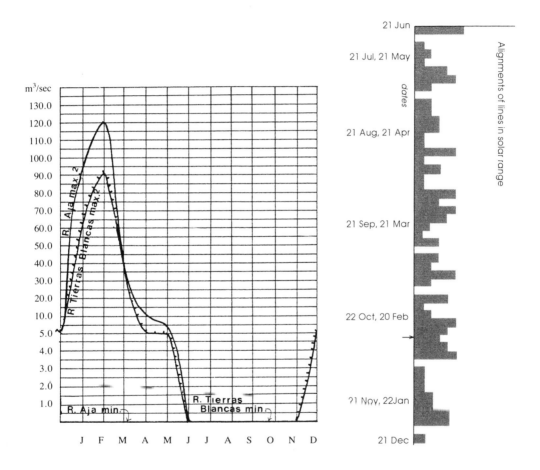

Figure 39. Water begins to flow in Nasca's canals about the first of November, as this graph of the discharge rate shows. Inset shows the increase in the number of lines pointing to the place where the sun rises and sets on the day when the trickle first begins. Graph from *The Lines of Nazca*, ed. A. Aveni, 1990, after Persis Clarkson. Inset by Julia Meyerson.

problem. When our 1984 Earthwatch field season rolled around, I invited archaeoastronomer and statistician Clive Ruggles of the University of Leicester in England to join us. Ruggles had already made a major contribution to archaeoastronomy by carefully remeasuring and analyzing Alexander Thom's alignments at megalithic sites in the British Isles. He argued that much of the precision moon-watching Thom alleged for the Bronze Age builders of Stonehenge and other megalithic sites was spurious. Ruggles's reinterpretation of megalithic astronomy seemed to me to be more in tune with what the prehistorians were telling us about the cultures who built stone circles and rows all over the British Isles and northwest Europe between 3000 and 2000 BC. Yes, these people were sighting the lunar standstills, but not precisely enough to predict eclipses or to detect tiny wobbles in the lunar course, which Thom had claimed. In Ruggles's eye, there were no Stone Age Einsteins bent on displaying a precise knowledge of mathematics, geometry, and astronomy for its own sake. These people were calendar makers. They were discovering the basic principles of short- and long-term temporal order that related the cosmos to everyday life. In Ruggles's opinion, there was far more religion than astronomy at Stonehenge.

Ruggles had recently embarked on a detailed study of alignments of stone rows and circles in western Scotland when I called him up and persuaded him to come over and run some tests of his own on the Nasca lines. He was glad to oblige, and he began by looking at the individual centers. Like me, he found that some of them exhibited line orientation clusterings in particular directions, so that we might be led to conclude their orientations had been deliberately laid out. Most of these centers lie in the northwest corner of the pampa, and Ruggles suspected, as I did, that the effect was due as much to local topography, which precluded the construction of lines in particular directions, as it might be to astronomy. He also confirmed the northward alignment preference as well as a slight eastward avoidance I had found, and he picked up our minor bump on the graph that corresponded to sunrises in early November when the sun crossed the zenith, along with a handful of other little peaks.

When Ruggles isolated the lines that connected ray centers from the sample, the concentration around 100 degrees azimuth (10 degrees south of east) became even stronger. But here he and I parted ways. Ruggles preferred the Pleiades as the likely target because its rising point more closely matched this orientation, and its setting point (in Nasca times) lined up with another clumping he found around azimuth 262 degrees. I was riveted on the hydrological connection, and besides, I didn't feel the solar correlation I had found needed to be all that precise, for if the ancient Nasca had discovered it, their insight would have come through noting the incipient flow of water over many seasons, events that surely would not have taken place on the same date every year. In other words, I would anticipate a sizable horizontal spread on the graph.

Rigor and statistics had brought both Ruggles and me around to the same conclusion: nothing that either he or I would have to say about the pampa as a calendar would ever bear the title "Nasca Decoded." The enigma of the pampa was far more complex, far too subtle for that. Our reading of the Nasca text showed it was anything but the biggest astronomy book in the world. Yes, skywatching was likely connected with some phase of the geoglyph project, and the sky-water association was the connection that made the most sense to me. Given the enduring popularity of Reiche's more deeply ingrained astronomical and geometrical theories about the pampa, I wanted to be careful when I wrote up the results not to overstate the importance of astronomical orientations. Yet her ideas, far more speculative than ours, would continue to stand in the literature as the ultimate raison d'être, the underlying motive of the people who erected the geoglyphs. The Nasca lines were written in the stars.

When Theories Collide

Our relationship with Maria Reiche would vacillate between lukewarm and cool during the eight field seasons our team spent at Nasca. Reiche's long association with the pampa, combined with the many arduous years she had logged walking and measuring the lines in solitude, had accorded her the status of reigning expert and given her some well-deserved proprietary rights as well. She took no better to strangers treading her turf than she did to foreign experts criticizing her ideas. Tony Morrison's two books on Nasca detail the long retinue of visitors to the pampa who tried to work with Maria, most of them for short periods and none of them very successfully: an Argentinean artist, a British journalist, and a series of American graduate students and anthropologists, most of them women. Reiche often said that her successor on the pampa would be a woman, one who, like her, would devote her entire life to independence, solitude, and to proving her astronomical theories about the pampa. Zuidema, Urton, and I, like astronomer Gerry Hawkins who preceded us, were professionally trained. We had ideas of our own, and being members of the opposite gender didn't help our cause.

At the outset, our relations were cordial. Reiche had willingly shown us her homemade setup at the Hotel de Turistas, even trucked us out to the Cantalloc fishing-rod geoglyph to demonstrate her theory on how the Nascas precisely laid out megaspirals. During our first couple of seasons, Urton and I would dutifully pay homage at the hotel each morning to clear with Reiche our plans for the day, as local custom required of all who would investigate the pampa. We needed her personal okay for each itinerary we made out to the desert, despite the permission papers we held from the Instituto Nacional de Cultura in Lima. Such was protocol in places where regional jurisdiction often overrides any authorization granted by higher officials in a distant capital.

"Today we're going over to the Pampa de Atarco" or "This afternoon we plan to head up the Quebrada Cangana de Majuelos to survey some of the lines near Cahuachi," we would say. After nodding approval, Reiche, her soft voice quavering, would usually launch into her whispered litany of pampa do's and don't's: "Make sure you don't walk on the pampa, stay only on the lines," "Don't touch any of the broken ceramics," and so on.

The better we got to know Maria, the more we seemed to become a threat to her. It was clear that our methods, our ideas, our attitudes, backgrounds, outlooks, even our gender, were grossly out of synch with her rule of the pampa. There would be no quest for Andean complementary dualism operating here, only universal astronomy and geometry. We knew we were in for a clash somewhere along the road through Nasca. It was just a matter of time before the conflict would unfold.

When Gary and I proceeded to draw up a large map of all the lines on the pampa, we used air photos as a rough guide. It soon became clear that many of the features we had explored at ground level were too faint to show up on the relatively high-altitude photos. We needed pictures taken from lower levels, and these simply didn't exist. So, in the summer of 1984 we decided to follow up on a suggestion archaeologist John Hyslop made to us: Do a low-altitude photographic survey of the pampa, like the one he had done when he surveyed the coastal ruins of Inkawasi up the coast to the north. Hyslop put us in touch with Gerry Johnson, an engineer at the University of Minnesota's Department of Civil and Mineral Engineering. Johnson had helped pioneer low-altitude surveys by employing a radio-operated Hasselblad camera suspended from a tethered helium balloon. When we wrote him into our next National Science Foundation and National Geographic grant application and received modest funding, Johnson arrived in Lima to meet our fourth expedition. He was accompanied by colleagues Doug Meisner of Minnesota's Remote Sensing Lab and Bill Johnson of the faculty of forest engineering at the State University of New York's College of Environmental Science and Forestry at Syracuse. With Gary's help, they lugged all the necessary equipment to do the survey, lacking only the gas required to elevate the balloon. Helium would be the usual substance of choice, but given the weight of the photographic equipment, Gerry had always pushed for more lift. The next most obvious (indeed the only) lighter-than-air alternative was hydrogen, which came with a major caveat because of its inflammability. Nonetheless, Gerry, with a linguistic assist from Urton, managed to get hold of a couple of four-foot-long tanks at a fertilizer factory on the outskirts of Lima, which they arranged to have transported six hours south to Nasca on a flatbed truck. In recognition of Johnson and company's association with this potentially deadly gas (especially when the tanks approached within 20 yards of any smoker in the group), along with the increasingly embellished story they told about how difficult hydrogen was to acquire in Peru, our three specialists earned the friendly nickname "the gasheads."

Carting all this equipment into the lobby of the Hotel de Turistas attracted a bit of attention. Had we come to duplicate Jim Woodman's balloon flight over the pampa? Were we looking for more evidence of Daniken's UFO runways or of secret treasures buried by the Incas beneath their tambos? The gasheads did a run-through of the equipment to be sure everything was in order, while the rest

Figure 40. Gerry Johnson secures the cable on the hydrogen balloon from which he suspended a remotely operated camera to snap the first low-altitude photographs of the pampa. Courtesy of Gary Urton.

of us helped by poring over the map to select frames and plot out a suitable place to begin the survey. We calculated how wide our field of view would be at elevations of 800, 1,000, 1,200, and 1,500 feet. Above all, we would need a calm, windless day to carry out the survey. Any gust above 15 mph, Gerry assured us, could blow the balloon dangerously off course. (Unfortunately, at this time of year gusty winds were quite commonplace on the pampa.) Six days of waiting for optimum conditions passed, and on the morning of the seventh, the weather observed at our daily 4 AM rising looked ideal for the launch of our Hindenberg of the Pampa (Figure 40). We grabbed the thermoses of hot coffee and some bread that the hotel had laid out for us, piled into the loaded van, and headed ten minutes up the Pan-American Highway, then off at the dirt track and into

Figure 41. In our first low-altitude shot of the pampa, at 1,000 feet, ray center 27 (circled) is clearly visible. Closer examination revealed features never before seen. From *The Lines of Nazca,* ed. A. Aveni, 1990, courtesy of American Philosophical Society, Memoirs, vol. 183.

the dry Río Socos bound for ray center 27 half an hour away. This was the ideal spot to begin because it was easy to get to, projecting outward from the pampa on a large sand dune overlooking the Río Nasca, and there was plenty of room on the dune to set up the equipment.

As the solar disk perched on the fingerlike hills that encroached onto the pampa from the east, the breeze picked up just a bit. It took about half an hour to inflate the balloon. Then, as the full-blown craft slowly rose, toting up the Hasselblad on its gimbal, Doug Meisner gradually let out the line (with an apparatus resembling a fishing rod), 300, 500, 700, slowly up to 1,000 feet. It was already beginning to be obvious that the impure hydrogen the fertilizer people had sold us would cheat us out of enough lift to get the balloon up to the desired height of 1,500 feet, so we settled for 1,000. The radio-controlled shutter began to snap away, garnering the first really close-up aerial view of a pampa ray center, a picture that would reveal several new lines as well as two spiral figures never before detected (Figure 41).

Our next ray center, No. 32, lay about half a mile to the west. As we started to walk the balloon along the pampa's edge toward it, a gust of wind sent the gimbal reeling out of control, alerting us that it was time to bring the apparatus in and put any further picture-taking on hold. But it was too late. The whole contraption jiggled wildly, then commenced a nosedive toward the middle of an ancient Nasca trapezoid a quarter-mile north of the Río Nasca's bank. As a few of my Earthwatchers instinctively dashed out onto the pampa to retrieve the craft they anticipated would strike the ground, we all heard a low-flying plane approaching us from the direction of the airfield. Eight AM seemed a little early, but still it wasn't a bad time for informed tourists interested in capturing high-relief photos of geoglyphs. As Meisner and Johnson reeled in the balloon, the plane passed over the chaotic site of our frantically aborted mission, and a stocky man in reflector sunglasses leaned out the open door and began to snap pictures—of *us*.

Disappointed, if relieved that no harm had come either to the geoglyphs or the camera, we collected ourselves and our goods and drove back to the hotel. Meisner and Johnson theorized along the dusty ride in the ever-increasing midmorning heat that our heavy hydrogen was as responsible for the accident as the unanticipated wind gust. Dusty and disheveled, we arrived by half-past ten and quickly convened a meeting to discuss our next course of action. Better not to reinflate tomorrow; we needed a few minor repairs, Gerry advised. Instead, why can't we proceed to our backup plan of making a photomosaic by using a side-mount camera system positioned on one of the locally chartered light aircraft? We could make a dozen or so traverses across the pampa at just above 6,000 feet. This would at least constitute an improvement over the government's spotty aerial photos.

We had extended the discussion through and beyond lunch, which we took in the hotel dining room, when suddenly a middle-aged uniformed officer, the hotel manager, and a burly man wearing sunglasses approached our table. "You're under arrest for trespassing," said the official in a firm voice as he handed us a document. Reiche had filed a *denuncia*, or legal denouncement against us, for willfully harming the pampa (violation of her rule against walking on the pampa) and for excavating without a permit (a total fabrication). Knowing arrest could be tantamount to extortion, we protested vigorously. "These are lies, all lies," a red-faced Gary Urton retorted, his Spanish by far the best among the group, as he hammered the royal decree with his index finger. Despite our protests, we were to remain in Nasca until the officials decided how to deal with us.

Next morning the Nasca town newspaper heralded, "American huaqueros found digging on the pampa." Fortunately, Peruvian officials would come to our rescue. That night we called Rogger Ravines in Lima and begged him to intervene. It would take the weekend for him to draft a document from the INC reiterating that we were research anthropologists and that excavation had no part in our program. (Urton's vociferousness would ultimately net us, in addition, an official written apology from the government of Peru.) At the local level, we talked to schoolteacher Josué Lancho and got him to go before the Nasca police to explain the misunderstanding. Even up to the last minute in this crisis, Gary and I had not put out of mind the notion of calling Colgate's dean of the faculty for bail money. This tense and nerve-racking ordeal lasted three days, a huge loss of precious time, and it was complicated by the responsibility we had for the care and feeding of our terror-stricken Earthwatchers and Colgate students.

What had happened? My theory is that Reiche and her caretaker sister, Renate (a retired doctor come from Germany to reside in Peru), had been egged on by the hotel manager, a nasty man with an apparent single-minded interest in exerting his will over the situation; the result was a joint attack against us. Not only had we failed to work under their complete supervision, but also our ideas, which included entertaining hypotheses other than her own, were perceived as a threat to truths Reiche felt she had already established. The run to retrieve our downed balloon provided the perfect opportunity for the conspirators to gather evidence that we were violating the pampa and therefore could be forcibly removed. We later learned that Reiche's airborne investigator had been tracking our every move in the course of his daily tourist-laden flights over the ray centers.

That scenario would replay a few years later with archaeologist Persis Clarkson. With her government permit in hand she, too, would be ordered off the pampa by Reiche's guards. The same police official who had harassed us threatened Clarkson with lynching, and Renate publicly accused her of stealing ceramic remains. The feisty young archaeologist retaliated by going public on Lima TV, radio, and in the newspapers. Wrote journalist Wendy Marston of the situation in *The Sciences* magazine, "No one—including Clarkson and Urton—denies the debt the world owes to Maria Reiche; she has lovingly tended an archaeological treasure. But the controversy over access to the site continues. And in the light of recent political upheavals in Peru, a more pressing question may be, How much longer will anyone be able to study the lines—with or without the Reiches' blessing?"[19]

There was one benefit from our temporary banishment from the Nasca pampa. It gave us a chance to take trips to some of the adjacent pampas out of Reiche's jurisdiction. Even the most superficial study of lines on other pampas had never been broached by anyone. On these side trips we managed to establish that all forms of Nasca lines as we know them are not unique to the pampa of Nasca. They are more visible there only because of the unusual nature of the elevated desert between the Ingenio and Nasca rivers. This zone is practically the only pampa along the entire coastal strip that is heavily laden with large, angled bits of desert-varnished debris. When these chunks are removed and piled up, the patterns they reveal are not only easily visible but also quite durable and long lasting.

On one occasion we walked the length of the pampa between the Pisco and Chincha valleys north of the Nasca pampa. Though this terrain is quite sandy, we discovered several lines, most of them 10 to 50 yards wide. In a few instances, the enclosed area was framed not by the space produced by removal of the fragmentary debris but rather by the addition of material from well outside to form the border. These figures are more like negative Nasca lines, rather than etchings. Still, the forms are the same. Wide avenues lead up to dunes that overlook the river valleys. In one center six lines emanated from a single point, and each terminated at a bend in a local irrigation canal. Indeed, many pampa roads lead to water.

Tying Land to Water

Think of all those subjects you studied in school: geography, history, math, physics, geology. These disciplines are all products of the taxonomy of an educational system handed down to us from the great European Enlightenment. Honed to be more specialized, they make up the floorboards in an expanding house of knowledge. Today we have begun to acquire fresh knowledge from the merging of these disciplines as we fill in the interdisciplinary spaces between the floorboards: neurophysiology, astrophysics, biochemistry. To explore the thousand-year-old ideas that underlie the patterns we were beginning to find on the pampa, we would need to take the same multiperspective approach that had helped Tom Zuidema and me to understand Cuzco's ceque system; that is, we would need to know something about land and water utilization in the fragile desert environment of the Nasca drainage basin then and now.

Two problems here: there were no chroniclers around to record what society was like at the time the Nasca people constructed the lines (they would come a millennium too late to tell any stories like those they told about Inca Cuzco), and there were no contemporary anthropologists studying the making of coastal calendars that deal with life cycles, distribution of resources, and so on. We also lacked a third necessity. Without the help of a seasoned field archaeologist, interpreting all those artifacts that lay out on the pampa (their dates and placement in the Nasca ceramic sequence, an evaluation of the condition and situation in which they were found) would prove fruitless. Any meaningful study of the pampa at ground level would need to involve geography, anthropology, ethnohistory, and archaeology and all of the subdisciplines between the disciplines, the very expertises working together that all previous studies seem to have lacked. Even more important, this interdisciplinary effort would need to address questions and set priorities viewed through the lens of ancient coastal societies rather than from our own generally culturally biased point of view.

I've already expressed how surprised I was when I first realized that practically nobody had walked the lines and studied them from ground level. Maria Reiche was the remarkable exception, but even she had paid little attention to the remains on the pampa and confined practically all her attention to discovering and clearing the geoglyphs of their contents (including potsherds). To solve the problem of the lack of archaeological know-how while we were investigating and mapping the lines, Urton and I contacted Persis Clarkson, then a graduate student at the University of Calgary, to explore the archaeological remains associated with the Nasca figures. Clarkson had been one of my brightest students at Colgate back in the mid-seventies. She had already traveled with me to Mexico to explore the astronomical orientations of Maya and Mexican buildings. Later she spent two years on a prestigious Watson Foundation fellowship working on Maya ceramics in Guatemala and added to that a couple of years of archaeological fieldwork in Ecuador and a few more exploring ancient Peru. With her discerning eye and hardy, persistent spirit, Clarkson was the ideal person to walk every square foot of pampa in search of samples of ancient remains that might shed light on the mystery of the Nasca lines. When she began working with us in 1982, Clarkson squared off the pampa on the 1:50,000 government maps and immediately plunged into a self-designed program with her typical vigor. Ultimately, she would walk hundreds of miles of pampa and record thousands of artifacts.

Clarkson found Nasca ceramics scattered all over the pampa. The majority were polychromes: flaring bowls, cup-shaped bowls, dishes, straight-sided jars, bottles with twin spouts. These were decorated with painted birds, fish, plants, human heads, and trophy heads, all ceremonial wares. As she filed records of the various shapes and decors into the imaginary boxes that make up the Nasca chronological ceramic sequence (see Chapter 3), a time scale began to reveal itself. Her dates spanned the Early Intermediate Period with its several Nasca phases (200 BC to AD 600) all the way up to the period of Spanish contact. She found an especially heavy concentration in the Late Intermediate Period (after AD 1000). The densest concentrations lay close to the Nasca River, an expected result since it is close to, though downstream from, most of the habitation and disturbed cemetery sites.[20] The Nasca sherds she found on the trapezoids backed up the earlier, more limited survey conducted in 1969 by astronomer Gerald Hawkins. One fairly large deposit, on a peak jutting out onto the pampa, may have involved a rite in which some of the finest Nasca polychrome pots had been deliberately smashed and dumped. (A reminder about using ceramic finds to date the lines: the age of an artifact found on a line cannot be older than the line, but it can be considerably younger. Even bottle caps from the nationally popular lemon-grass-tasting, yellow soft drink Inca Cola have been found adjacent to ceramic remains. This is especially so if the lines were maintained or ritually cleansed periodically. In this case, a linear feature could be much older than the stuff situated on top of it.)

Clarkson's most surprising conclusion was that on the one hand, potsherds found on the animal figures correlated best with an Early Intermediate chronology (which is precisely when the subject matter painted on the pots matches best with what we see etched on the pampa), but on the other hand, the low yield of Early Intermediate ceramic fragments in midpampa, where most of the straight lines are located, placed the latter in the Middle Horizon (AD 600–1000) and

Late Intermediate (AD 1000–1450) periods. This pointed to a later construction date for the lines, a result that agreed with the many instances in which we found straight features overlying animal figures (e.g., Figure 12). In fact, Clarkson's data indicated that the figures predated the lines by 500 years or more.

Ceramics were not the only remains Persis found on and about the Nasca lines. She also cataloged stone circles, cairns, even a few walled structures. The stone circles look like big campfire sites (Figure 42). Made up of fist-sized boulders piled one or two courses high, they average six feet in diameter, big enough to get inside. Clarkson recognized a resemblance between these circles and the North American Plains Indian tipi rings, where the stones served as weights to anchor a cloth shelter held up by a post. The location of most of the circles in gullies and at the bases of sandy ridges along with the utilitarian ceramics (water jugs and dishes to eat from) found in and around them supported this idea. Furthermore, circles often turned up in the environs of line centers. Maybe the line workers or visitors used them for protection. Having been out on the pampa working in the heat of midday, I have often craved cover from the sun as well as from the frequent dust storms that strike without warning. Her idea made sense to me.

Figure 42. There is more to the Nasca pampa than lines. Archaeologist Persis Clarkson's survey revealed that cairns and stone circles like this one are abundant. Were they used for shelter by people who visited the lines? Photo © Persis Clarkson.

The many cairns Persis found were piles of flat rocks and had about the same dimensions as the rings, though somewhat taller. At six feet, the tallest of them is easily visible a long way off. Many have fallen over, their stones scattered about the vicinity. Walking the lines to their points of termination, we encountered a number of these cairns positioned on the tops of natural hills from where the lines radiate (Figure 35). We had also seen them at bends in zigzag features (like the ones on the Cantalloc fishing rod) and at spots where lines abruptly widened or narrowed, an observation that John Hyslop had also made in his study of Inca roads. As we walked the pampa's many straight lines, we found it easy to focus our attention on the hills toward which we were being led by sighting cairns atop them in the distance. Whenever we descended into a quebrada and lost sight of a line, we would inevitably recover our orientation by spotting a cairn beside the line on the opposite bank. I have never been an advocate of the theory that what works for me also worked for the ancients, but in this particular instance it is difficult to get away from the notion that cairns are practical and orientational— guideposts on the interstate highway of the pampa. Locals call them *markas,* piles of stones constructed specifically for marking or sighting.

Could the stones that make up the cairns have been deposited one at a time by itinerants? All over the Andes, stone piles confront the traveler. Natives call them *apachetas,* and they appear at significant places in the landscape. In Cuzco they are at the point of the horizon where the city first becomes visible to those who climb over the mountain passes that descend into the valley. For luck they say travelers should carry a stone from wherever they come and deposit it in the pile as they pass, thus building a lithic hegemony with the world outside.

Clarkson also found contemporary materials associated with some of the hill-top cairns, which led her to think that not all of them might date to antiquity. For example, she found evidence that itinerant gold miners had camped there-abouts. Near the edges of the pampa lie rectangular walled structures, some having been used in recent times to herd goats. At least one of them (adjacent to line center 37 and previously noted by Gary Urton) is close to the transpampa Inca road and could have served as a tambo, or resting place, for weary pre-Columbian travelers.

Upon returning to the lab, Clarkson helped apply a new method for getting a handle on when the Nasca lines were constructed, a method that might help circumvent the issue of whether the lines were repeatedly cleaned or swept, be-cause it depends not on an analysis of the ceramics but instead on tests made on the broken stones that had been removed from the surface of the pampa and piled at the edges when the figure was constructed.

The dark color of the pampa comes from a varnish that forms on the exposed surface; the lighter colors of the geoglyphs represent unvarnished material (see Figure 5). This desert varnish forms when iron- and manganese-rich surfaces are exposed to air and become oxidized. Microscopic quantities of organic material from plant or bacterial remains can get trapped beneath the thin layers of varnish. The carbon remaining in these deposits can be radiocarbon dated. Suppose a Nasca line builder overturns a chunk of rock. Long protected from contact with the air, its upper surface slowly begins to weather. If we can date the organic matter that first appears on its surface, we can in effect discover when the sample was disturbed.

Working with Ronald Dorn, an Arizona State University geographer who pioneered the method, Persis submitted several samples collected on various areas of the pampa near the geoglyphs for radiocarbon dating. The results from the two independent dating techniques confirmed approximately what archaeologist William Duncan Strong had found 40 years earlier, when he arrived at a radiocarbon date for a fragment of post pulled from a hole at the intersection of a pair of trapezoids: the Nasca figural drawings sampled were made around the same time that similar figures and patterns were being painted on the ceramics, about AD 360, give or take 75 years. (The date assigned the remains of the post was about AD 550, and it likely may have been reused.) This analysis also implied that the figures were made before the straight lines. At this writing, however, the efficacy of Dorn's method has been challenged.[21]

Clarkson also collected a few samples of varnished rock fragments that made up the roofs of two subterranean aqueducts at the eastern end of the pampa.[22] Her results, again about AD 550, confirmed the findings of archaeologist Katharina Schreiber and Josué Lancho, who studied shifts in settlement patterns in the area through the collection and analysis of Nasca potsherds and location of sites. The people who built the straight lines on top of the pampa and the people who constructed the straight underground channels may have been contemporaries, possibly the same people. Schreiber and Lancho's settlement maps are compelling.[23] They reflect where people had access to water and when. The early Nasca sites are all located upstream because that is where rivers flow most of the time, but late Nasca sites are positioned downstream, where water is absent much of the time. By the time the Inca show up on the pampa, habitation sites flourish in many locales where there is no water. None of this makes sense, Schreiber and Lancho argue, unless these cultures were building underground aqueducts to access water. The same patterns and conclusions seem to hold up in the adjacent river valleys of Taruga and Las Trancas, but anthropologist Monica Barnes and her colleague David Fleming have challenged these conclusions. They base their faith on a different kind of evidence. They have amassed statements from historical documents that suggest the Spaniards might have brought the so-called *qanat,* or underground canal technology, over after Columbus, though documents describing aqueduct construction in Nasca are still wanting.[24]

Can everyone be correct? Perhaps there was an ancient irrigation system in place, and then another completely independent (yet almost identical) foreign one was brought over. Could it be that the stones Clarkson sampled from the underground chambers had been reused components from an earlier open canal irrigation system, an indigenous system that had been expanded and improved? If so, the microbiotic matter that makes up the desert varnish would have been deposited on them years, perhaps many centuries, before the stones were put in place.

Though he never worked directly with us on the pampa, I had always considered John Hyslop the reigning authority on Inca roads, until his tragic death in 1993. The knowledge he imparted to us, always willingly and generously, would go a long way toward contributing to our conclusion that above all, the Nasca lines were built to walk on rather than to gape at. Hyslop was a young maverick archaeologist who spent three years, 1979–1982, cruising the ancient Inca highways of Peru (most of the 23,000 miles of them) on a motorcycle. Before his early death, he produced one of the most important works on the Inca empire, a book entitled *The Inka Road System.* In it he detailed his archaeological survey work on the roads and their associated sites. Because Hyslop's time in the field coincided with ours, we crossed paths often. He told us of his attempts to trace the old Inca coastal road through the vicinity of the pampa. Some of the features of the road system up and down the coast from Nasca bore a suspicious resemblance to what we had seen when we walked and surveyed the Nasca lines (Figure 43). By 1982 our group had collectively walked more than 100 miles of pampa, and it had become resoundingly clear that the many, often multiple, deep footpaths we encountered along the lines could not be attributed to locals cutting across the pampa (personally, I never observed a single Nasca inhabitant on the pampa proper in the twenty or so years that span my visits there) or to tourists, few of whom ventured out into the desolate midpampa region. Clearly people in the past had trod this surface and produced these well-worn tracks.

One feature shared by Nasca lines and Inca roads is that both exhibit pairs or even groups of parallel features (Figures 43 and 44). Hyslop described and illustrated a road segment on the southern entrance to the Zaña Valley on the north coast that consists of three parallel lines separated by hummocks of cleared ma-

Figure 43. Nasca lines and Inca roads have many similarities. Compare the pair of cairns that mark the termination point of an Inca road *(above)* with those, indicated by arrow, that signal the end of a Nasca trapezoid *(facing, top)*, or the straight border of an Inca road *(left)* with a Nasca line *(facing, bottom)*. Photos on this page by John Hyslop; top photo on p. 169 from Servicio Aerofotográfico Nacional, Peru; bottom photo on p. 169 © Persis Clarkson.

terial. Gutiérrez de Santa Clara, the Spanish chronicler, described how such a road might have been used:

> Two collateral roads were on both sides of the (coastal) royal road and they too had two strong and wide walls. And when the Inka passed on these roads, he went on the middle one and was followed by those who were responsible for carrying his litter. They were 600 men who alternated carrying it on their shoulders. There were also many important Indians of his royal court who accompanied him. They were carried by many Indians on their shoulders because they were great lords and chiefs of different people who were given permission to travel in a litter. . . . The other multitudes of Indian workers and bearers went by the other two adjoining roads. And none of them passed to the middle road unless the Inka called them.[25]

Hyslop's description and the photographs he showed us reveal that the clearing, edging, and dimensions of many of the lines that we examined on the pampa are virtually identical to Inca roads. Some of Hyslop's roads even take on trapezoidal proportions, with cairns at the points where changes of width occur. He shared with me a page of his field notes (dated August 1979) depicting a section of road in the Chicama Valley (also on the north coast). It opened into a trapezoid 40 yards wide and 300 yards long, which widened to 60 yards at its wider end. This base, which lay toward the valley, was marked by a pair of piles of sand and rock positioned precisely at the point where it exited into a road 30 yards wide that took the traveler down into the Chicama. We found likely traces of this same road at Nasca, our transpampa line, one of the rare linear features we mapped that we could not trace to a line center.

If speech is an acoustical acting out of language, then walking is a spatial acting out of place, an appropriation of topography.[26] We were now fairly certain that all those other lines, at least the straight ones enclosing the multiple pathways, served some purpose relating to movement: walking, running, dancing. At least this hypothesis fit the facts much better than the notion that the lines were built to be seen from above. But why would the people of Nasca care to tread on the desolate pampa?

New wine in old bottles: I found an interesting case of ceremonial line walking in an article from the thirties by the Belgian anthropologist Alfred Métraux. It concerned the pathways trod by the Chipaya Indians, an Aymara-speaking people of highland Bolivia. Like spokes on a wheel, these pathways converge on isolated rock cairns, leading the walker straight to them without regard for the roughness or incline of the ground. Métraux's description bears a strong resemblance to our line centers. Tony Morrison, who visited a number of these rock

Figure 44. This triple Nasca line is five miles long, and it runs straight over a mountain. Many of the Inca roads also appear in triplicate. According to the chronicler Gutiérrez de Santa Clara, the king traveled on the main road, while his retinue and commoners used the adjacent paths. Photo Servicio Aerofotográfico Nacional, Peru.

shrines, pointed out that Métraux called the accessways "paths," as distinct from "lines," but then, remember, the latter label appears in Nasca only after the advent of aviation and aerial photography.

Locals call the conical piles of stone and earth (of about the same dimensions as the Nasca stone cairns) *mal'ku,* after the earth spirits who were venerated there. These mal'ku represent the effigies of various earth spirits, each with its own name, and they all lie on straight lines a few miles from the nearest village, from where pilgrims journey to place offerings in chambers at their bases.

When Morrison visited the mal'ku, one of his Aymara informants told him that just before a fiesta held on January 2, the worshipers would proceed to a shrine to fast. They would encircle it on their knees. Later, when the fast was broken, they would shatter the bowls that once contained their food and present them to the shrine as *jik'illita* (money fragments). Morrison also found many instances among the Aymara of pathways called *t'aki* that led to shrines at the tops of the highest hills, with intermediate shrines established along the path,

Figure 45. Lines similar to Nasca's are still used today. Here villagers and musicians in contemporary Bolivia return from ceremonies they performed at the end of a straight line. Once they ascended the line to the hilltop (rear left), they worshiped the mountain gods, asking them to send rain. Photo © Johan Reinhard.

particularly where shallower hills intervened. The similar custom of erecting a *calvario,* or Christian cross, on the highest hilltop in sight of a village may be of colonial origin.

Later the explorer-anthropologist Johan Reinhard would successfully extend the search for the contemporary use of straight lines. One example he studied occurred in two areas of a little village near La Paz, Bolivia. Villagers would walk half a mile along a line to an adjacent hilltop shrine, dancing and worshiping the mountain gods along the way, asking them to send rain (Figure 45). Later families would walk the line again and assemble in a miniature mock field dotted with symbolic crops made of stone. They would use miniature replicas of plows and pretend to plant the area, again making offerings for the success of the crops. At another village 150 miles to the south, villagers convey themselves along a similar straight line two miles long that divides the village into two moieties. Representatives ascend a 3,000-foot mountain via the line, carrying sea water and calling to the clouds for rain. Then they return via a different route along the ridge, where they perform rituals at designated spots along the way at critical points in the agricultural cycle.[27]

When I gave a progress report to the anthropology department at the State University of New York at Albany, archaeologist Dwight Wallace told me about yet another radial road system. He had been excavating the pre-Inca complex of La Centinela in the Chincha Valley north of Nasca.[28] John Hyslop had once commented that the straight roads that extended out from the large adobe pyramid there "were enough to make any Andean archaeologist wonder about their relationship to the Inca ceque system."[29] Hyslop had followed the four paths that led outward several miles from the giant pyramid. One led across the pampa to the Pisco River valley, passing a number of scattered stone piles along the way. (Were they shrines along the road?) He found remains of corn, fish bones, and a few pieces of textile scattered among the stones. Three of the four roads ended at habitation sites, which led him to think that these paths, unlike those of the Chipaya, may have been of practical, economic importance, rather than purely ritualistic.

All of these descriptions, particularly the contemporary ones, reminded me of Cuzco's ceque system: the radial lines are like ceques, and the stopping points where people deposit offerings are their huacas. Earth spirits, praying to the gods for rain, pathways to gain access to the gods: these religious and agricultural motives began to fuse together. This was the proverbial iceberg's tip, for we would soon learn that the straight line as a principle of organization had even deeper pan-Andean roots.

A Place for People

Anthropology is a profession whose revelations can be painful, capable of dealing unnerving blows to the psyche of the society that practices it. Claude Lévi-Strauss once said that the work of the anthropologist often exposes us to a denial of what we thought we knew, to a negation of our most cherished ideas and habits by other peoples' ideas and habits best able to rebut them. Following the anthropologists' cardinal rule of getting to know people well before attempting to explain why they behave as they do, in 1982 Gary Urton initiated a much-needed study of seasonal calendars among the coastal cultures of Peru. Because we were testing the astronomy and calendar hypothesis on the pampa, this seemed like a good idea. His study was based on both an analysis of old archival documents and several months' residence in the southern fishing port of Chala. Gary went out on a number of fishing launches for all-night trips (experiencing many episodes of seasickness) to talk to pilots about the stars known to local mariners. What he uncovered revealed a continuity between the calendars present there and those used to regulate activities in the highland regions, but as one might expect, the ecology of the desert coast and the delicate transition region between coast and highlands (where Nasca is located), with its markedly different seasonal pattern, promotes a different way of ordering temporal events. Marine cycles, periods of flowering of the landscape, and the availability of water are among the most important environmental correlates that make up these calendars.

Among groups exploiting resources in the higher reaches of the coastal valleys, Urton found more complex calendars, "subsistence" calendars he called them, because they reflected the impact of a number of vital ecozones on one another. Astronomy was a part of these subsistence calendars, too. People make calendars to reach out to the future, to time the arrival of impending social and natural events. But we can know the future only by paying close attention to the patterns of the past, and when we organize our world around the reliable repeatable phenomena that occur in nature, we must be able to tie events of social significance to those that follow the unending rhythm of cyclic time. For example, the appearance and disappearance of the Pleiades were tied to combined agricultural and fishing cycles in many of these communities. The April 10 antizenith sun passage in the Moche-Huanchaco calendar of the north coast also coincides with the beginning of the disappearance period of the Pleiades. This use of the Pleiades' period of absence from the sky as a rough indicator of an interim period of ecological significance, along with the connections of Pleiades phenomena with the zenith and antizenith sun passages, is reminiscent of the old calendar mapped into the ceque system of Cuzco. Urton also found that these people sighted the first and last seasonal appearance of Orion's Belt, the Southern Cross, and several dark cloud constellations as timing devices in their subsistence calendars. In each instance, these seasonal boundaries marked by the stars formed what he called core periodicities (e.g., the time when river water flows). Upon these timings, more elaborate calendars were built, thus enabling organized societies to improve their use of even more diverse ecological zones. As he put it, "A coastal society's ability to efficiently coordinate the resources and human activities of its river valley would have been a determining factor in the relative success or failure of its cultural tradition."[30]

As important as Gary Urton's work on the coast of Peru was in giving us ideas to explore about the connections between Nasca ecology, astronomy, and the lines, it would be his work at Pacariqtambo (a small village about eight hours away by potato truck from Cuzco) between 1981 and 1984 that would be even more seminal, for it would offer a detailed motive for why people walked the lines.

We don't often think of our garbage as a collection of memories of what happened in our kitchen yesterday or of emptying it as a sacred rite, but in many cultures the act of cleaning is far more than the simple tidying up of an area in preparation for future activity. "Cleansing" would be a better term for the process, as anthropologist Mary Douglas describes it.[31] It has to do with restoring a sacred place to a state of purity by removing all pollution, all matter that might lend some earlier, less sacred identity to the place, for such a previous association might oppose the order sought through the rituals about to be conducted there. The people of Pacariqtambo divide their community plaza into ten rectangular strips called *chhiutas* (divisions), one for each of the ten ayllus that make up the town. Representatives from each of the ayllus are required to sweep the chhiutas clean of debris and maintain them, especially when annual religious festivals take place there. For example, on one of the Catholic saints' days that comes at the end of the planting season, Urton witnessed how the ayllus divide up the preparatory duties of cleansing and repairing the town hall, the church, and its surrounding adobe wall. Out of respect for the image of the saint, which is carried and accompanied by a retinue of barefooted devotees across the plaza, the way must be swept clean. So, on the morning of the festival, representatives from ayllus whose chhiutas border one another come and stand in the plaza. They gaze at the partitioned wall together and negotiate by eyeball, accompanied by dialogue, exactly where each representative will clean (Figure 46). Urton describes what he saw: "At least one member of each one of the nine groups goes to the center of town and sweeps up the debris within his *chhiuta,* loads it into a carrying cloth, and dumps it off the plaza grounds."[32] Although the lines divide

Figure 46. Along this partitioned wall of the plaza at Pacariqtambo, representatives of kin and work groups still gather to eyeball long narrow strips of the plaza that identify their social status. Contrast the whitewashed, roofed segment on the right with the less well appointed segment on the left (*top*). Caught up in his own dust, one of the representatives can be seen sweeping his strip (*bottom*). Photos courtesy of Gary Urton

ing the chhiutas are not marked out on the grounds of the churchyard and plaza, the adobe wall shared by each of the ten cleared strips was maintained section by section, one-tenth of it freshly whitewashed, another tenth with new roofing tiles, a third in a relatively unkempt condition, and so on. On the next religious occasion, ayllu representatives reestablish their contiguous chhiutas all over again. This is hardly the way family groups belonging to one of our churches, synagogues, or mosques would share in tidying up its interior. Can you imagine your family dusting off and sweeping its own designated pew? We would probably time-share, one family taking on the duty for the entire congregation at Easter, another at Christmas. But as Lévi-Strauss warns, we must be prepared to see our ideas negated.

We have already learned that representatives of ancient Cuzco's 40 "families" conducted a ritual plowing in the plaza of Hurin Cuzco, but strips of clean-swept turf in contemporary highland Peru are a long way in space and time from ancient strips on a coastal desert. Still, there are closer parallels. At least at the time of the conquest, coastal societies were organized around ayllus and moieties, and similar forms of social organization could have been tied to comparable land structures, even if they were not linked directly and historically. This is where archival documents come in. One of the earliest colonial reports, the 1593 Visita de Acari (or "visit to the town of Acari," one of many ordered by the government to assure that bureaucratic procedures controlled the natives and to see to it that their labors continued to benefit the Spanish crown), would forge the missing link between Pacariqtambo and Nasca Urton was seeking. Found in a musty archive in Lima and written by one of the officials in charge of relocating the Indians, the Visita made it clear that there were ayllus along the coast and furthermore that they were divided between hanan and hurin (upriver and downriver) moieties, just as in Cuzco. The report told of many people living in the Nasca valley who belonged to ayllus of different towns along the coast; for example, thirteen men from the ayllus of Acari's upper moiety had married Nasca women, which is why they came to Nasca in the first place. All of them were involved in labor and other tributary activities under the mit'a, or shared-labor system of obligation. Urton also rooted out the last will and testament of the wealthy landowner García Nasca (dated 1569), after whom the modern town of Nasca was named. It says that Nasca ayllus were grouped into four suyus, or *parcialidades*. These ayllus, too, participated in the shared-labor system while working Don García's vineyards.

The Nasca pampa was slowly beginning to crystallize as a space of far greater significance than a barren desert. It was beginning to emerge as the dividing place between two sets of moieties à la Cuzco. Like Pacariqtambo's plaza, the area bordering the two vital watershed areas of the Ingenio and Nasca was a space for negotiating agricultural and ritual activities, a space for organizing people in a symbolic way through its territorial divisions.

If this space in-between coordinated any shared activity among the parcialidades that bordered one another in the Ingenio and Nasca valleys, the construction, use, and maintenance of irrigation facilities would likely have figured in that activity. Chronicler Cobo tells us that highland irrigation projects under the mit'a system operated just like Pacariqtambo's plaza. Each ayllu was given a section or line of an irrigation channel, and the group workers of that ayllu, along with their wives and children, were required to complete that specific section. Another document Urton found, concerning a dispute over water rights, specifically mentions "mit'as de aguas" (water-sharing obligations) in the Nasca-Ingenio zone. When one hacienda owner in the upper valley (hydrologically the more strategic place to live) was accused of using more than his share of water, the owners of haciendas in the lower Ingenio devised a clever time-sharing solution that involved taking turns by segments proportional to the area of land they held: "So that there will be a sufficient amount of water to reach our haciendas, the hacienda owners higher up must be compelled to recognize the allotment of the said water; thus, there should be approved and set aside customary days for turns ["días communes de mit'as"] both for the haciendas above and for those lower down, which is a distance of three leagues [about nine miles] . . . and the *mit'as* that you [judge] assign should run without confusing anyone, as is done, and as has been done, in all these valleys of Nasca."[33]

Anyone who visits the Nasca area and sees how precipitously water runs down to the pampa will get a sense that controlling that precious liquid would have been foremost in the minds of the people who hoped to thrive there. Was the irrigated land in the Nasca valley actually divided into strips (like Pacariqtambo's plaza) that were incorporated into the performance of mit'a labor? We have no direct evidence, though one chronicler tells us that when the Inca king Huayna Capac conquered the coast, he moved thousands of Indians from diverse ethnic groups to that region, and then he settled them into five strips averaging three miles long by half a mile wide running perpendicular to the nearby river.

We did find an ancient plaza not far from Nasca that had been divided into visible strips. While studying the seasonal calendar and astronomy of fishermen in the coastal village of Chala, about 100 miles southeast of Nasca, Gary had heard about a place called Quebrada de la Vaca, an archaeological site dating from Inca times (an Inca road passes nearby) that looked a lot like the divided plaza he had been studying at Pacariqtambo up in the highlands. Quebrada is a walled trapezoidal area, 30 by 45 yards, with a row of chambers on its longest side. The space within is subdivided into eight strips, each about 30 yards long and 5 yards wide, carefully demarcated by lines made up of small round pieces of stone (Figure 47). The eight lines are split into two zones of four by a sort of alleyway running up the middle, making nine strips in all. Structurally this is very similar to the plaza or churchyard in Pacariqtambo. Gary speculated that the chambers at Quebrada were for storage and the large open area was used by the local ayllus for ritual activities, perhaps having to do with the harvest:

> Half of the chambers would have been used by the *ayllus* of the upper moiety, the other half by those of the lower moiety. The evenly divided strips in front of the chambers could have served for the cleaning and drying of the wheat or for other communal/agricultural activities. Presumably, the *ayllus* would have also been responsible for the maintenance of the plaza/chamber complex itself. In this work, their interactions may have produced episodes of cooperation and confrontation similar to those in modern-day Pacariqtambo during the sweeping of the *chhiutas.*[34]

Figure 47. An ancient public space divided into long rectangular strips, Quebrada de la Vaca dates from Inca times. Its form is reminiscent of Pacariqtambo's divided plaza, where each strip is ritually maintained by members of a given land-owning kin group. Photo by author.

But why flexible strips with negotiable boundaries at Pacariqtambo and fixed or frozen rectangular divisions bounded by stone lines at Quebrada? Why assume society then and now are exactly the same? Perhaps when the Inca took over they kept the situation as they found it, fixing the boundaries permanently as a measure of control over the local inhabitants, as states are wont to do. Still, parallel rectangular strips, permanently marked out or not, aren't the same as radial Nasca lines, and the vast open area of desert on which we find the lines doesn't have much in common with either a storage area or a plaza at the center of a town. Maybe the relationship is purely a formal one, perhaps even a deceptive analogy, argued Urton's critics. He countered that in the Inca empire both radial and grid structures were used to partition the land to indicate the distribution of water rights. Radial division of space was used by the elites, who tended to view imperial organization from a central point; Cuzco is a good example. Grid systems seem better suited for the lower classes. But let's not lose the main point: either system can be maintained at the same time by different ayllus within the same territory. So, the parallel-strip system of organizing irrigation might have been developed in the Nasca and Ingenio valleys among members of ayllus and suyus who worked there, while the pampa (the space in-between) was the locale for coordinating the evidently more complex regional hierarchical relations. Whatever went on in midpampa—ritual battles, confrontations, assemblies, offertory rites such as those Cobo mentions for the ceque system—maintaining, sweeping, and cleaning these lines would have been a part of the process of social interaction among the ayllus of all the areas under the dominion of local elites.

By paying attention to Andean institutions, Andean customs (the ayllus and the mit'a system of shared labor, dividing land into narrow chhiuta and suyu strips, and the process of maintenance), Gary Urton's work had succeeded in putting people onto the pampa. His was a social theory that offered a motive for making the lines, a theory that could not have been imagined without knowing something about those who lived and still live there. Our vision of the pampa began to transform into both a practical and a symbolic focal plane for working out problems of space and resource distribution among the valley's residents. Our explanations were a far cry from what the astronomers and engineers were searching for, and they had little to do with rooting out universal lost knowledge. We never fancied our ideas would gain wide popularity, but if you value, as I do, learning how people in other times and in other places went about solving their social problems by recourse to methods our sophisticated culture hasn't even dreamed of, it sounds pretty exciting.

When Pilgrims Came

The pampa of Nasca tells a story about the everyday lives and needs of the people who lived close by. Where an anthropologist left off, an archaeologist would pick up the slack. Shortly after Gary Urton and I began our surface study of the pampa, we learned that archaeologist Helaine Silverman, then a graduate student at the University of Texas, had been excavating at the ruins of Cahuachi on the south bank of the Nasca River. Helaine is one of the most vivacious, effervescent personalities I've ever met. Her enthusiasm about archaeology, vocally expressed in her thick, fast-talking New York accent, spreads like wildfire to all her students. (She is now a professor at the University of Illinois.) So I wasn't surprised when she expressed a willingness to collaborate with us. When she did, she immediately became absorbed with Gary's ideas on the pampa as a divided space used for expressing social action and interaction. Archaeologists use the term "ethnographic analogy" to describe the way modern information from field studies in anthropology is used to test a hypothesis gleaned from ancient archaeological data.[35] Silverman would use it to build a pretty strong case that Cahuachi was, at least in its principal stages of occupation, a pilgrimage center. Its plaza appeared to have experienced the same kind of ritual cleansing Urton had observed in the plaza of Pacariqtambo and that may have occurred on the Nasca lines. Based on extensive test excavations over 85 percent of the area, Silverman had become convinced that Cahuachi may have been a nice place to visit, but nobody really wanted to live there. As shown in Figure 38, Cahuachi fronts one of the heaviest concentrations of line centers, though it never had a large residential population.

Another important aspect of Cahuachi Silverman discovered is that the river adjacent to it is almost never dry, regardless of the season. It is a natural huaca where water comes magically to the surface, as she puts it. Was it possible that pilgrims traveled to Cahuachi for this reason, viewing the area as a sacred place where the underworld, the source of fertility, and the world of the living meet and unite?

Why so many mounds? Silverman thought of three possibilities. They may have been the result of a large social group's repetitive cycle of worship at the site. (I thought about the way Maya worshipers in highland Guatemala in their successive ritual rounds are required to travel to four different peripheral shrines at each of the cardinal points and of the Aztec sacrifice of children in the month of March to bring the rains, which took place at seven different strategic mountain locations circumscribing the ancient capital of Tenochtitlán.) A second possibility is that different ayllus were required to worship, each at their own sacred place or huaca. The ceque system of Cuzco is the obvious prototype for comparison here. Finally, the various mounds all may have functioned differently from one another, perhaps reflecting some sort of social hierarchy. She argued for all these explanations as the best fits with what we know about Andean social organization. For example, in the highland pilgrimage of Qollur R'iti, people travel to a mountaintop shrine to demonstrate group prestige. Together they proudly represent their hierarchical place in the local community, rather than in some large undifferentiated group, as is the case in most Christian pilgrimages. When they return home, they need to vie with rival social groups to retain their prestige and status. There is other evidence of communal activity that focuses on Cahuachi. The Great Cloth, a complex masterpiece of weaving 20 feet long and 1.5 feet wide, was excavated at Cahuachi back in the fifties. Its production seems to have involved considerable teamwork, employing a number of weavers with different

---

Pilgrims the World Over

Undertaking a journey en masse to a distant sacred and venerable place for devotional purposes is a far cry from the sorts of activities we individually minded moderns indulge in, but in the religious systems of many societies around the world, such acts hold center stage. Mecca and Jerusalem come to mind. In Roman Catholic Europe, journeys of penance were conducted throughout the Middle Ages. They were especially popular in Jubilee years, specially designated years of indulgence that offered people a means of remitting the penal consequences of their sins. When the Black Death ravaged Italy in the late 1340's, Pope Clement VI broke the rule that Jubilee years should be held once a century (the first one took place in 1300). In crisis, he proclaimed 1350 such a year and granted all who would make the journey to Rome absolution from their sins, which he believed had perpetrated the scourge that had wiped out a third of the European population in less than a year. One chronicler wrote that around Easter of the Holy Year, the roads to Rome from all directions were clogged with pilgrims. Ironically, concentrating a million people in the heart of the Eternal City only renewed the force of the epidemic. (For more on pilgrimages, see Chapter 6.)

skills. No one knows how it was used, but the way it was carefully folded and buried by itself suggests that it might have been a sacred object used in rituals at the pilgrimage site.[36]

Were any of Cahuachi's pyramids linked to the lines directly? Surveying in the area behind the Great Pyramid, Silverman noted a significant number of lines as well as figural drawings (Figure 48). They had also been described by Persis Clarkson in her dissertation. If what Urton had discovered about the plaza strips at Pacariqtambo was applied to Nasca, that is, if the lines were ritually

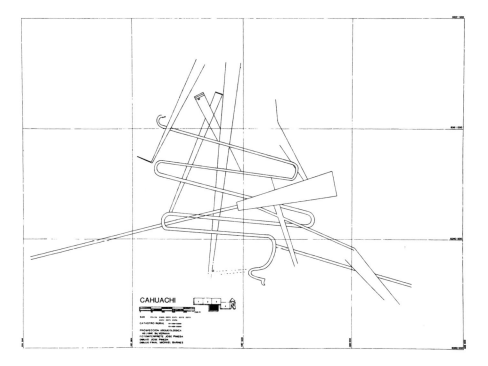

Figure 48. Helaine Silverman mapped this complex of Nasca lines behind the Great Pyramid of Cahuachi (shown melting away in the inset). The heaviest concentration of lines occurs on the pampa fronting the same pyramid. Map and photo by Helaine Silverman.

maintained and swept clean periodically, then earlier ceramic fragments would have been removed from them, leaving only the remains of recent activity on the surface for modern archaeologists to retrieve. If this habit of ritual cleansing had been abandoned, say in the Middle Horizon (AD 600–1000), then we would expect to find sherds from that time (and later) in greatest abundance. In fact, Silverman also noted that the straight features on the Ingenio side of the pampa were heavily strewn with ceramics. So the whole business of making lines may have been a continuous process, some lines being constructed earlier than others.

The name "Cahuachi" itself bespeaks pilgrimage. The word "qhawachi" means to make them see, make them observe, an act that obliges someone to observe. Cahuachi, then, may have been a locus for ceremonial activity having something to do with observing and predicting, a place where priests foretold seminal future activities having to do with agriculture and the regularity and sufficiency of the water supply so vital to crop production in the circumpampa area. From the elevated shrine, they could observe the entire pampa with its lines, along with the surrounding mountains and their deities, all the parts of a puzzle that Johan Reinhard would convincingly demonstrate had a connection with rain and fertility. Silverman saw Cahuachi as an arena for resolving social tensions that resulted from the sort of status-seeking enterprise often attached to pilgrimages. It wasn't out of the question, she believed, that ritual battles were performed there, even the taking of trophy heads. Did different ayllus construct and sweep their own Nasca lines the way they created and maintained the chhiutas at Pacariqtambo, to fulfill their ritual obligation under the mit'a system? Were the ayllus of Nasca responsible for their own huacas and ceques? Maybe, as Helaine suggested, the maze of lines we see today is the product of the repeated reenactment of hundreds of years of selective line making and sweeping, some lines being more pertinent than others at different times. To disentangle what the pampa meant at any given time, we need to read between the lines.

Pipelines on the Pampa

I was first turned on to the idea that the Nasca ray centers and the flow of water on the pampa might be connected when I came across a little-known report on desert ecology in southern Peru, written by a Florida geographer back in the late sixties. It included a map of the Pisco River valley showing faint markings just outside the limits of irrigation: six straight, narrow lines radiating from a single point. Followed outward to distances up to five miles, each one of them intersected a major irrigation canal at a point where it distinctly changed direction. "This seems rather more than mere coincidence and suggests the possibility that many of the linear markings may be related to surveying in connection with the construction of irrigation systems," wrote geographer Alan Craig, who conducted the survey.[37]

No commodity in Nasca is more important than water. The Nasca pampa is bordered by two of the principal tributaries of the Río Grande, and the quebradas that cut across the pampa drain water from the mountains into the Nasca River. In this narrow coastal strip between the high Andes and the Pacific Ocean, where it almost never rains, the precious liquid plummets from 10,000 feet to sea level over a mere twenty miles in places. It is difficult to imagine any steep coastal worldview in which water, its origin, movement, and function, would not play a central role. One of the predominant themes of virtually every conversation Gary had with his informants in the Nasca and Ingenio valleys was rain and the abundance or lack of water in the rivers. No wonder. At the most practical level, the seasonal and long-term variations in the flow of these descending waters are vital to the survival of all the people who live on the coast.

Is there direct evidence that the lines of Nasca themselves were associated with water? Father Alberto Rossel Castro was first to carry the Nasca lines and water into the realm of the practical. Just as the subterranean aqueducts (which he called *galerías filtrantes,* or filtration galleries) subdivided the land below ground into an irrigation network, so too did the geometrical figures parcel out the land above ground, he claimed. Rossel conceived the lines as a direct component of an irrigation plan. Even today, he tells us, the land around Nasca is divided into trapezoids or triangular parcels (called *kollo* in Quechua) that resemble the shapes and dimensions of Nasca ground drawings. (A typical plot, he says, is 850 yards long and up to 100 yards wide.) Often the skinny angle of a triangular plot connects to a water source, and the land is heaped up around the border to conserve moisture within the parcel so that a better crop can grow. In ancient times, Rossel imagines, the pampa was verdant, for once the parcels were laid out, the infertile soil native to the pampa was removed and replaced with more enriched loam. Rossel even had an explanation for why all the giant geometrical figures are close to the rims of the river valleys. It is because they physically served an agricultural function—they were cultivated fields. The animal figures near and often between the large geometrical features also possess agricultural significance: the spider is a symbol of fecundity, and the vulture a precursor of rain. Persis Clarkson spoke at length with a British-Peruvian farmer who had been born and raised on an hacienda in Peru. He owned a vineyard near Nasca, and he told her about the fertility of the pampa soil, which actually turns out to be quite suitable for agricultural purposes. "I don't claim that he meant all of the pampa," Persis told me, "but he did point to the plowing northwest of line centers number three and four [at the far eastern end of the pampa] as indication that people are willing to farm the area as soon as the government irrigation project comes through."

I had always thought Father Rossel a bit of an agriextremist; that is, until Helaine Silverman pointed out to me that she and colleague David Browne had encountered a type of cleared space that looks quite distinct from the Nasca geometric features, rather more like a mock field. These spaces usually occur close to the edge of the pampa, nearer to the actual crops. She calls them *campos barridos*, or swept fields. Her archaeological dating of the campos suggests that this Nasca mode of marking out space may have been practiced as early as late pre-Nasca times (before 100 BC). These campos may have signaled the beginning of the Nasca geoglyph tradition, so there may be a symbolic botanical twilight zone between the land of the living in the valley and the sterile and lifeless pampa.

Water in Nasca comes not from the sky but from the mountains, and Andean anthropologists and historians have gathered plenty of information about the importance of the mountain peaks that overlook most of the sites. When Urton began his fieldwork in the area around Nasca, he spoke with the locals about the hills surrounding the pampa. The prominent white mountain Cerro Blanco to the east (it actually resembles a giant sand dune, peaking at 4,500 feet above the level of the pampa) was seminal in local rites for inducing the rains. A number of residents of Nasca town claim that this hill was a "volcano of water"—that it actually erupted and spewed water. Another local legend implicates Viracocha in the creation process. Witness this story told to Gary, which appears in his field notes:

> In ancient times, before there were aqueducts in the valley, a great drought oc-
> curred and the people had no water for years. The people began crying out to
> their god, Viracocha or Con. They cried and screamed the word *nanay* [Quechua
> for pain]. . . . The people went en-masse to the foot of Cerro Blanco, which was
> their principal *templo* or *adoratorio;* this was the place where they spoke to the
> gods. At that moment, Viracocha/Con descended from the sky to the summit of
> the mountain and heard the weeping of his people. He was so moved by their
> cries that he began weeping, and tears flowed from his eyes. The tears ran down
> Cerro Blanco, penetrated the earth, and these tears were the origin of the
> aqueducts.

To induce rain during dry periods, a man is sent with a jug to the coast, to a place where the waves crash onto the rocks. He gathers up the foamy seawater, races to the top of the hill overlooking the pampa, and sprinkles its contents on

Nasca's Underground Puzzle

The mystery of the Nasca underground aqueducts involves a classic example of the age-old debate about diffusion versus independent invention. We've heard it before: pyramids in Egypt and pyramids in the New World, similar words in the Indonesian and Peruvian languages, festal periods in calendars in the Near East and Mesoamerica that happen at the same time. Thor Heyerdahl brought it all to a head in the fifties with his controversial book *Kon Tiki*. His story goes: If I can build a raft out of materials native to the coast of Peru and sail across the Pacific Ocean, then it is likely that my ancient predecessors did the same, bringing with them ideas about how to build, how to worship, how to keep time, and so on. This monomyth of the origin of culture has its nineteenth-century precedents in the lost continent of Atlantis and the lost tribes of Israel (see Chapter 4). The issue in Nasca is this: Were the straight underground irrigation channels in the valleys adjacent to the pampa invented on the spot, or did the idea come over with the Spanish invaders? Archaeologist Katharina Schreiber of the University of California at Santa Barbara, assisted by Nasca teacher and historian Josué Lancho, argues that the nature of the stonework and the building materials that line the canals are totally unlike the filtration galleries of Europe. They date the aqueducts to the middle of Phase 5 in the Nasca ceramic sequence (approximately the sixth century AD), coincident with a time of widespread drought beginning about AD 560. This overlaps with the time the majority of the pampa figures were erected. Some investigators have challenged the notion that Nasca subterranean irrigation is a unique pre-Hispanic invention.

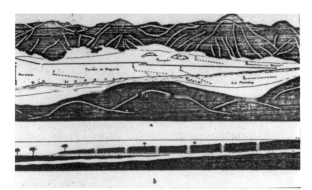

Map of aqueduct system from T. Mejía Xesspe, "Acueductos y caminos antiguos de la hoya del Río Grande de Nazca" [1927], *Actas y Trabajos Cimtíficos del Congreso Internacional de Americanistas* (Lima) 1 (1942): 559–569. (A cross section of one aqueduct is shown at bottom.)

the summit. Within two weeks, rain is sure to come. But beware of spilling the sea foam on the climb up to the summit, for then a deluge will ensue.

Johan Reinhard has climbed more mountains and studied more diverse South American mountain cults than anyone I know. He believes that the Nasca people thought their deities resided in the mountains and that they controlled meteorological phenomena.[38] His Nasca theory views the lines as areas where the locals staged their water and fertility rituals. We should think of the lines as conveyances *to* the ray centers and other sacred places on the pampa, rather than as pathways that extend out from the ray centers, as if to point to something, he argues. (Persis Clarkson calls the centers "terminals," in the transportation sense.) Reinhard found evidence from the chronicles that just a few hundred years before the Spanish occupation of the valley, ancient Nascans thought of the great sand mountain of Cerro Blanco as their principal huaca. They devoutly worshiped it as a means of providing water. But our survey showed that not a single line out of a sample of several dozen in the vicinity was oriented anywhere close to the direction of Cerro Blanco. If anything, it seemed the line builders deliberately avoided aiming lines at the great white mountain. Maybe this *was* a connection.

After half a dozen field surveys, the bond between line centers and water on the Nasca pampa also was beginning to tighten. For one thing, the ray centers seemed to be situated at strategic points where water issued out onto the pampa. Then there were the trapezoids. At least one and often many more of them were directly linked to each line center (e.g., Figure 37). Often a line would turn into a trapezoid a long way out from a center. While the lines that emanated from the centers usually cut across the dry quebradas, the large trapezoids attached to the lines seemed to be situated in the spits of elevated land that lay in between. Often their axes were parallel to the direction of the flow of water. No surprise here: the physical layout of the pampa is dictated largely by the flow of water, and the elongated spaces of land between quebradas generally follow their direction.

Intrigued with the water connection, I set out to explore it further and decided to make a histogram just like the one that I used to explore possible astronomical orientations for the lines (Figure 39). This time I would plot the angles formed by the lines and the direction of flow of water (rather than using true north). The results for all the wide features on the pampa surprised me (Figure 49). As I expected, sharp peaks occurred at 0 degrees (upstream) and 180 degrees (downstream). Now look at the cross-stream directions, the number of features aligning perpendicular to the direction of flow (90 degrees and 270 degrees). Here's the surprise: there are practically no figures aligning with the cross-stream direction looking northwest (220–320 degrees), but the southeast cross-stream direction (40–140 degrees) shows a huge bulge right around 90 degrees. What can this mean? I speculate that the line builders were attempting to establish some sense of local direction, or handedness, when it came to conducting their ritual to acquire water from the gods. Suppose, for example, that a walker were to enter from a line into the widening space of a trapezoid. It may have been necessary to approach the terminal point of the figure, that is, the bank of the quebrada, in such a way that the upstream or water source direction would be on the right rather than on the left; conversely it might have been forbidden to situate the upstream direction to one's left and the downstream to the right.

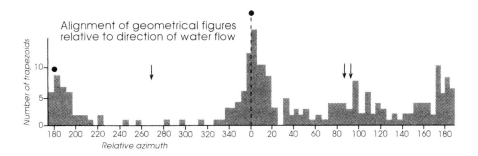

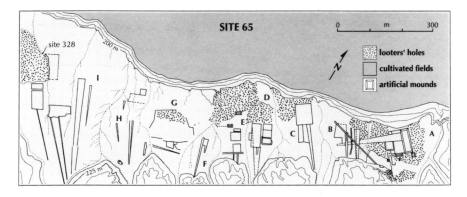

Figure 49. Are Nasca trapezoids right-handed? *Top:* When we graphed their alignments against the direction of water flow, we discovered this skewed pattern. Although many trapezoids align with the direction of water flow (dotted line), a significant number seem to be situated perpendicular to the flow direction, with upstream on the right (double arrows) as opposed to downstream on the left (single arrow), where there are few lines represented. Drawing by Julia Meyerson. *Bottom:* In Helaine Silverman's plan of a complex of geoglyphs abutting the Río Grande Valley we can actually see a large number of trapezoids lining up perpendicular to the river (upstream lies to the right). Courtesy of Helaine Silverman.

Which way should I face when I worship? This question underlies the rules of communication between people and their gods in many cultures. Which way must a priest or worshiper turn to perform a private or public ceremony, a consecration, or a sacrifice in the proper manner? We all know Muslims need to face Mecca, and many old Christian churches align in the direction of sunrise, reflecting the pagan custom of facing the sun god. The Etruscans believed directions were set not according to man but rather to the world itself. There was a front and a back, a left and a right, to Etruscan sacred space, oriented to the home of the gods who lived in the sky: "Four parts did it have: that toward the east *antica,* and *postica* that toward the west; the northern part on the left, the southern on the right," wrote Isidorus, the Roman historian. Other historians tell us precisely what the Roman augur (literally, one who divines by the observation of the course of birds in flight) did when he laid out a temple: "Birds to the left and augury to the left: that is what permits us to act, . . . and when you look south for the seat of the gods, the east is on your left, the west is on your right. I believe it is for this reason that the augurs on the left are to be better than those on the right."[39] The idea of the lucky right and unlucky or "sinister" left that most of us have heard about turns out to be a Greek idea that got switched around long before it ever got handed off to the Romans. Of course, these are all examples from other cultures. We don't know whether the ancient Nascans considered themselves lucky or unlucky depending on which way they entered a trapezoid, but our measurements suggest that the direction of entry (or exit) does seem to have mattered.

When I told this story to Katharina Schreiber, she offered the more practical impression that the wide ends of trapezoids usually point to places where one can climb down to the valley below. Perhaps these wide trapezoids, entered via skinny lines at their narrow ends, served as a guide to people using them as pathways across the pampa, she suggests, telling them that they were close and on the right track. Explorer David Johnson goes farther.[40] He believes the lines, especially the trapezoids, map subterranean rather than surface water sources. He finds that aquifers enter the valley at points where geologic faults or formation changes occur, thus implying that the ancient Nasca people knew something about the underground geology of the region. Geoglyphs, he claims, occur in areas where aquifers flow, and their form is part of a hydrological mapping code; for example, long triangles identify aquifers, and zigzags mean "no water here." All of the knowledge, Johnson asserts, was derived through ancient dowsing, the same method he initially used to reach his own conclusions. An interesting hypothesis, but its validity needs to be tested by careful examination of all the data.

Desert Zoo Parade

Nasca's straight features (the trapezoids, lines, and ray centers that interconnect them) seem to exhibit some organization, but the eye catchers, the large drawings of animals and plants (highlighted in Figure 8 and further displayed in Figure 50), defy all explanation. On the one hand, most of them are concentrated on the northeast corner of the pampa, close to the south bank of the Ingenio River. Few appear elsewhere. On the other, most of them seem to lie under the lines. In fact, I haven't observed a single instance of an animal figure that covers over a line or trapezoid. Very few straight lines join up with the animals. The monkey is an exception, but how do we know the connection

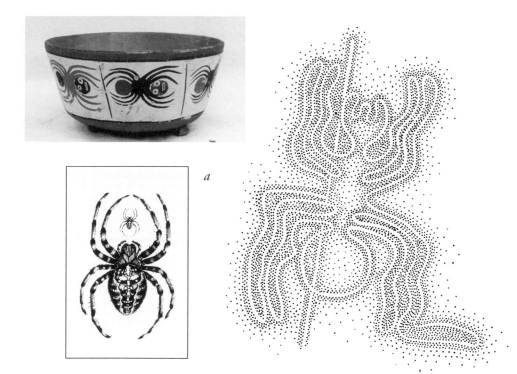

a

Figure 50. This menagerie sampler shows a handful of biomorphs etched on the pampa (for more animal etchings see Figure 8).

a: The wasp-waisted spider. Maria Reiche has argued that it is an effigy of our constellation of Orion. Drawing by Julia Meyerson. *Insets:* the real thing (*Grzimek's Animal Life Encyclopedia* [New York: Van Nostrand, 1972], vol. 1, p. 398; artist unknown) and a representation on a ceramic vessel (photo courtesy of Donald Proulx).

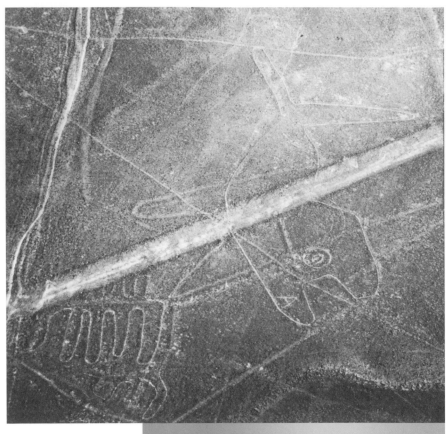

b

b: A shark or whale with a spiral eye. Photo by Evan Hadingham. *Inset:* ceramic representation. Photo courtesy of Donald Proulx.

wasn't made at a later date? True, three straight lines do intersect the spider (one of them appears in Figure 50a), but twelve others from the same ray center do not—pure coincidence. All of this evidence would make one think the biomorphs, as the archaeologists like to call them, are a local phenomenon, scribblings on the desert blackboard that have nothing to do with the straight features that go from one end of the pampa to the other.

The biomorphs may date from an earlier time. Persis Clarkson's survey of the ceramics bears out this conclusion. She assigned a date of AD 660–1000 (or later) to most of the lines and a much earlier one (AD 200–600, or even earlier) to the animals. On the contrary, Helaine Silverman's survey of geoglyphs in the Ingenio Valley points us in a different direction. She thinks the lines and the animals are contemporary. As she told me, "The Nasca lines are pure Nasca." The problem remains unsolved.

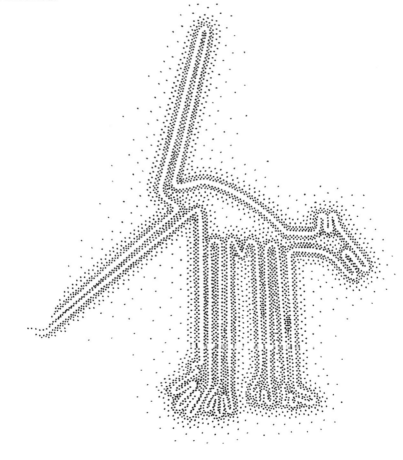

c: A cartoonish dog or fox tiptoes over the landscape.
Drawing by Julia Meyerson.

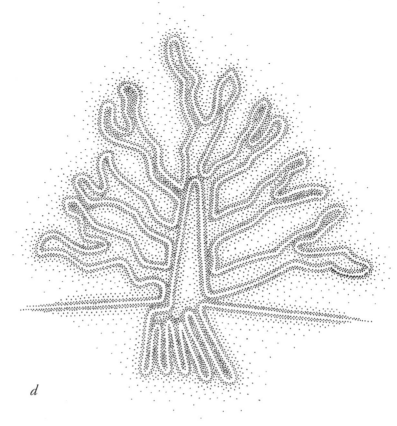

d

d: A pair of plants: a tree and a tuber? Andean plants with extensive tubers include potatoes and oxalis tubers (related to sorrel). Drawings by Julia Meyerson.

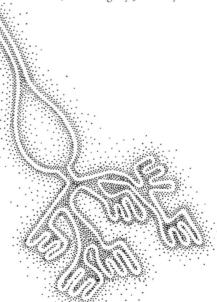

What do the animals represent? Are they totems, effigies of animals that give clans their identity, the way Detroiters identify with the Tigers or Chicagoans with the Bulls? What kinds of creatures make up these bizarre unilineal earth etchings? The vast majority are birds. Largest of all is the one whose profile is situated at the far east end of the pampa (Figure 8*a*). At first I couldn't make heads or tails of this avian creature. Then Susan Yung, one of my sharp-eyed

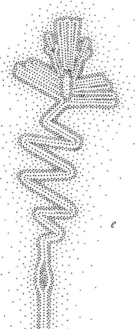

e

e: The bird with the long zigzag neck is related to the cormorant. Drawing by Julia Meyerson. Next to it is a bird similarly rendered on a Nasca pot. *Below:* Pelican and guanay to left; cormorant lower right. Drawings by Guy Tudor from E. Blake, *Manual of Neotropical Birds* (Chicago: University of Chicago Press, 1977), vol. 1, plate 2.

Colgate students who had spent quite a lot of time browsing encyclopedias of native coastal animals, had a hunch that it was a frigate bird. The real one positioned next to it in Figure 8*a* looks pretty convincing. The male of the species inflates his red throat pouch like a balloon to attract his mate.

Other avian creatures exhibit the same hooked bill seen in Figure 8*a*. A pampa rendition of one of them, about two-fifths of a mile long, displays two characteristics we have already observed in the lines (Figure 50*e*). First, it is four-fifths beak attached to a neck that zigzags back and forth several times, a stark contrast with its dead-straight bill. Second, this bird has a fan-shaped tail, and its legs, punctuated by knobby knees, are fully extended and its wings swept back. Like the Nasca ray centers, all parts of the bird's anatomy seem to extend radially outward from a common point, giving the impression that this bird is not positioned for flight, even if its representation looks like a ground-based view. Observe the way the beak, legs, tail feathers, and wings on both the condor and the

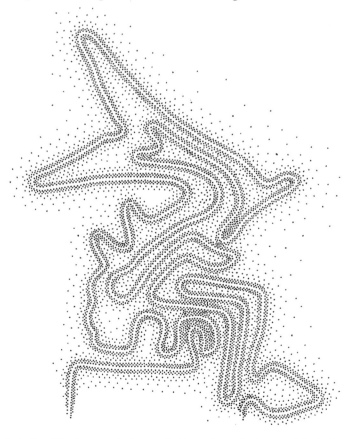

f: Into the belly of the beast or the heart of a flower (p. 197), the same labyrinthine quality appears in the monkey's tail. Drawing by Julia Meyerson.

hummingbird also seem to radiate outward from a focal point, an earmark of the Nasca pampa artistic style (Figures 8*b* and 8*c*). Bird expert Guy Tudor suggested to me that the best long-necked candidate to fly the pampa is the guanay, a relative of the cormorant, among the most valued Peruvian shorebirds (Figure 50*e*). The tons of guano (used for fertilizer) they produce still coats the coastal islands with a snow-white layer. The anhinga, a freshwater swamp bird, is another candidate.

What could have motivated desert artists to take such license with the bird's neck? I can think of two possible reasons: Ornithologist Robert Murphy has written that "all cormorants dive and plunge in zigzag lines."[41] Second, when cormorants eat fish, the neck often vibrates in an S or Z form.

Let's trace out an even rarer bird (Figure 8*g*). This one is a little over 125 yards long, formed by a mile-long line that starts at the eye and ends at the beak. It has a 40-yard bill, but there is something very unreal about this avian critter. The

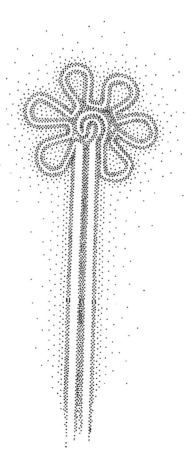
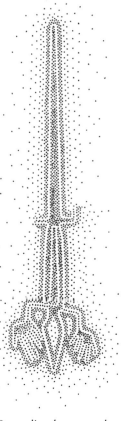

g: Pampa lizard, now partly
destroyed. Drawing by Julia Meyerson.

wings are segmented and pressed back against its skinny linear body in a rectangular, geometrical pattern. This bird, too, is clearly plunging, diving. The pouch below the neck makes the pelican a logical candidate. (There are at least two other pampa pelicans, by the way; see Figure 8.) Here the pouch doubles as a trophy head, a deliberate play on image. Some of the other animals also show trophy heads worn about the neck, a native tradition dating back to 1000 BC. These mummified human heads were believed to be sources of spiritual power, perhaps emphasizing fertility, for the shape of the figure often resembles an egg case. Having seen the condor, that great Peruvian scavenger, soar on powerful wings over the pampa, I can understand why natives say its image brings together all levels of the landscape (Figure 8b). When it sits, its toes branch out like the dunes on the river's edge. Its dark back is slanted like the side of a mountain, and the white collar below the crested head is like the snow at the mountain's summit, observes anthropologist Joseph Bastien.[42] No wonder they say the condor is a mountain god.[43] We can still predict the rains by timing its appearance and disappearance on the pampa. By contrast, the hummingbird, once thought to be a messenger from the gods, is a tiny darter common to Nasca household gardens; in Figure 8c it seems poised in midair as it draws nectar from an abstract straight line on the pampa (not shown).

Two species of native long-tailed monkeys match the coil-tailed one we find on the pampa: the woolly monkey, which lives on the east slope of the Andes, and the spider monkey, which looks just as skinny as its Nasca counterpart (Figure 8f). The protruding ears resemble those of the squirrel monkey also found in some parts of the country, but the squirrel version lacks the prehensile tail. Finally, there are three rather odd properties associated with our 80-yard-long primate on the pampa: its tail coils up instead of down, it's hunched over in an impossible position, and it has only nine digits.

Like the monkey, the comical minicanid (only 30 yards long) seems to be walking on its toes (Figure 50c). It was made by clearing a thin line that begins and ends at the back of the creature. This figure has been called a dog, even a frightened cat, but I think the long pointed nose gives it away as a fox. At least two kinds of foxes that resemble this drawing prowl the pampa today (especially in the vicinity of chicken ranches): the crab-eating fox and the South American fox. Johan Reinhard recalls the legend told by the sixteenth-century Spanish chronicler Father Avila in which the fox helped the mountain god construct the first irrigation system in Peru,[44] and Gary Urton has identified one of the dark cloud constellations of the southern Milky Way with the fox.[45] They call the celestial canid Atoq, a dark spot in the southern Milky Way located between our constellations of Sagittarius and Scorpio.

By now you will have noticed that there is something incongruous about practically every figure. The fox is no exception. Its catlike tail points up, and once again the number of digits is strange. It has three (or four); foxes have five. Let's not overlook the slim-waisted spider, a 50-yard masterpiece of symmetry that looks to be crawling across the desert when viewed from above (Figure 50a). Astronomer Gerald Hawkins suggested that it is the male of a rare Amazonian species that reproduces by transferring its sperm to the female via the tip of one of its legs (we can see why).[46]

Although many Nasca figures exhibit a continuous contour line starting at one of the extremities, the pointy-headed lizard, a slender flower, and a pampa fish have something equally curious in common, a property also reflected in the spirals (Figures 50f and 50g). Look at the way the contour line penetrates the belly of the beast. Sue Yung convinced me that this particular fish was not a killer whale, a sticker frequently applied to it in many popular works. Whales have only four fins, and our Nasca figure has seven. Clearly this is not a deep-sea fish. In fact, the overall anatomy of a common sand shark, with seven minor fins and a caudal fin, fits this desert denizen just fine. What's that object hanging from the neck of the other shark (Figure 50b)? Oviparous sharks lay eggs in a case on the ocean floor. By contrast, ovoviviparous babies hatch in the mother's oviduct, and they do not leave the body until they are more fully developed. The artists may be playing up the likeness between a trophy head and the egg sac carried beneath the mother, with the hatchlings depicting the facial features of the mummified head.

Science writer Evan Hadingham ties the display of trophy heads to the infamous practice of head hunting by the Jívaro of highland Ecuador, first revealed to the modern world in the twenties, though now the custom is no longer practiced. The virility of a Jívaro male was measured by the number of enemy heads he amassed (reminds me of the World War II fighter pilots who would paint a symbol on their airplanes for every enemy craft they downed, or the college all-stars whose football helmets are plastered with decals). The man who murdered an adversary in warfare would acquire the power of the foe's soul and with it the soul's power of fertility. In one Jívaro fertility rite, the warrior would hold the cured and preserved shrunken head aloft while his woman clung to him as the power of fertility passed from the deceased soul through his body and into hers. We don't know whether this strange dualism connecting warfare and fertility surfaced in the Nasca culture, but there is plenty of circumstantial evidence to suggest that collecting heads was a Nasca passion. Drawings of trophy heads accompany the pampa geoglyphs, and severed heads are portrayed on Nasca pots, their eyes closed and their lips sewn shut with thorns. Still other scenes on ceramics and textiles going back to Paracas times show monsters gripping clusters of heads by the hair. Mummified heads and head effigies also often accompany grave goods in Nasca burials.

The marine animal in Figure 50*b* lacks that in-and-out labyrinthine quality displayed in Nasca's double spirals (Figures 9 and 11) and even in a few trapezoids. This creature looks more like a shark or a whale with the head of a cat, and it is executed in a style so radically different from the others that I am convinced it was made by a different group of artists. Maybe that's why it is etched at the remote southeastern end of the pampa, adjacent to the Nasca River valley rather than the Ingenio, where most of the other figures are positioned. First of all, the figure is closed; second, it looks sketchier; and third, the spiral eye is made from an entirely separate line.

There are comparatively few plant drawings at Nasca. Most delicate is the labyrinthine six-petaled flower, whose guideline penetrates the stamens. Reinhard identifies this hook, which also appears in other geoglyphs, with a design representing a cave below the summit of a mountain.[47] Lined up between the labyrinthine lizard and cartoon bird character in Figure 8*e* is a strange-looking plant whose roots are drawn in the same back-and-forth style as the wings of so many of the birds (on the right in Figure 50*d*). Investigators have variously labeled it a seaweed or a huarango, the so-called Indian carob (which resembles an olive tree), but this plant also may be the yuca, which appears on Nasca textiles (Maria Reiche calls it "plant with roots"). Persis Clarkson identifies the plant at the bottom of Figure 50*d* as a jiquima (called jicama in Mexico), again based on descriptions and depictions of it in Nasca ceramics and textiles. A thick root whose texture resembles that of a potato, it is eaten raw.

In addition to plants and animals, there are also humanoid geoglyphs out there. Reinhard has paid some attention to the oft-unreported figures of this kind carved on the Nasca pampa as well as in northern Chile.[48] He associates many of them with a "staff-carrying deity" (for instance, the 20-yard-tall man in the top hat who appears on the pampa near the town of Palpa just north of Nasca). Because of similar elements such as trophy heads and plants that he has found in these same figures on ceramics and in textiles dating back to about 200 BC, Reinhard links them to fertility and meteorology. The celebrated owl man (frontispiece) carved on the slope of a hill, rather than on the usual flat surface of the pampa, has been linked in popular literature with extraterrestrials. (His wide-eyed countenance and up-raised right arm beckon to his cohorts to land their spaceships!) I cannot deny its authenticity, but I have always thought this figure exhibited a rather modern look. Besides, the symbol that appears on the Peruvian flag and the name "HERNAN" carved not so far away look suspicious.

Persis, who has checked out a number of these humanoid figures, including the owl man, believes they could well be contemporary with the other pampa figures.

By now I've given enough details and descriptions of plants and animals, spirals and zigzags, trapezoids and triangles, to reveal what became obvious to me as early as my first field season at Nasca: though we still can't agree on when the biomorphs were laid down, there is a connection among all the Nasca etchings, not so much a physical as a stylistic connection, a way of representing the figures. Let's try a riddle: Why is a spider like a spiral, or a cormorant like a zigzag? Like the creators of medieval allegory, clever Nasca artists seem to be veiling concepts and ideas in shapes and forms that have something in common, something worth recognizing. These figures, I think, have a lot more to do with the observation of and commentary upon nature than with displays of a precise knowledge of geometry and encoded secret information. For example, take the idea of animal locomotion. When a spider spins a web, it first sends out a bridge line between the two objects that will anchor the web. From these points, the arachnid establishes other foundation lines. It constructs several radii, knitting them together with a thread that spirals outward from the hub to the periphery. Then it meticulously works the viscid thread spirally back inward. A work of art perfectly balanced and symmetrical, the web belies its true function, to snare the spider's prey.

Of zigzag and cormorant I have already spoken. These birds fly along the coast in search of food. After surveying the situation, they execute a series of zigzag turns as they zero in on a school of anchovies. Having spotted their quarry, the birds descend in a spiral terminated by a vertical plunge into the water, where they further pursue their prey. The lizard reveals a zigzag pattern of movement too. It wriggles rather than walks as it lifts its body off the ground with its legs. It moves forward by alternating legs so that the front foot is displaced by the rear, just like a snake walking.[49]

The ornithologist Albert Woolfson talks at length about both spiral and zigzag search patterns executed by domesticated birds. For example, a bird placed several miles from home flies in a spiral that widens with each revolution.[50] This same labyrinthine pattern (the one we find in Nasca double spirals) also penetrates the belly of the shark in Figure 50f and other creatures, as if to mimic the sinuous course of the intestines.

Keen twenty-first-century observers of nature will wonder: Why did the ancient Nasca choose these particular animals to decorate their pampa? Thinking they are like us, we might tend to look for clues such as, Were all these animals part of the food chain? The answer is no. Are they all predators? Again, no. In fact, some are not even indigenous to the pampa (the monkey and the spider reside in the Amazonian jungle over the mountains far to the east). By now you might be able to guess that for me, a safe assumption would be that our biology, our taxonomy or classification scheme, indeed our entire outlook on nature, is very different from theirs. That a spider spinning its web and a predatory bird zeroing in on its quarry execute similar motions would not constitute useful information in understanding what spiders have to do with birds as far as a modern bio-taxonomist is concerned. When I gaze at the animals on the pampa I get the sense that the people who made them were seeking a different kind of order from that pursued by our biologists. To put it simply, the message on the pampa was not intended for us.

There is scarcely a bestiary in world mythology that doesn't harbor a compound animal, and Nasca's desert menagerie seems no exception. There's a shark or whale with the head of a cat, an insect with birdlike qualities, and a tweety bird with a monkey head (Figures 50*b*, 8*d*, and 8*e*). "If you don't know what a Griffin is, look at the picture," says Lewis Carroll in *Alice's Adventures in Wonderland.* This winged quadruped has the body of a lion and the wings and head of an eagle. It hates horses and will tear apart any human being that comes within reach of it. So reads a medieval catalog of strange beasts that includes the manticore (part lion, part man), the yale (a hideous critter with the face of a boar and the tail of an elephant; it comes equipped with adjustable horns), the jaculus (a serpent that flies), and the high-maintenance leucrota (it's as big as a donkey, has the head of a horse, the chest and shins of a lion, the haunches of a stag, and the voice of a human that broadcasts its message through a toothless mouth that runs from ear to ear).[51]

Clearly, the imaginary zookeepers of long ago weren't out to emphasize biological accuracy. They seem to have been more concerned with using exotic descriptions and pictures as a way of searching for a relationship between man and animal, often with the motive of teaching religious, moral, or political ideals. Thus the horselike characteristics of the centaur enhance the manliness of ordinary man, for the horse is virile. He excels in battle, has the capacity to sniff out combat, gets excited by the trumpet's call to battle, and spurs to charge at the sound of the war yell. Lions are brave, goats and eagles have sharp eyes, dogs harbor healing tongues, donkeys are stubborn, and vultures have foresight. It's the quality, the power inherent in the beast, that matters, and mixing and matching are okay. Here is a way of exploiting an animal at first sight entirely alien to us. Whatever their message, the biomorphic figures on the pampa give me the gut feeling that the secret that lies within them is closer to Alice in Wonderland than to Darwin's origin of species.

Geoglyphs on Other Coastal Pampas

On the Atacama Desert on the north coast of Chile lie hundreds of geoglyphs. Long chains of llama and human stick-figure effigies, circles, and various geometries make up the bulk of the designs. Unlike the Nasca figures, most of these are situated on hillsides and therefore are more easily seen at ground level. One of the more supernatural-looking humanoid drawings is more than 100 feet long. It may be related to the staff deity who appears on ceramics, especially from Tiahuanaco. It has a catlike head with huge whiskers perched on its rectangular body, arrows for arms, and appendages coming out of its hips (a tiny four-legged animal is outlined at the end of one of them). Little piles of stones form the creature's eyes, nose, and mouth. Looking somewhat like the Nasca figures are the geometric patterns, interlocked rectangles resembling a crossword puzzle. Most of the Atacama Desert geoglyphs are along llama caravan routes interconnecting coastal oases with the highlands. They may have been placed there as protective symbols or to guide the merchant traveler on his way (See P. Clarkson, 1998, "Designs on the Desert," *Discovering Archaeology*, May–June, pp. 84–89).

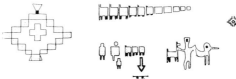

Illustrations by L. Núñez A., "Geoglifos y tráfico de caravanas," in *Homenaje al Dr. G. LePaige* (Antofagasta, Chile: Universidad del Norte, 1976), courtesy Universidad del Norte.

Air Nasca Lives

Most of the recent interpretations of the Nasca lines (Johan Reinhard's, Josué Lancho's, and of course our own) point to the local population's ground-based subsistence activity, like irrigation and farming. People walked the lines; they maintained them; they may have assembled on them, perhaps using them as pilgrimage accessways to the Cahuachi pyramid to pray to the rain god. Still, the explanation that captivates the public eye remains a consequence of modernity willfully projecting itself upon other cultures of the past. Most people who don't know the pampa still think of it as the largest astronomy book in the world.

By the late eighties, Maria Reiche, then an octogenarian debilitated by Parkinson's disease (she died in 1998 at the age of 95), felt the need to name a successor. She set out with her younger sister's help to create one in her own image. Phyllis Pitluga, an astronomer at Chicago's Adler Planetarium, first came to Nasca in 1983. She followed the universal itinerary: the touristic 30- to 45-minute flight, an audience with Maria, who told of her quest for the lost astronomical and mathematical knowledge preserved in the giant etchings, and a trip to the needle-and-thread geoglyph to see how the Nasca did it. A few weeks after Pitluga returned home, she received a letter, postmarked Nasca and addressed to "The Woman Astronomer, Chicago Planetarium, USA." Maria had a dream: Phyllis would be anointed her successor. Later, Reiche sent a taped message framing her invitation to the tune of "Daisy, Daisy, give me your answer do," with the name "Phyllis" appropriately substituted. Within two years, Pitluga had a Fulbright and was spending time under Reiche's tutelage replicating and extending her alignments with the transit and seeking novel ways to reframe the astronomical hypothesis: "My approach right now is to start with the working hypothesis that all long, straight, narrow lines are sight lines for astronomy," she told an interviewer, as the story of Pitluga and Reiche's partnership intrigued the press corps.[52] To prove her serious intentions, Pitluga enrolled in archaeology courses at the nearby University of Chicago.

Phyllis Pitluga was convinced that astronomy transcended the lines; there was astral meaning in the biomorphs, too. By the end of the decade Maria Reiche's official successor started reenvisioning the work on the spider her mentor had begun 30 years earlier. She reported, "The figure so well matched what the stars of Orion were doing as seen from the focal point over a few hundred years' time—it was strong, overwhelming evidence of the relationship of one set of lines to another in terms of dating, showing the kinds of changes that my theodolite [a surveying instrument] and calculations were showing."[53] The "focal point" is one of the ray centers from which Pitluga singled out only those lines that cross over the spider. Though her three lines point to stars in Orion, they are part of a ray system of fifteen lines. She hadn't looked at the other twelve.

To match animal figures with constellations, Pitluga used Gary Urton's work on the dark cloud constellations of contemporary highland Andean people as a springboard, conjuring up what seemed to me a rather complex model of the geoglyphs: the Nasca plant and animal figures all line up with the dark cloud constellations of the Milky Way, she contended. The long axes of certain "quadrangles" (or zones) were connected with the figural drawings and aligned with the rising and setting of the Milky Way at dawn at the time of the harvesting and planting seasons. (I had already concluded that Milky Way alignments didn't correlate with the directions of straight Nasca lines.) I must admit that Pitluga's presentations at professional meetings in the late eighties and nineties were impressively convincing. Accompanied by sophisticated computer graphics and color slides, they were a model of style, and her idea of a grand plan involving high intellect seemed appealing. But I really had trouble finding good evidence to back up what she contended. Pitluga never laid out the criteria for selecting the lines she chose to measure, nor did she pay much attention to the archaeological data Clarkson and Silverman had unearthed. Her case did little justice to other information about the coastal cultures, save applying, with subtle contortions, Urton's representations of constellations from the highlands. As historian Jacquetta Hawkes might ask: was she getting the pampa she desired?

Meanwhile, the idea that the lines were meant to be seen from above was given fresh impetus by another Maria, a distinguished Peruvian anthropologist and ethnohistorian with an unpronounceable moniker, Maria Rostworowski de Diez Canseco.[54] Rostworowski had been impressed by Silverman's ideas about the pampa as a pilgrimage site. Perhaps, she speculated, the pilgrims created the geoglyphs to announce the arrival on the pampa of Kón (Con) Viracocha, the ubiquitous winged figure that flies across the surface of so many Nasca pots. There a priest and his faithful would gather to wait for him. Rostworowski analyzed a well-known return myth told by three different chroniclers. The story goes that the flying god Con is the son of the sun and the moon (he also figured in Gary Urton's and Johan Reinhard's investigations). He was responsible for transforming the once lush landscape into a desert, thus forcing all the people to the fertile river valleys to seek sustenance. Later, when the gods of Pachacamac came on the scene from the north, Con fled by marching out to sea. Then one day he flew up into the sky, pledging to return to these lands. We've heard myths like these before, the Quetzalcoatl myth in Mexico, for example: different sets of gods change the landscape as they replace one another, offering a novel way of accounting for ecological disasters. Because all versions of the myth describe

Con as having no bones, Rostworowski was led to equate him with the figure of the supple-looking flying deity with a catlike face portrayed extensively on Nasca ceramics (Figure 17). How could the airborne supernatural be sure he had arrived on his home turf and that his people would help him? According to Rostworowski, believers in the cult of Con would undertake pilgrimages to the pampa, where the lines represented the entrance to the pampa of the various kin groups. They would assemble on the huge trapezoids and construct the animal figures as a way of signaling the deity, who said he would make his arrival from the north. (Most of the animal drawings lie at the north end of the pampa.) In this Maria's eyes, each figure represents a distinct lineage or perhaps one of the ayllus of Con-worshiping artisans. So the pampa becomes a medium of communication not only among all the people who worshiped at Nasca but also between the people and their gods.

Crossing the Desert One More Time

Ancient Peru and ancient Egypt—I have trod the turf in both places, and I can't get away from the feeling that there's a parallel between ancient Nasca and the remains of the Nilotic peoples who constructed the first wonder of the world. Both labored hard and long to exploit the delicate environment of that narrow fertile ribbon that threads its way through an otherwise vast wasteland. Like the Egyptians, the ancient Nascas climbed up onto the dry desert and used it as a place for expressing themselves and their beliefs. Whatever else the Nasca lines were about, I am convinced that they had a lot to do with acting out social and religious rites.

"Once you fly over the lines, you will be convinced forever that they were made to be seen from above." How many times have I heard visitors to the Nasca pampa utter that statement with conviction? I must say with equal certainty that once I walked the Nasca lines, I was convinced that all of them were meant to be trod upon. For me they remain dead-straight pathways crisscrossing over the pampa. Still others, like Paul Kosok, remained forever impressed by seeing a moonrise or sunset along a line, insisting that all of them were cosmic pointers. An eye to the sky can go a long way toward convincing one of the validity of an astronomical theory.

That was them; this is us. Think for a moment about the significance of these subjective reactions, including my own. How we experience the lines could have little to do with what the lines meant, how they functioned, the motives of the people who constructed them. In fact, it is presumptuous for us to think our perception has any arguable connection with that of the people who lived in ancient Nasca. The data we had gathered (information left behind by the ancient Nasca culture) helped us to realize just how different ancient and modern societies really are. But let me go farther. I think those who persist in promoting the idea that the Nasca lines were constructed by primitive intellectuals, cardboard ancestors of contemporary people or descendants of alien beings who mated with terrestrials, insult the indigenous cultures of Peru. Such notions border on racist, because they deny these people the capacity to create something uniquely complex.

I have tried hard not to allow a single one of our hypotheses concerning the construction and use of the lines to be developed and presented outside the context of what we know about Andean culture. That's the hallmark of this chapter, in which I have attempted to tell all about our work. I have tried to let the data speak for themselves. First we began by separating out the straight features, then we found that the several hundred lines we surveyed crisscrossing the pampa were actually connected by several dozen radial centers. The radiating arrangement developed into a meaningful system only when we began to look at the ancient Andean native record. There we found several cultural components that might have been part of the system: ritual walking, irrigation, fertility, the radial pattern of organization of the landscape, and the division of territory into cleared strips. These ideas converged to give us an explanation for the lines in cultural context.

The radial idea came to mind first, simply because we know it as a basic spatial principle of organization in the only pre-Columbian Andean population center where we have some reliable information. The ceque system of Cuzco was part of a network of radiating territorial kinship divisions marked out on the physical environment, with special attention being paid to irrigation and the flow of water. It is but one manifestation of the well-developed Andean idea that has no parallel in the cultures of the West, the idea of hierarchical dividing, splitting, or bifurcating of kin groups, water, information on a cotton quipu, and so on. In Cuzco the radial ceques were both a prescription and a framework for worship, ritual, and kinship; they even divided time and the seasonal calendar. On the pampa we found radial patterns too, but they were visible in a different way from what we saw in Cuzco, where a ceque is traced by noting its component huacas. On the coast the medium was different. Here was a sandy, flat desert covered with dark rock fragments, rather than a deep valley encapsulated by rocky hillsides. But the message was the same: organize the world in a way that simultaneously focuses and disperses human energy and resources—organize it radially.

The key to comprehending the meaning of the Nasca lines lay in focusing on the organizing principle, the way the topography is carved up, rather than the way it looks to us. Here is where Gary Urton's contemporary studies at Pacariqtambo entered the picture. He was able to reveal a living scheme for how Andean people mapped territorial divisions and how they used the resulting space to organize their society. Each rectangular strip, or chhiuta, is the product of the activity of an ayllu, a group of people defined on the basis of the land they hold, their bloodline, and their labor and ceremonial obligations. Another concept without parallel in our culture, the ayllu is the same unit that was central to social life in ancient Cuzco; ayllus connote social spaces. When representatives of a given ayllu showed up in the center of Pacariqtambo on the day of a festival, invariably they were there to perform a prelude as important to them as the main event: to sweep clean their specially designated strip of the plaza. Could they be performing an act of cleansing similar to what once took place on the pampa a millennium before their time? If the answer is yes, then we can think of both chhiutas and Nasca lines as mechanisms by which social groups map out the division of responsibilities, by dividing up their public spaces, by moving over them, and by sweeping them.

More than this, the coastal chroniclers tell us that the division of labor and other tributary obligations similar to the social organization of contemporary Pacariqtambo also existed in the Nasca valley. Just as in Cuzco then, the Nasca pampa emerges as the dividing place between two sets of moieties. The river valleys were deliberately partitioned so that the organization of agricultural activities (constructing, using, and maintaining irrigation facilities) was coordinated in a symbolic way through the division of the space between the two vital watershed areas. This is what the pampa of Nasca was for.

Considerations like these pulled us farther into the subject of water and irrigation. The ecology of the Nasca region is and always was delicate, a transition zone between two extremes: the highlands to the east, the Pacific Coast on the west. It scarcely ever rains in Nasca. All the water that flows in the canals comes from the rain that falls in the mountains far away to the east of the pampa. If there is one dominant commodity tied into all the data we collected at the Nasca line centers, it is water. Most of the 62 line centers we charted lie along the major riverbanks, on or near tributaries, or at the base of the last hill in a chain that descends out onto the pampa. The line directions fit both parallel and perpendicular to stream orientations. The watery connection is no coincidence, especially when we keep in mind that irrigation principles also lie at the core of the ceque system of Cuzco.

The aquatic link, to which we always seem to return when contemplating Nasca phenomena, may even tap into the sky, for just as a small portion of the ceque lines of Cuzco seem to be astronomically oriented, we find the same to be true at Nasca. A slight excess of lines pointing in the direction of sunrise and sunset on the days of passage of the sun across the zenith makes good hydrological sense. Not only is this solar event well documented in the Andes, but it also would have been an ideal way to anticipate when water would first appear in the canals. Even today the arrival of water in Nasca is the single most important event in the local agricultural cycle.

People really did walk straight lines in ancient Peru. The chronicler Cristóbal de Molina tells us that in Cuzco both messengers and royal sacrificial victims from all regions of the empire followed ceques into the capital city. On their way back home, he says, many people did not follow the ordinary roads but pursued straight-line paths instead. The collective, ritual movement of people on the lines became a central element in Helaine Silverman's idea that Cahuachi functioned as a sacred pilgrimage center, even receiving offerings long after it had been abandoned. Cahuachi, at the pampa's edge, was both a place of assembly and a focus for ceremonial activities where people worshiped the gods in anticipation of signs of agricultural fertility, signs that would assure the regularity and sufficiency of the flow of water. Silverman also argued that the social organization involved in ritually maintaining Cahuachi's archaeological features was based on principles like the ones Urton found in contemporary Pacariqtambo. The high degree of concentration of lines in the area along the north bank of the Nasca River immediately opposite Cahuachi's largest pyramid supported her idea.

Water, walking, astronomy, kinship, divisions of labor and ceremonial responsibility, sweeping, radiality—a strange set of explanatory bedfellows, but there is a place for all of these human actions and concepts in the story of the Nasca lines. It is a complex story but nonetheless a story we can believe and one that is far more interesting than extraterrestrial visitations. Whatever the mosaic of explanations, however all the parts fit together, our cardinal rule has been that everything must make sense in the context of what we know about Andean culture in general and about Nasca culture in particular. We can no longer view the Nasca lines simply as the largest astronomy book in the world, the product of a massive superhuman work effort undertaken as a single-minded grand project. The builders had no need of our cultural trappings. They used little advanced technology (though they were expert weavers, potters, and metallurgists), no sophisticated knowledge of mathematics and geometry in the Western sense, no maps or blueprints in order to create what we see.

I am reminded once again of Claude Lévi-Strauss's words about how studying other cultures forces us to expose what we cherish to the buffeting of ideas and habits of others best able to rebut them. Oddly enough, we have ended up illuminating the people who built the lines in a more alien light than any of our predecessors on the pampa. By discovering an ancient people of Nasca so different from ourselves, perhaps unwittingly Urton, Zuidema, Silverman, Clarkson, Ruggles, and I (along with a host of others who helped out along the way) may have succeeded in making the Nasca lines an even more fascinating enigma.

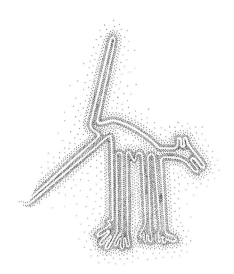

PART FOUR. RECESSIONAL

> I've been to Nasca so many times . . . always coming out
> of the sky, that the locals have nicknamed me E.T. They
> wonder why this smiling, tall, blue-eyed woman keeps
> returning. It's really very simple: I return there as if to an
> old friend.
>
> **Photographer-artist Marilyn Bridges**[1]

High on a mesa in the Sangre de Cristo Mountains overlooking Las Vegas, New Mexico, about an hour's drive from Santa Fe, artist Charles Ross has spent the past 23 years bulldozing a perfectly aligned north-south channel 500 feet long and 100 feet deep. Ross is building his own version of a kiva, a subterranean circular chamber used by ancient Pueblo peoples of the U.S. Southwest to worship their gods. When he completes it, the giant gouge in the earth will serve as the principal baseline of a work of earth art he calls *Star Axis* (Figure 51). Visitors who enter the stainless-steel tunnel, stand in the exact center, and peer through the distant opening at the other end will lock their gaze on the North Star, Polaris. As they ascend eleven stories of stairways to the top of the mesa, they will witness the gradual enlargement of the opening and the changing view of the celestial axis through time. Along the way, dates engraved on the steps tell them when a particular star field was (or will be) as they see it, when people first came to America, when the Pueblo ancestors of the Hopi built the kivas, or when the fourth millennium will begin.

Across the continent in the middle of 57 acres of landfill in the New Jersey Meadowlands, Nancy Holt engages an equally monumental task. Within eyeshot of New York's World Trade Center on one side and the New Jersey Turnpike on the other, she is busy transforming a 100-foot-high, earth-covered pile of pure waste into *Sky Mound*. When she is done, visitors will be able to stand at the center and view sunrise at the solstices and equinoxes in carefully calculated notches between steel poles perched on artificial peaks shaped out of the periphery of the mound. At noon on the summer solstice, a spherical steel cage will throw a circular shadow precisely onto a steel ring implanted in the ground.

Figure 51. *Top:* We still move the earth. Bulldozed out of a thousand tons of rock carted to the site, Robert Smithson's *Spiral Jetty* is probably the most celebrated minimalist piece to emerge out of the rebellious and restless generation of sixties and seventies earth sculptors. This is what it looked like before it was inundated by the rising waters of the Great Salt Lake just a few years after he built it. Photo © Kunstraum München, from *Peruanische Erdzeichen,* ed. H. Kern (Munich: Kunstraum München, 1974). *Bottom:* A generation later, Charles Ross created this work of art as a space to see in; when you look along *Star Axis* from the base of the tunnel, you can see the sky turning about the celestial pole precisely aligned with the time-altered physical environment created by the artist. *Star Axis,* by Charles Ross, in B. Oakes, *Sculpting the Environment* (New York: Van Nostrand Press, 1995), copyright © 1995 by Baile Oakes. Reprinted by permission of John Wiley & Sons, Inc.

Sound sculpture is the medium Douglas Hollis seems to be exploring. On the shores of Lake Washington in Seattle, he has achieved the orchestral culmination of a decade in his *Sound Garden*. Visitors wind their way up a meandering brick path in a lakeside park while they listen to tones that resonate from a field of aluminum wind pipe organs. Described as the sounds of whales and warblers, the harmonious acoustics combine in different ways depending on the speed of the wind and where the listener stands in the field of silvery wind-vane structures.

The Spring, by Peter Richards, in the Artpark near Lewiston, New York, may have been inspired by the nearby Niagara River Gorge. Adjacent to a hydroelectric plant, the project began ten years ago as part of the recovery of a trash-filled, overgrown spring that once attracted summer visitors, until it became a receptacle for materials discarded by technological expansion in the area. Richards supervised the cleaning and rebuilding of the park, and its centerpiece is now the rechanneled waterway. A springhouse made out of river gorge slabs and framed by a pair of protective earthen mounds stands in the midst of it. From it a channel in the shape of a double helix carved into a solid flat rock spills pure water onto a boulder that Richards had removed from a nearby glacial moraine. Aquatic plants and animals populate the spring's course.

For those of us especially sensitive to the way art can change with the seasons, consider the Kansas wheat-field sculptures of Stanley Herd. He changes the flat contours of his 30-acre canvases with a two-bladed plow, creating a variety of sculptures by cutting the wheat to varying heights, first one way, then another. Plantings of flowers add a dimension of color, and dark outlines are etched into the landscape by dragging out dirt with a plow. To appreciate Herd's temporary crop art, whether it be his half-mile-square portrait of Will Rogers, or a still life that includes ears of corn and a loaf of bread aptly named *The Harvest* (before it was harvested), or *Little Girl in the Wind* (a portrait of a Kickapoo Indian woman), you need to visit the local airport in Lawrence and hire a pilot and a plane. Only then can you answer the question that Herd says he had been pondering since his early youth, plowing the Kansas wheat farm where he grew up. It is the question that drove him to take creative turns with plow and mower: "I wonder what it all looks like as seen from above?"

Practical engineering, architectural planning, and art all merge in Viet Ngo's designs of wastewater treatment plants. To recover resources once lost, he grows lemna plants, small floating flora that thrive on ponds in diverse climates all over the world. The plants filter and neutralize pollutants in wastewater and stabilize bioreactions in the pond, giving back pure water to the environment. They control odor and render the waste area more pleasing to the eye. Their high protein content makes lemna a potential food source for the future. The design of Ngo's lemna systems incorporates an aesthetic component, especially when it comes to ways of controlling the flow of water over vast acreage. If you view his Devil's Lake, North Dakota, installation (completed in 1990) from an airplane, you'll immediately notice an intricate pattern of green rectangular serpentine, zigzagging channels. "It always amazed me," he writes, "when forms that have been prevalent through the ages, such as the serpent form of Devil's Lake, seem to spring out of the land when they are part of a design that seeks balance with the processes of the Earth. In the case of Devil's Lake, there is a little more technology involved, but the product is linked to the past."[2]

Ngo speaks for each of the modern earthmovers whose works I've just profiled (a handful among many I could have mentioned), who seem to be pursuing ways of forging links between the technological present and a past consisting of an almost pious reverence for the sacred landscape. Peter Richards thinks of himself as a public artist, a social interpreter of the relationship between things, people, and places. His *Spring,* by being made of things forged by earth and the hands of people, offers participants the opportunity to recoup the history of the place where they live. Doug Hollis says he wants people to experience natural phenomena and at the same time learn that they are an integral part of those phenomena by provoking an interaction via their "sensory instruments." If you ask Nancy Holt why she would bother to track the sun, the moon, and the stars from a trash heap turned planetarium amid a panoply of train tracks, highways, and oil storage tanks, she will tell you (as she told me) it is because she wants to recover the feeling she gets every time she stands atop solstitially aligned Monk's Mound in ancient Cahokia in southern Illinois or on Ohio's Hopewell octagon to sight the northern limit of the rising moon. The tradition associated with what lies beneath the Indian mounds provides a stark contrast in Holt's eye to the cultural castoffs interred beneath her observatory on the Meadowlands. Likewise, the *Star Axis* of Charles Ross recovers lost time by bringing the stars down to earth, distilling them into an environment that otherwise seems changeless.

Many of these works and artists seem to be responding to a perceived ecological crisis. Most of them convert wastelands into wonders of art anchored in a contemporary, holistic view of the world—what physicist Fridtjof Capra characterizes as a "deep ecological paradigm." This is a way of thinking that attempts to perceive how each thing is embedded in its natural and social environment, from the raw materials that go into it to the way it was manufactured to how using it "affects the natural environment and the community by which it is used."[3] Whether the tradition be Christian, Buddhist, or Native American, what underlies the earth art movement is a kind of religious or spiritual awareness threaded by a communal vision of the real world based in the natural environment that transcends the human individual. These public design projects, dipping deeply into the past for many of their conceptualizations, espouse values that are less centered in human need and focused more on preserving earth and all of its attendant life forms, just as we imagine our predecessors did.

"Looking at the splendid heads of the four horses I was suddenly overcome with emotion. I felt a deep and clear certainty that here was the work of one of the great masters, a Leonardo da Vinci," French cave art interpreter Jean Clottes wrote in 1995 shortly after he discovered the 30,000-year-old cave paintings in Chauvet, France.[4] With that thought he traded the uncouth thick-skulled Stone Age people imagined in the first half of the twentieth century for the highly advanced, sensitive, and articulate version of them that we have implanted in our minds in the second half. Today they are us, and in the megaterrestrial works of art our earthmovers make out of the contemporary landscape, we become them.

I think many of the new-millennium interpretations of the Nasca geoglyphs share in the overtones of this sort of dialogue with our predecessors via an earth transformed. That is why, in this final chapter, I began by talking about some of these examples of grand-scale earthmoving that, at least in form and structure, evoke thoughts of the wondrous remains we've been probing on the pampa. Listening to the explanations offered by careful observers of these contemporary works might help us gather insight into ways of achieving that delicate balance between understanding both the motives of our ancient ancestors and the prevailing tendency we have to paint them in the hues that emanate from our contemporary sphere of concerns.

"The further down the line one looks the greater its definition. Yet the greater the distance the less the definition of detail. The lines are both general and more distinct as lines in direct proportion to the distance focused by the eye. The gestalt becomes stronger as the detail becomes weaker."[5] Those remarks resonate from a generation of artists who preceded the landscape sculptors of the nineties in search of ecological holism, a generation concerned with breaking with the tradition of art as a purely visual medium that offers practically every experience on a 90-degree plane placed between the viewer and the world. For the American sculptor Robert Morris and his colleagues, the Nasca lines symbolize a form of public art that offered a dramatic counterpoint to "seeing is believing." Aerial photography may give us our desired viewpoint, reflected Morris after a lengthy visit to the pampa, but the experience from the ground has nothing to do with seeing things. A highway sign may warn the eye that a curve in the road is imminent, but the curve itself can be felt only by moving physically through every sinuous bend and turn of it. Like the monkey's tail and the other labyrinthine figures we can follow with our eyes in aerial photos, these figures, once confronted at ground level, offer a different experience for a different set of senses.

The minimalist art Morris espoused drew inspiration from plans drawn on flat surfaces and extended itself to exploring the relativity and irrationality of space from different points of view and with different senses. Many of the familiar museum installations of the sixties and seventies tried to mediate what we see in flat space with what we experience when we enter the universe of a particular work in three dimensions. They involved enclosed "spaces for the self." Our course of movement and position altered the conditions of perception. The concern with environmental backdrop would take its place in the earthworks first fashioned in the sixties. Given our increased ecological awareness, today they enjoy a resurgence. While at work in Nasca, I often recalled many of these contemporary outdoor installations, especially Nasca-inspired works like Walter de Maria's mile-long pair of parallel lines 12 feet apart chalked out across the Mojave Desert in 1968, and Robert Smithson's *Spiral Jetty,* a spiral of black stone 1,500 feet by 15 feet, its earthen base bulldozed out of the shoreline of Utah's Great Salt Lake in 1970 (Figure 51). The labyrinth, one of Nasca's most prevalent forms, was a paragon of mid-seventies minimalist earthworks. As one artist commented, "The personal and involved experience you acquire within it is so entirely foreign to the more comprehensible view from above which reduces it to simple planar curves."[6]

The Pilgrim Enters the Labyrinth

"Historically, the maze is both the metonym of the search for oneself and the metaphor of both complexity and confusion. . . . An inner space . . . isolated from its surroundings by a separating wall that runs all around it, [it is] the most perfect embodiment of the initiation process."[7] Hermann Kern, director of Munich's Kunstraum Museum, wrote this when he curated an exhibition on labyrinthine art at Milan's Palazzo della Permanente in 1981. Visiting labyrinths around the world, he discovered that among Hopi, Pueblo, Pima, and Papago people in America, as well as those in Europe, India, and Indonesia, they serve as a fixed element in the choreography of movement, as winding courses through which chains of dancers proceed.

History's most famous labyrinth is the one associated with the Cretan legend of Theseus and the Minotaur. As described by the Roman historian Plutarch in the first century, the labyrinth of powerful King Minos of the island of Crete was so contrived that anyone placed within it would find it impossible to get out. The tortuous turf was inhabited by a grotesque and ferocious half-man, half-bull monster called the Minotaur, who destroyed anyone who violated his domain. Having defeated the Athenians, Minos exacted from them the following tribute: Every nine years they were to send seven young men and women to the island to be cast into the labyrinth. Never did a soul survive who plied the maze until Theseus, son of Aegeus, king of Athens, volunteered to be one of the fourteen, if only to alleviate his father's depression over the continuing obligation. Once he arrived in Knossos, the Minoan seat of power, he fell in love with Ariadne, the king's daughter, who conspired against her father by providing Theseus with a sword to slay the monster and a thread to unravel from the entrance as he made his way into the maze. In a fierce battle, Theseus slew the Minotaur, traced his way back to the labyrinth's entrance, and broke the tribute. Victorious and together, Theseus and Ariadne set sail back to Athens.

Happy ending? Not in a Greek tragedy. As he approached home port, Theseus forgot to hoist a white sail as he had promised to telegraph news of his success to his waiting father. Thinking the worst, the despondent king drowned himself in the sea that would ultimately bear his name. Happily for posterity, along the way husband and wife had acted out their story to islanders they visited. Until recently, natives of the Aegean islands were still said to perform the convoluted crane dance, in which they imitate the motion of Theseus going through the labyrinth. Many an expedition since the Napoleonic explorations of antiquity has set out to discover the actual labyrinth (none has been successful).[8]

Fast-forward a dozen and a half centuries, and a different perspective appears. The French architectural historian Emile Mâle has called the twelfth century one of France's finest periods. Few of us can appreciate the religious atmosphere breathed by the twelfth-century European suppliant, at a time when Chartres and other great cathedrals began to rise skyward. The Christian faith was blossoming, and forgiveness, sacrifice, and abnegation were the moral order of the day. Dedicated to the cult of the Virgin and located on the site of an underground spring that served as the seat of a pagan water cult, Chartres magically took shape out of communal enthusiasm. From everywhere they came: "People could be seen harnessed to wagons loaded with stones, wood, wheat, everything which could advance the work on the cathedral," with their offerings, forgiving their enemies.[9]

The main axis of the cathedral is oriented to the west, the direction of the setting sun, a symbol of death. The pilgrim who journeyed to the holy place was confronted with an emotion-inspiring display of grandiose Gothic architecture, sacred sculpture, and stained glass. The portals depicting the life of Christ, the creation in Genesis, and scenes of confession and martyrdom offered a full theological narrative of the pursuit of the good life to both literate and illiterate itinerants. These sculptural scenes could relate to every person, for they depicted citizens from all walks of life, from the royal sector to the guilds to the peasant class—draper, tanner, stonecutter, banker, barber, cooper, fisherman, and farmer. All were portrayed in Christian dedication. Once inside the cathedral, the pilgrim would confront a different kind of imagery. Groups of good citizens donated the stained-glass windows that illuminated and amalgamated French history with the stories of the Bible via picture rather than word, colorful scenes depicting the tree of Jesse, pilgrims traveling to the shrine of Saint Thomas, the veneration of a local saint, the parable of the prodigal son, and Charlemagne conquering the enemy.

In the midst of it all lies a labyrinth, a common feature adorning the floors and walls of many of Europe's medieval churches. The one at Chartres is 40 feet wide, laid out in blue and white stone into the floor of the central nave of the cathedral (Figure 52). The labyrinth consists of eleven turns and is about 150 yards long. Locals call it the road to Jerusalem; they say its center is "heaven" or simply "Jerusalem," which may offer a clue to how it functioned. Journeying on one's knees through the labyrinth as a penance was a likely prescription for a symbolic alternative to making an actual pilgrimage to Jerusalem. Such atonement could be offered to individuals too infirm or too poor to get involved in

Figure 52 The labyrinth of the French medieval Cathedral of Chartres. Like the spirals on the Nasca pampa, it may once have conveyed pilgrims from near and far. Photo by author.

the real thing. At another level, the church labyrinth may be merely a symbol of the complex and intricate pathway through life to salvation that every Christian confronts, with its requirement to stay unswervingly on the Way and to remain free of sin. (Eleven, they say, is the number of sin and imperfection.) Though its purpose is yet debated, the labyrinth was part of the Chartres program of sacred art and architecture that bound the social order together into an idealized image designed to show how all the classes that make up the world complement one another.

Visitors to Great Britain will recall the turf-and-hedge masses that still adorn many gardens there, and France's Tuileries, Chantilly, and Versailles all exhibit topiary labyrinths as a complement to English hedge trimming. They may be an outgrowth of the mazes found on mosaic floors from the time of the Roman empire. That many of them are located near ecclesiastical sites suggests, on the other hand, that they descended from the one at Chartres; at least many seem to have been constructed as early. In the eighteenth and nineteenth centuries mazes were a part of the popular pleasure gardens that adorned fashionable health resorts. In Elizabethan England they were used in games, like threading the maze, and largely for the entertainment of children. Oddly enough, most of these mazes, like the Nasca labyrinthine figures, have no bifurcating paths or dead ends; as Ariadne's thread implies, there is only one way through to the center. Perhaps the participants were blindfolded, suggests W. H. Matthews, who wrote an entire book on mazes.[10]

Whether you walk one of them or follow the design of one with your finger, the mazes I've talked about aren't all puzzles (multicursal or branched pathways designed to confuse those who try to find their way through them by continually forcing choices that might end in a cul-de-sac). In the unicursal labyrinth, the complexity comes in the many bends and turns, the zigzagging and meandering back and forth encountered by the sojourner, whatever the designer who constructed it had in mind.

A close Andean parallel to the labyrinth of King Minos was excavated in the mid-eighties by UCLA archaeologist Christopher Donnan at the pilgrimage center of Pacatnamú on the north coast of Peru. This was once the seat of a moon cult, according to the chronicler Antonio de Calancha. Even in the time of Pizarro, pilgrims journeyed there from afar with offerings of gold and silver. Pacatnamú's principal structure is an adobe-walled square about the size of four football fields. It consists of several open courtyards and elevated platforms accessible from a single entrance through corridors with walls above eye level that run back and forth in a confused manner. One of the chambers is barely large enough to hold two or three people. One can reach it only via a square spiral that winds ever more tightly through 360 degrees about it. At its center lies a tiny room, from which archaeologists excavated a small textile showing the design of the labyrinth.

Donnan speculates that the unroofed labyrinth was deliberately devised to disorient those who penetrated it. Like the labyrinth of Chartres, it prepared the pilgrim for the religious experience he or she would confront in the sanctuary, an experience that may have been like the one acquired by walkers on the fishing-rod spiral or the monkey's tail. Evan Hadingham points out that unlike the Western concept of religious architecture, which stresses mass congregation, Pacatnamú's enclosed labyrinth seems better suited for individual experience. Could it be that early Andean coastal religion was more solitary and meditative in character? The creation of most Nasca figures from a single line wide enough for only one person to tread lends some credence to this idea.

How difficult it is to imagine what a walk on a pampa labyrinth or a pilgrimage to nearby Cahuachi might have been like; the very idea of a pilgrimage is so far out of our field of human experience. The Koran tells us that a pilgrimage to the Kába, the earthly house of God in Mecca, is the duty all the people owe to Allah. It is thought that 10 percent of the world's 700 million Muslims actually make that journey at least once in their lives. The hajj, as it is called, takes place between the eighth and thirteenth days of the twelfth month of the Islamic year. Like Jerusalem at Easter time, the complex journey brings masses of people together in sacred space and time. As the line passes sacred stones outside Mecca, the visitors vow abstention from all worldly action, even from sex. They remove all their jewelry and put on special garb, white sheeted robes for the men, plain dresses for the women. They ritually wash and cut their hair and nails. Entering into the Kába, they are led through sacred zones arranged in concentric circles, touching various sacred objects as they go. They kiss a black stone (meteorite) and drink some sacred water. Many perform multiple circumambulations to imitate the original actions of their prophet Muhammad. Then the pilgrims depart to the Mount of Mercy several miles east of Mecca to pray at the spot where the prophet last addressed his followers, before moving on to the next site in the chain of events. At Medina they throw pebbles against the pillars on the very site where Abraham hurled stones at the Devil, who tempted him to disobey God's command to sacrifice his son. A ritual sheep slaughter precedes the return to Mecca via the house in Medina where Muhammad once resided. The process of pilgrimage can take weeks to fulfill. The hajj binds people together in a universal consideration of their faith, one that transcends local, parochial expressions.

The Hindu pilgrimage is even more complex. It, too, incorporates a variety of landscapes and movements, all of which attempt to span the hierarchical caste system. In the sacred center of Benares, pilgrims undergo self-purification by bathing in the waters of the Ganges. Each pilgrim constructs a personal sacred geography linked by visitations to a multitude of holy sites and shrines. The followers of Buddhism, rich and poor, travel all the way to those places in Nepal, northern India, and elsewhere that were said to have witnessed the most significant events in the life of Buddha. In a sense, the pilgrim traverses his or her terrestrial spiritual biography. Whether at St. Peter's in the Vatican, the Kába in Mecca, or Cahuachi on the pampa of Nasca, the religious tradition of the pilgrimage is often connected with great architecture of an important shrine, which serves as a symbol of group identity, even if the principle that holds people together varies across cultures; for example, the great cathedrals that served as the focal points of Christian pilgrimages were centers of a collective piety in an age when the very idea of atheism would have been inconceivable.

Isn't it a little dangerous to generalize, though—to think all pilgrimage sites really carry the same meaning to all who would visit them? Do all patriots who pass before Rushmore's lithic presidential countenances feel the same way about their country? Do all Catholics who journey to the Vatican from, say, Germany, Mexico, or the United States share in the same feelings regarding their shared faith? No more than those who walk the wall of the Vietnam War Memorial or the fields at Wounded Knee, I would think. Indeed, people have been known to disagree radically on what these sacred places symbolize. They often become sites of debate and discussion, even protest. Likewise, the great pilgrimage sites, including Nasca, become spaces for working out cultural identities, for reshaping and rewriting histories, for bringing people into dialogue with one another.[11]

Around the World on Straight Lines

Walled enclosures usually imply defense, keeping the enemy without, but they also can signify sanctuary, keeping the sacred within. Opinion about the walled enclosures in the Hopewellian octagon earthwork of Newark, Ohio, today leans toward the latter characterization. At least that is the way contemporary archaeologists view it. The parallel walls are above eye level, 680 feet long and 150 feet apart, leading from the huge enclosure to the Ohio River. The main Newark complex consists of a 20-acre circle joined by a narrow passageway to a 50-acre octagon penetrated by openings at the vertices (Figure 53). As at Nasca, both geometry and astronomy figure in the design plan. The radius of the circle (1,050 feet) is exactly the length of each side of the octagon. Also, the main axis of the complex points close to the place on the horizon where the moon would rise at its northernmost standstill. Actually, there are more than a dozen earthworks in the area dating from AD 600 that consist of a circle adjacent to a square (or a square with sides kinked outward to form an octagon) linked by a causeway. In a few cases the circle and square touch, and in still other cases they interpenetrate. Some of these earthworks have more than one circle. Two of the complexes duplicate some of the same properties, which makes it likely they are not accidental.

Figure 53. Earth geometry reaches a grand scale in octagons and circles at one of Ohio's Hopewell sites. Photo by Rick Pirko.

I found the most interesting parallel of all between Newark and Nasca surfacing in a recent discovery by Brad Lepper, the archaeological curator at the Ohio Historical Society. Lepper traced a perfectly straight, long road connecting the Hopewell enclosures to an almost identical site in Chillicothe, Ohio, 60 miles to the southeast on the banks of the Scioto River. Following up on nineteenth-century records that mentioned a walled passageway leading a few miles out of one of the complexes, Lepper picked up the remains of a road at four points going out from one direction. (One key to his discovery was an old 1848 map published by the same E. G. Squier who pioneered archaeological investigations in the Andes.)

Lepper's projection of the route led directly to the High Bank Works, another circle (also 1,050 feet in diameter) and octagon pair. That the High Bank Works is aligned at 90 degrees to the axis of the Newark mounds suggested to him that one of the complexes might have been meant to complement rather than repro-

---

North American Earth Geometry

Geometrical design patterns are conveyed in other early works of Native American earth architecture. The Poverty Point site on Bayou Macon, a tributary of the Mississippi in northeast Louisiana, probably consisted of an octagonal set of earthen ridges or embankments. Today only five walls remain; the eastern side was cut away when the Arkansas River shifted course around 400 BC, a century or two after the ridges were built, and later Bayou Macon wore off the northern segment. Locals knew about the ridges that ran through their fields, but no one realized that they formed a neatly arranged geometric pattern until 1953, when archaeologist James Ford, who was mapping the area, acquired aerial photos from the Mississippi River Commission of Army engineers. Wrote Ford, "It was only when Poverty Point was viewed from the air that the spectacular configuration of the ancient settlement became apparent." Only when he excavated the site did Ford discover its immense geometry. Originally some of the ridges were 10 feet high, and the outer octagon measured three-quarters of a mile in diameter. The native people who built it moved 530,000 cubic yards of earth, 35 times the cubage of Khufu's pyramidal wonder of the world. Ford and his team believed dwellings were once situated on the ridgetops, for the soil there had been stained with what

---

was left of countless charcoal fires, and the fill beneath contained the remains of kitchen and other utensils. Clearly, the Poverty Point people had gone to a good deal of trouble to build an orderly, well-planned city. The results must have been spectacular. Like Ohio's octagons, the ridges are broken by aisles that lead to the 1,600-square-yard interior area. Poverty Point has invited the eye of many an astronomer who has searched in vain for targets that match the directions of these interstices, though one alignment does correspond pretty closely to winter solstice sunset. Lower Mississippi Valley archaeologists haven't agreed on the purpose of the octagons, but the height and multiplicity of the walls at Poverty Point have led some of them to suggest that the threat of warfare furnished one of the basic mechanisms for the longevity of hierarchically ranked social systems among these people, and it was also this threat that led them to build and maintain defensive earthworks.

(*Anthropological Papers of the American Museum of Natural History* 46, no.2 [1956]).

duce the other. A remnant near the Newark end of the line revealed two 12-inch-high walls 200 feet apart. (Lepper thinks the entire length of the road was enclosed.) Why did Ohio's Hopewell people build this road? This question is difficult to answer, for like the Nasca, the architects of the project were long gone from the scene by the time the first European explorers arrived. "Routes of pilgrimage, sacred roads" was all the pioneers who moved westward through the area could elicit from the natives. Lepper speculates the Newark to Chillicothe road may have been a spirit path that united the two, perhaps through a common religious ritual having to do with the worship of their dead. "It is conceivable," he writes, "that Newark and Chillicothe were great religious centers and that pilgrims came here from across North America to leave rare and precious offerings of copper and mica."[12] (Both minerals have been excavated there.) Sacred roadways would have facilitated such pilgrimages, their straightness perhaps serving, as at Pacatnamú, to condition the mind of the participant to an anticipated out-of-the-ordinary experience. As at Britain's Stonehenge, the orientation or alignment might have fixed the timing of ceremonies within the long-term calendar.

Stonehenge, too, is accessible by an earthen bordered causeway. It meanders from a source three miles away on the north bank of the Avon River. When I last walked it, in the spring of 1996, I approached the main causeway of the site up the hill from the northeast. I distinctly recall seeing the upright megaliths gradually emerge out of the rolling landscape, coming into full view only on that last half-mile or so of the course up to the Heelstone. Lighted by a setting, midsummer full moon, it would have been an inspiring sight to any pilgrim who might have journeyed there.

Back in London, I left some extra time for book browsing off the Strand. When I asked one of the store clerks how to get back, he directed me to the nearest tube station. "But can I walk it?" I inquired, hoping to spend more time window shopping on the way. At this he became confused and uncertain, so I questioned one of the customers. He insisted on directing me to a different tube station where I wouldn't need to change trains, even if it would land me a couple of blocks farther east of my hotel destination. Politely I extricated myself from my self-appointed travel agent, cut to the nearest intersection, and whipped out my London street plan, as confused a maze of winding streets as might be anticipated in any urban scheme that evolved from a fossil medieval town that had once grown helter-skelter. I had seen such a nonplan before, taken to the extreme in Venice, Bruges, and Avignon. Attentive to the map, by performing a multiplicity of acute and obtuse angular turns, I gradually wove my way back to the hotel, a mere twelve blocks from that intersection, as it turned out.

My London walking experience made me realize just how out of touch with our immediate surroundings we moderns can be, even as we wind our way on foot through the city. We've all become so lulled into dependence on wheeled vehicles. In the course of researching and writing this book, I've often thought about how caught up we are in the field of proximate objects through which we move; we pay little attention to the natural landscape, the mountains, streams, and stars that set the large-scale stage behind the drama of our lives. To go from here to there, we only need gain access to the nearest portal, the doorway of our car or yellow taxi, or a hole in the ground accessed by a descending staircase. That gets us there automatically.

Alfred Watkins would have agreed. A country boy who lived outside London in the late nineteenth and early twentieth centuries, he prided himself on not being caught up in the loss of identity with the environment that comes from immersion in the complex rhythms of modern urbanism. His involvement in the flour-milling business gave him the opportunity to travel the English countryside, and his trips often took him quite deliberately, like my own London walk, to some out-of-the-way places. Watkins also did a lot of landscape photography in the course of his travels, eventually developing a national reputation for picture books, which he put together in the early twenties. It was his "great leap of cognition," as biographer Paul Devereux puts it, that led him to concoct a work that would bring him signal (and controversial) fame.[13]

Watkins had a vision of "a network of lines, that stood out like glowing wires all over the surface of the country, intersecting at the sites of churches, old stones, and other spots of traditional sanctity," all of them laid out by ancient surveyors using ranging lines and sighting poles.[14] He describes as a sudden "flood of ancestral memory" the realization on a warm summer day in 1921 that many ancient sites in the landscape lie on long straight lines, "tracts of open ground" or "leys," after the Saxon word, as he misnamed the alignments. Then he got hold of a piece of string. He laid it on a map and connected a church to an old Roman camp to the top of a hill to a Stone Age barrow to a set of crossroads to a group of stone markers, all with a single straight line that passed unimpeded over hill and vale. Next, Watkins eagerly took off to the sites and walked several of these imaginary beelines from point to point. Ultimately, he published a book entitled *Early British Trackways* in 1922, which attracted considerable attention. Ley-line aficionados, as repulsed by the fast-paced urban scene as Watkins, formed clubs and took to the countryside for outings, their picnic lunches packed in the boot of a Model T, to explore antiquity's link with the here and now.

Projecting his own habits and traits on those of his subject matter, Watkins first thought of ley lines quite practically as travel routes of merchants, one for the conveyance of precious metals, one for other goods, until he recognized that many were astronomically aligned (midsummer solstice was a popular orientation). Did ley lines perhaps possess more of a geomantic, magical, or religious (rather than a practical) function?[15] He developed a nomenclature for the kinds of markers and various types of purposes for the forgotten leys that linked them.

Out stormed the critics. They would declare ley lines a romantic form of escapism from the age of industry and technology foisted upon an uncritical public by a charter member of the lunatic fringe. Archaeologists rightly insisted that we can't connect lines between remains that date to different epochs (a Roman encampment and an arrangement of prehistoric piled stones likely have no connection). They were followed by the rigorous statisticians, who pointed out that given X number of points spread about a landscape with a tolerance of $\therefore \triangle X$, it is possible to find Y lines connecting at least Z of them (and Y is a very, very big number). Conclusion? It's all chance coincidence.

Finally, there was the argument of impracticality: the shortest route between two points is not necessarily the most efficient. One of the leys crosses five rivers and a mile of swamp in just eleven miles. Perhaps, rather than being simple trackways, leys traverse such impossible terrain because they were part of a system of landscape geometry, one of Watkins's followers suggested. Archaeologist Christopher Chippindale cites this development as the jumping-off point for a variety of mystical inquiries, including the linkage of ley lines with UFOs.[16]

Three generations later, Watkins's ley lines, though a bit more out of the limelight than when they raised an academic furor in the twenties, still live on.[17] Like their South American counterpart, they too would be impacted by the Stonehenge controversy of the sixties. Astronomy- and geometry-based theories go together, as we have seen both in the ley lines and on the pampa.[18] They seem to serve as a way of popularizing the rediscovery of the mythology of landscape. For example, British author John Michell connects the seven sanctuaries that surround the church at Glastonbury into a configuration resembling the Big Dipper. He links the Bear with Arthurian legend prominent in its vicinity, even tying the name of King Arthur with the etymology of the words "Great Bear" and the old constellation form of a wagon, or "Wain," to the one pulled by Arthur, as ploughman, about the North Pole.[19]

As I write in the late nineties, this idea of recovering the old spirited version of the sacred landscape has enjoyed an unprecedented resurgence, and it remains the subject of many texts sold in occult bookstores. What to the reasoned critics is a wishful flight to an imagined perfect past is to devout believers a revelation of a more direct pipeline to the supernatural than that offered by conventional religion. From straight lines to geometrical figures to biomorphs (England has

England's Geoglyphs

A medieval travel guide lists among the wonders of Britain (in addition to Stonehenge) the White Horse at Uffington, Berkshire, in the south of England. Measuring about 365 feet in length and made by laying chalk into a dug-out trench, it is among the oldest of the many hill figures that dot the downs. Some say that its long sleek body, pointy ears, and whiskers rather more resemble a cat. No one knows who built it, but historians have noted the similarity between the figure and horses imprinted on Iron Age coins going back 2,000 years. Archaeological dating based on the study of silts has recently pushed the time of origin back 1,000 years earlier than that, to the Late Bronze or Early Iron Age. At Dorset resides the Cerne Abbas Giant, similarly constructed, which dates from about AD 500. Some women still believe that sleeping with the giant is a cure for infertility. Like some of the more modern figures and symbols carved on hillsides, these geoglyphs may have served as emblems for the inhabitants who resided below them.

Cerne Abbas Giant, Dorset. Courtesy of Fortean Picture Library.

them too) to labyrinths, every conceivable kind of hypothesis that has been raised about Nasca can be found resurrected in these other ancient marvels that tantalize the inquiring eye. This is why I think they are worth parading by my readers, but only rarely, as in my final example, will we find living testimony that might help us discover their secrets.

The Blythe Intaglios: North America's Geoglyphs

In 1932, on a flight from Las Vegas to Blythe, California, just about the same time Peruvian pilots had spotted the Nasca lines, pilot George Palmer thought he caught a glimpse of a gigantic humanoid figure with outstretched arms sketched on the desert floor. Disbelieving his first impression, he banked his plane into a sharp turn, lowered his altitude, and retraced his course back over the desert. This time, not only did he confirm his discovery, but also he found two additional human figures along with two animal figures in the vicinity. The Blythe intaglios, as they came to be known, are among some 200 geoglyphs etched on the flat terrain that borders the lower Colorado and Gila rivers of southwestern Arizona and southern California. Some were made by the now familiar process of removing desert-varnished pebbles from a paler undersurface. Others were created by rock alignments that outline the figure.

In addition to humans and animals, the figures near Blythe also include abstract designs such as spirals, crosses, and circles.[20] The humanoid stick figures, which range in length up to 100 feet, now number more than 50. (Some of them are mentioned in turn-of-the-century reports filed away in Washington, D.C., in the Bureau of American Ethnology.) All have the same pose: legs together, arms outstretched or bent slightly downward (though many figures lack a head or an arm). Usually the genitals are clearly indicated, even the pubic hair in one case, and the wavy aura of a bride of Frankenstein hairdo emanates from the head (Figure 54).

There are about half as many animal figures; horse, lizard, rattlesnake, scorpion, thunderbird, fish, and quail are the most common. A 150-foot slithering snake with an enlarged head, inlaid rocks for eyes, and a wiggly tongue has nine bumps on its tail. A nest of nine baby snakes 3 to 6 feet long, made of heaped-up gravel, accompanies the mother on her desert trek. Cleared circles make up the greatest share of the abstract figures; there are 50 of them, the largest measuring 270 feet in diameter. The smallest ones, up to 9 feet wide, are often positioned near the animal and humanoid figures. They seem set apart from the other figures, at least as far as their function is concerned. The tamped-down nature of their etched surfaces makes it clear that people once walked over them. Many of

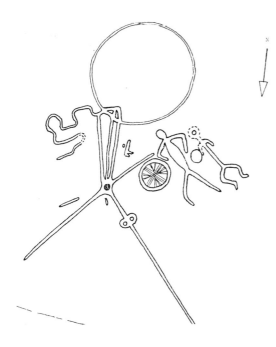

Figure 54. This is one of the more complex intaglios, or incised figures, on the lower Colorado and Gila River desert that features three common patterns: a dance circle, twin humanoid stick figures, and a geometrical pattern (in this case, a birdlike design with radial spokes). Unlike the Nasca geoglyphs, we have direct testimony from living descendants of the Mojave, Halchidoma, Quechan, and Maricopa people about what these figures meant and how they were used. From Boma Johnson, "Earth figures of the Lower Colorado and Gila River Deserts: A Functional Analysis," *Arizona Archaeologist* 20 (1985), courtesy of the Arizona Archaeological Society.

the paths deviate via straight or slightly curved lines leading into and out of the closed loop.

The Nasca remains and their designers are separated by centuries, but the desert figures of the American Southwest have histories not so far removed from the present. "I knew the meaning of certain circles worn in the flat ground, adjacent to the many water holes, about which I had vainly speculated," wrote one visitor to the desert in 1886. "They were extempore dancing grounds of the Chemehuevis." Then in 1910, a Diequeno informant told an anthropologist, who was examining one of the circular paths, "Each village has a circular dance ground, kept in readiness, where dances take place. This is sprinkled and packed down to keep the dust from rising." In former times, these dance circles "were surrounded in a wall of brush." This was placed upright and held in place by large rocks and "served to keep the wind away."[21]

Many of the modern dances that accompany Mojave festivals (the corn dance, the turtle song dance, the creation ceremony dance) call for two lines of participants to revolve counterclockwise in a circle about a drummer–song leader who sits in the center. Some of this ceremonial dancing is associated with healing the sick by removing a malignant influence. One of the circles is attached to a set of meandering access paths that emanate from a radial center well outside the circle (Figure 54 offers a perfect example). Two humanoid figures accompany these geoglyphs. According to archaeologist Boma Johnson, who has worked on them for more than 20 years, the large figure may be the creator god, the adjacent one his evil twin. Early anthropologists mention Yavapai ceremonies in which the sick person is placed in the center of a circular healing area at the beginning of the ceremony. Dancers then move around the circle to invoke the spirit. Are the human figures with missing body parts, often located near the circles, the effigies of the victims? Johnson's opinion: "One can imagine dancers circling around the dance circle, while another dancer moves over the complex path, eventually approaching the elbow of the creator in petition for a healing blessing for the sick person."[22] In the center of one of the circular paths, said one informant, a hole was dug out, a young girl placed in it, and the remaining space filled with warm sand. They tattooed the young girl's face, then they sang about food to see if she could withstand hunger, though they refused to feed her. Around the girl in the hole they danced for a week, a puberty rite.

Circles made of rocks piled up, rather than cleared away as if to make a path, were called "power circles" or "vision quest rings" by one informant. They have still another function: as enclosures. Informants say that one who desired strength or spiritual vision would (after fasting and undergoing other rites in preparation) sit for some length of time in the center of one of these rock rings, which were specially built in locations known to contain power.

Some of the etched scenes on these sacred grounds represent the backdrop for the reenactment of stories important to the heritage of southwestern people. The giant humanoid figures, for example, have been linked with Native American creation myths. The Mojave say their ancestors created a giant effigy of their god Mustamho to elicit his support in getting rid of an evil giant who had been terrorizing them. (The Hopi Fire Clan version of the story is that the effigies are their own clan deities erected by them to keep the rival Water Clan, whom they had earlier driven out, from returning.) The sixteen paired human figures, one of which is usually dismembered, according to the Pima-Papago people, evoke still another legend about an evil giant who had the unfortunate habit of eating children. The killing and dismemberment of the evil giant by his twin brother is a legendary event still commemorated in the desert figures. In the dance ceremonies attached to the creation celebration, concentric paths outside the figures represent the world, and the line along the middle is the Milky Way, over which dancers trace the routes of the gods who created the world.[23]

I envy Boma Johnson and the other scholars who have studied these desert effigies, for unlike those of us who have worked at Nasca, they have been able to find a strong correspondence between the archaeological and historical records, thanks to the close temporal proximity of the two. Even though the lower Colorado and Nasca valleys are worlds apart culturally, the landscapes are not so different. The Blythe intaglio studies offer motives for native people to create such giant figural drawings. Though they (along with the other case studies I've mentioned) offer us little more than an analogy, they can teach us a lot about the complex social customs and motives of the people who made them—their dance patterns, their myths of origin, the way they raised their children, how they healed their afflictions, how they conflicted with neighboring peoples.

Getting the Nasca Lines We Deserve

Let's think of the Nasca geoglyphs as an audacious adventure in changing the look of the face of the earth. If we do, then the birds, the spirals, the trapezoids, and the patterns of lines on the pampa do have something in common with all the other earth-moving projects I've talked about in this chapter: the Blythe intaglios, the Newark to Chillicothe beeline expressway, the chalk-filled effigies above the English downs, even the modern minimalists' wheat fields and converted trash heaps that opened this chapter. But when we penetrate below the skin of each terrasculpture, when we quest for a motive, we always seem to discover that a single rationale for enhancing the world's lithosphere will never suffice. We learn, too, that the most tantalizing of all the explanations can also be the most porous. What is true of the Blythe figures, that the motives for carving giant humans and circles can be totally unrelated, even at the same location, is a scenario I had long suspected when I compared the Nasca animals to the straight lines.

So, are the Nasca lines the eighth wonder of the world? Given that they are one of a kind and the persistence of the belief (despite our counterdemonstrations) that a staggering effort was involved in making them, my answer is an emphatic yes. Just look at the way their existence has stretched our imaginations. To comprehend them, we've raised every imaginable explanation conjured up by the whole of humanity, from runways for spaceships to runways for Olympians, from op art to pop art to astronomical observatories. As much as the lines have awed me, I have also marveled at the imaginations of the people who have experienced them, at the capacity we all have for seeking reflections of ourselves in the bright pink sand. Where the astronomer sees the pampa as a celestial textbook, the artist views it as a canvas for creative expression, the anthropologist as a social or sacred place for coordinating activity among people.

The multitude of journeys to Nasca I've recounted remind me of the parable of the three blind men who encounter an elephant. One grasps a tusk and runs his hand along it, concluding that all elephants surely must be long, hard-shelled animals that taper smoothly toward one end. Positioned at the posterior end of the pachyderm, the second blind man grabs the tail and runs his hand over it. He conjectures that the elephant must be a relative of the snake, except that it has leathery skin and a tuft on its rear end. Standing between the other two, the third blind man feels only the soft underbelly of the beast. He reaches the conclusion that an elephant is a pliable, wrinkled living wall, mammoth in extent. So too, astronomer, artist, anthropologist, and others all seek explanations of the unknown that can be framed within the context of what is familiar to them. What else can we do but judge a thing by our own field of experience?

To understand the Nasca lines, we need to escape from the straitjacket of our own universe of discourse. This was the credo that motivated me to work with a diverse group of people, each knowledgeable in his or her own background. We may not have decoded the mystery of the Nasca lines, but I believe we've surely learned that the maze of lines and figures etched in a seemingly confused array across the desert floor is neither whimsical nor chaotic. The pampa isn't just a conglomeration of dysfunctional doodles on a gigantic scratchpad. There is order, a pattern and a system, behind the geoglyphs.

Rapidly vanishing, the features that we can still see today have offered up clues to the expression of ideas and beliefs of the people who lived in the delicate ecological framework of the south coast of Peru.[24] We found it necessary to labor hard to push open the doorway to the past just a tiny bit, but I think we have illuminated, even if only in the dimmest light, the patterns of behavior of a culture still all too unfamiliar to us. The order we discerned began to look like just the sort of order we might have expected ancient Andean coastal people to seek, an order that involved water, sky, mountain, and earth. People used the pampa to organize themselves. Their perambulations to and fro across the desert wasteland were directed to their mundane activities and to their worship of their sacred places.

Remember the saying, "Every age has the Stonehenge it desires—or deserves"?[25] The lesson learned from Stonehenge, indeed from the deepest study of all the great feats of human engineering we like to call the wonders of the world, is that to know their meaning we must know about the people who built them. To know Nasca means we must become acquainted with all Andean peoples past and present. Unless we do, we are destined to get the Nasca lines we deserve.

NOTES

1. Introduction

1. Maria Reiche, *Mystery on the Desert* (Stuttgart: Offizindruck AG, 1968), p. 10.

2. Wonders of the World

1. P. Clayton and M. Price, eds., *The Seven Wonders of the Ancient World* (London: Routledge, 1988), p. 12.

2. M. Lehner, "Some Observations on the Layout of the Khufu and Khafre Pyramids," *Journal of the American Research Center in Egypt* 20 (1983): 7–22.

3. E. Banks, *The Seven Wonders of the Ancient World* (New York: Putnam's, 1988), p. 49.

4. B. Trell in Clayton and Price, eds., *Seven Wonders*, p. 83.

5. Higgins in Clayton and Price, eds., *Seven Wonders*, p. 132.

6. D. Carroll, *The Taj Mahal* (New York: Newsweek, 1972), p. 95.

7. S. Schama, *Landscape and Memory* (New York: Knopf, 1996).

8. R. Dean, *Living Granite* (New York: Viking, 1949), p. 17.

9. Ibid., p. 75.

10. J. Harriss, *The Tallest Tower* (Boston: Houghton Mifflin, 1975), p. 227.

11. Dean, *Living Granite*, p. 16.

12. Conceived by eccentric sculptor Korczak Ziolkowski, the 87-foot-tall visage, which represents but a small part of the whole, was dedicated in June 1998. Ziolkowski's children, who have carried on the work of their father since his death in 1982, anticipate that it will take at least 50 more years to complete the privately funded Crazy Horse Monument, which will show the chief mounted on his stallion, extending an arm the length of a football field out over the Black Hills.

13. Scott Raymond has done a detailed study of all the ancient food sources of this area, "The Maritime Foundations of Andean Civilization: A Reconsideration of the Evidence," *American Antiquity* 46, no. 4 (1981): 806–821.

14. Though rainfall averages less than 25 millimeters a year, today the south coast still occasionally experiences El Niño, an insurgence into the cool Humboldt current of a warmer stream from the equator, which lies 15 degrees to the north. This produces heavy rain over the coast, often of devastating proportions. The phenomenon is named "the child" because it tends to occur in the season close to the celebration of the birth of Christ.

15. Generally scholars used to use the term "Nazca," with a *z*, when referring to the place and "Nasca," with an *s*, when referring to the culture. I have adopted the latter throughout, as it now seems to have become the standard. Recently, residents of the town took down their sign with the *z* spelling and replaced it with the *s* spelling.

16. For details on the deposition process, see R. Dorn and T. Oberlander, "Microbial Origin of Desert Varnish," *Science* 213 (1981): 1245–1247. The oxides are largely iron and manganese.

17. J. Reinhard, *The Nazca Lines: A New Perspective on Their Origin and Meaning* (Lima: Los Pinos, 1987), p. 32.

18. G. von Breunig, "Nasca: A Pre-Columbian Olympic Site," *Interciencia* 5 (1980): 209–219.

19. M. Spencer, 1983, "Bean Sprouts New Theory," *South American Explorer* 9: 7.

3. Nasca before Columbus

1. H. Silverman, "The Nazca Lines as Cult Archaeology, Economics, and Politics," in *Broken Images,* ed. D. Parker (Manchester: Cornerhouse, 1992), p. 13.

2. In archaeological parlance, this corresponds roughly to the Early Intermediate (AD 1–600) and to the beginning of the Middle Horizon (AD 600–1000) periods of the currently accepted relative chronology (though not all archaeologists accept these dates). See J. Rowe and D. Menzel, *Peruvian Archaeology, Selected Readings* (Palo Alto: Peek, 1967), pp. 293–320. For a thorough study of Nasca ceramics, see D. Proulx, "The Nasca Style in Art of the Andes," in *Pre-Columbian Sculpture and Painted Ceramics from the Arthur Sackler Collection,* ed. L. Katz (Washington, D.C.: A. Sackler Foundation, 1983), pp. 87–106.

3. M. Moseley, *The Incas and Their Ancestors* (London: Thames and Hudson, 1992); L. Lumbreras, *The Peoples and Cultures of Ancient Peru,* trans. B. J. Meggers (Washington, D.C.: Smithsonian Institution Press, 1974).

4. Moseley, *The Incas and Their Ancestors,* p. 141.

5. A. Sawyer, "Mystery of the Ancient Nazca Lines," *National Geographic Society* 147, no. 5 (1975): 726.

6. K. Schreiber, *Wari Imperialism in Middle Horizon Peru,* Anthropology Papers 8 (Ann Arbor: Museum of Anthropology, University of Michigan, 1992); W. Isbell and K. Schreiber, "Was Huari a State?" *American Antiquity* 43, no. 3 (1978): 372–389.

7. G. Hawkins, "Ancient Lines in the Peruvian Desert," *Smithsonian Astrophysical Observatory Special Report* 906-4 (1969), p. 16.

8. One of the best detailed accounts of the Andean conquest story is that of John Hemming, *The Conquest of the Incas* (New York: Harcourt Brace, 1970).

9. Ibid., p. 42.

10. The room measured 22 feet long and 17 feet wide.

11. P. Cieza de León, *La Crónica del Perú* [1550], ed. J. Muñoz et al. (Lima: Biblioteca Peruana, 1973).

12. Hemming, *Conquest of the Incas,* p. 64.

13. J. Murra, *The Economic Organization of the Inka State* (Greenwich, Conn.: JAI Press, 1980).

14. B. Cobo, *Historia del Nuevo Mundo* [1653], Biblioteca de Autores Españoles 5 (Madrid, 1956); translated by J. Rowe, *Ñawpa Pacha* 17 (1979): 27.

15. Garcilaso de la Vega, *Royal Commentaries of the Inca* [1609], trans. H. Livermore (Austin: University of Texas Press, 1966), vol. 2, pp. 230–232.

16. The translation is by Gary Urton, in *The Lines of Nazca,* ed. A. Aveni (Philadelphia: American Philosophical Society, 1990), pp. 197–198.

17. Ibid.

18. J. Hyslop, *The Inka Road System* (New York: Academic, 1984).

19. F. Salomon and G. Urioste, trans., *The Huarochirí Manuscript* (Austin: University of Texas Press, 1991), p. 15.

20. Ibid.

21. Ibid., Ch. 31, sections 425–426.

22. Hemming, *Conquest of the Incas*, p. 348.

23. D. Durán, *The Book of the Gods and Rites and the Ancient Calendar,* trans. F. Horcasitas and D. Heyden (Norman: University of Oklahoma Press, 1971), p. 470.

4. Seeing Is Believing

1. Astronomer Gerald Hawkins to T. Morrison, *Pathways to the Gods* (Lima: Andean Air Mail and Peruvian Times, 1978), p. 48.

2. M. Hodgen, *Early Anthropology in the Sixteenth and Seventeenth Centuries* (Philadelphia: University of Pennsylvania Press, 1964).

3. R. Silverberg, *The Mound Builders* (New York: Ballantine, 1974), p. 27.

4. G. Stocking, *Race, Culture, and Evolution* (New York: Free Press, 1968), p. 16.

5. Dégerando's principal work, *The Observation of Savage Peoples,* trans. F. T. C. Moore (Berkeley: University of California Press, 1969), intended to give advice to the French expeditions of the time, lays out a scientific method for acquiring information on native cultures. Critical of his predecessors, he wrote, "They habitually judge the customs of savages by analogies drawn from our own customs, when in fact they are so little related to each other" (p. 67).

6. A. von Humboldt, *Researches Concerning the Institutions and Monuments of the Ancient Inhabitants of America, with Descriptions and Views of Some of the Most Striking Scenes in the Cordilleras* (London: Longman et al., 1814), p. 408.

7. Stocking, *Race, Culture, and Evolution,* p. 70.

8. I was surprised, while browsing a local library a few years ago, to discover that the prolific Squier had even managed to produce a 500-page volume on the archaeology of New York State.

9. E. G. Squier, *Peru: Incidents of Travel and Exploration in the Land of the Incas* [1877] (New York: AMS Press, 1973), pp. 222–223.

10. Later in life Bingham entered politics, becoming governor and then U.S. senator from the state of Connecticut.

11. H. Bingham, *Lost City of the Incas: The Story of Machu Picchu and Its Builders* (New York: Duell, Sloan, and Pearce, 1948).

12. Ibid., pp. 164–165.

13. Vilcabamba on the eastern slopes of the Andes was discovered much later by explorer Gene Savoy, as was the administrative capital of Huanuco Pampa, a virtual replica of Cuzco. Machu Picchu was actually listed in property documents, a fact that even may have been known to Bingham.

14. L. Monzón, *Relación Geográfica de Indias* [1586] (Madrid, 1881), vol. 1, p. 210.

15. A. L. Kroeber and D. Collier, *The Archaeology and Pottery of Nazca, Peru,* ed. P. Carmichael (Walnut Creek, Calif.: Altamira, 1998), vol. 2, no. 2, p. 90, based on notes taken about 1924.

16. M. Bridges, *Planet Peru: An Aerial Journey through a Timeless Land* (New York: Aperture, 1991), pp. 106–107.

17. P. Kosok, *Life, Land, and Water in Ancient Peru* (New York: Long Island University Press, 1965), p. 31.

18. T. Mejía Xesspe, "Acueductos y Caminos Antiguos de la Hoya del Río Grande de Nazca" [1927], *Actas y Trabajos Científicos del Congreso Internacional de Americanistas* (Lima, 1942) 1: 559–569.

19. Kroeber and Collier, *The Archaeology and Pottery of Nazca, Peru,* pp. 39–40. Schreiber, in her "Afterword: Nasca Research since 1926" (same volume), tells us the lines had been mentioned in government documents as early as 1839.

20. Quoted in T. Morrison, *The Mystery of the Nazca Lines* (Suffolk: Nonesuch, 1987), p. 24.

21. H. Horkheimer, "Las plazoletas, rayas y figuras prehispánicas en las pampas y crestas de la hoya del Río Grande," *Revista Universidad Nacional de la Libertad* 2, no. 1 (1947): 41–65.

22. P. Kosok and M. Reiche, "The Mysterious Markings of Nazca," *Natural History* 56 (1947): 200–207, 237–238. Oddly enough, Gerald Hawkins experienced his intuitive flash at Stonehenge in much the same way. He and his wife witnessed sunrise over the heelstone in June 1961. Stirred by what he saw, he says that he was suddenly struck with the possibility that all of the stones at Stonehenge might have been conceived with an astronomical master plan.

23. Ibid., p. 203.

24. Ibid.

25. Kosok, *Life, Land, and Water,* p. 54.

26. Humboldt, *Researches,* p. 131.

27. M. Reiche, *Mystery on the Desert* (Stuttgart: Offizindruck AG, 1968), p. 10.

28. Morrison, *Mystery of the Nazca Lines,* p. 131.

29. Ibid., p. 21.

30. Among these were one of sixteen zigzag segments of a single feature, a line emanating from a trapezoid, one side of each of two trapezoids, one side of a triangle, and four other scattered lines.

31. Morrison, *Mystery of the Nazca Lines,* p. 40.

32. Morrison, *Pathways to the Gods,* p. 41. Lancho is the author of an excellent brief history of Nasca, *Ensayo histórico de Nasca* (undated), which unfortunately has appeared only locally and in Spanish. In it he gives the obligatory full range of theories on the lines and highlights the hydrological hypothesis, which he would develop later in a small, privately issued pamphlet.

33. In addition to our own, I know of at least two other modern attempts to make Nasca lines, in each case using a plan of existing figures and attempting to duplicate them. Spanish schoolteacher Joan Ventura i Ballbé (*Proyecto Colibrí* [Catalunya, Spain, privately printed, 1996]) chalked out one-to-one copies of a 30-yard whale, a 60-yard hummingbird, and a 50-yard spider in about six hours apiece with a crew of half a dozen people. Debunker-magician Joe Nickell ("The Nazca Drawings: Creation of a Full-Sized Duplicate," *Skeptical Inquirer,* Spring [1983]: 36–47) executed a copy of the condor, also in chalk, in about the same time. Of course, none of these figures needed to be cleared, which would have taken much more time.

34. In addition to me ("An Assessment of Previous Studies of the Nazca Lines," in *The Lines of Nazca,* ed. A. Aveni, [Philadelphia: American Philosophical Society, 1983], pp. 16–18),

critics include Evan Hadingham, *Lines to the Mountain Gods: Nazca and the Mysteries of Peru* (New York: Random, 1987) and Gerald Hawkins, "Ancient Lines in the Peruvian Desert," *Smithsonian Astrophysical Observatory Special Report* 906-4 (1969).

35. M. Reiche, *Mystery on the Desert* (Nasca, 1949), p. 18 (not to be confused with the 1968 edition).

36. Ibid., p. 26.

37. Cf., e.g., L. Lumbreras, *The Peoples and Cultures of Ancient Peru* (Washington, D.C.: Smithsonian Institution Press, 1974); A. Pezzia, *El rayado descomunal nazquense* (Ica: Instituto Nacional de Cultura, 1979), pp. 114–123. Maria Reiche's *New York Times* obituary (15 June 1998) states that "all of the animal figures are indeed representations of heavenly shapes."

38. A. Thom, *Megalithic Sites in Britain* (Oxford: Clarendon, 1967), p. 27.

39. H. Kern and M. Reiche, *Peruanische Erdzeichen* (Munich: Kunstraum München, 1974), p. 12.

40. Ibid., figs. 64–66.

41. M. Spencer, "Bean Sprouts New Theory," *South American Explorer* 9 (1983): 8.

42. Morrison, *Pathways to the Gods*, p. 53.

43. Hawkins, "Ancient Lines in the Peruvian Desert," p. 2.

44. Hawkins never published a record of precisely which lines he had measured, but he kindly provided me with a copy of his map, made by the Servicio Aerofotográfico Nacional, from which he selected lines for his study. This map was very helpful in our investigations. It charts out somewhat more than half of the total lines visible in aerial photographs of the same region of the pampa fronting the Ingenio River on the south.

45. Hawkins, "Ancient Lines in the Peruvian Desert," p. 27.

46. Hawkins, "Stonehenge Decoded," *Nature* 200 (1963): 306–308.

47. Hawkins, "Ancient Lines in the Peruvian Desert," p. 29.

48. Ibid., p. 40.

49. Morrison, *Pathways to the Gods*, pp. 62, 64.

50. Among Nasca researchers who have followed the astronomical paradigm to its limits is Lorenzo Rosselló Truel. He has concocted an elaborate scheme, which after a full reading of his work ("Cantogrande y su relacíon con los centros ceremoniales de Planta en 'U'" [Lima, 1997]) I still do not understand. Basically, he argues that certain bright stars (e.g., Spica, Canopus, and Arcturus) form a system of fundamental template-like lines and angles in the sky that are duplicated in patterns in the human-made trapezoids and other works of architecture here below. He also claims that these patterns (which were used as a means of social classification) functioned as indicators of the 26,000-year precession of the equinoxes, which, he argues, was known to the ancient Nasca people.

51. P. Tompkins, *Mysteries of the Mexican Pyramids* (New York: Harper, 1976), p. 304. Other influential works by Peter Tompkins include *Secrets of the Great Pyramid* and *The Secret Life of Plants*.

52. J. Woodman, *Nazca Journey to the Sun* (New York: Simon and Schuster Pocket Books, 1977), p. 39.

53. Ibid., p. 201.

54. G. von Breunig, "Nasca: A Pre-Columbian Olympic Site," *Interciencia* 5 (1980): 211. A Harvard psychiatrist thinks military rather than athletic training was involved: "These markings served as efficient (ceremonial) paths for unwittingly exercising the late maturing

frontal lobe system (FLS) of the pre-Inca Nazcans, who had to survive in warlike competition with other tribes in an inhospitable desert environment." A. Pontius, "Nazca's Prehistoric Fostering of Frontal Lobe Functions: A Positive Ecological Effect on Neuro-Development," in *Archivum Oecologiae Hominis* (Vienna, 1978), pp. 135–143.

55. E. von Daniken, *Chariots of the Gods* (New York: Bantam, 1968).

56. Ezekiel 1: 15–21.

57. W. Stiebing Jr., *Ancient Astronauts, Cosmic Collisions, and Other Popular Theories about Man's Past* (Buffalo, N.Y.: Prometheus, 1984).

58. R. Charroux, *The Mysteries of the Andes* (New York: Avon, 1974). Evan Hadingham has traced the idea of "beacons for the gods" back even further, to works of the mid-fifties, when a few authors threatened to sue Daniken for plagiarism (*Lines to the Mountain Gods,* p. 54).

59. Charroux, *Mysteries of the Andes,* p. 173.

60. Ibid., pp. 179–180.

61. J. Hawkes, "God in the Machine," *Antiquity* 41 (1967): 174–180.

62. Daniken, *Chariots of the Gods,* p. vii.

63. "Boom Times on the Psychic Frontier," *Time,* 4 March 1974, pp. 65–72.

64. Archaeologist Helaine Silverman, who was present in 1988 when this episode took place, tells the following story: "The inspector of south coast archaeological monuments of the National Institute of Culture and I were driving along the Pan-American highway one afternoon when we espied people doing something on the pampa. Inasmuch as no one is permitted on the pampa without a permit and the whole pampa has been declared an 'untouchable national reserve,' the Inspector stopped our vehicle and walked over to investigate. There he was informed of the project to memorialize Maria. It was immediately apparent that there were geoglyphs in that exact spot and that the perpetrators were altering the pampa surface. An inquiry ensued and tempers flared. Whereas for the archaeologists the issue was the preservation of the pristine pampa surface, in Nazca the matter became a catalyst for simmering political disagreements. The several political factions in town lined up on different sides of the dispute" ("The Nazca Lines as Cult Archaeology, Economics, and Politics," in *Broken Images,* ed. D. Parker [Manchester: Cornerhouse, 1992], p. 12).

65. Lumbreras, *Peoples and Cultures of Ancient Peru,* p. 126.

5. Sacred Landscapes

1. S. van den Bergh, "The Nasca Geoglyphs: An Astronomical (?) Mystery," *Vistas in Astronomy* 35 (1992): 273.

2. B. van der Waerden, *Science Awakening 2: The Birth of Astronomy* (Leiden: Noordhoff, 1974), p. 58.

3. J. P. Perez, in J. Stephens, *Incidents of Travel in Yucatan* [1843] (New York: Dover, 1963), vol. 1, p. 280.

4. Panacas are royal ayllus. An ayllu is a social grouping based on a combination of factors, among them shared land ownership, kinship, and obligations connected with labor and religious worship.

5. B. Cobo, *Historia del Nuevo Mundo* [1653], Biblioteca de Autores Españoles 5 (Madrid, 1956); translated by J. Rowe, *Ñawpa Pacha* 17 (1979): 27.

6. These were collana ("first or most prominent," said to be maintained and worshiped by

the primary kin of the Inca ruler, that is, by the aristocratic class), payan (worshiped by his subsidiary kin, formed by the union of collana men with noncollana women who were chosen as subsidiary wives), and callao (tended to by that segment of the population not related to the ruler). The worship assignments rotated sequentially (from collana to payan to callao and back to collana) from one ceque to the next all the way around the horizon, in a clockwise direction in the suyus of the northern moiety of Hanan Cuzco and counterclockwise in the southern moiety of Hurin Cuzco.

7. Cobo, *Historia del Nuevo Mundo,* p. 25.

8. Cobo also says that Ravaypampa, the next huaca in the direction of Cuzco on the adjacent ceque, is a "terrace on the slope of the hill of Chinchincalla." Likewise, the huaca Puquincancha, which we were also able to locate, limited our view on the ceque adjacent to the south.

9. B. Bauer and D. Dearborn, *Astronomy and Empire in the Ancient Andes* (Austin: University of Texas Press, 1995), photo 8, p. 78. More recently see, B. Bauer, *The Sacred Landscape of the Inca: The Cuzco Ceque System* (Austin: University of Texas Press, 1999). I am indebted to Brian Bauer for making material available to me in advance of publication. Susan Niles also has done some excellent archaeological survey work on the ceque system. See her *Callachaca: Style and Status in an Inca Community* (Iowa City: University of Iowa Press, 1987).

10. Probably from V. M. Maurtua, "Discurso de la sucesión y gobierno de los Yngas" [ca. 1570], *Juicio de límites entre el Perú y Bolivia: Prueba Peruana* (Madrid: Chunchos, 1906), vol. 8, pp. 149–165. Although the Cuzco pillars are long gone, Brian Bauer and David Dearborn claim to have found the remains of a pair of solstice pillars 32 meters apart on the Island of the Sun in Lake Titicaca, where, legend has it, the sun was born. From a platform (the remains of which they also claim to have found) outside the walls of a sanctuary, commoners could have viewed the sun setting behind elite personages situated in the plaza within the walls, a hierophany demonstrating that indeed the Inca were the children of the sun.

11. Cieza de León, *La Crónica del Peru* [1550], ed. J. Muñoz et al. (Lima: Biblioteca Peruana, 1973), p. 214. Other chroniclers who mention the sun pillars include J. de Betanzos, *Suma y narración de los Incas* [1551] (Madrid: Edición Atlas, 1987), translated by R. Hamilton and D. Buchanan as *Narrative of the Incas* (Austin: University of Texas Press, 1996), and P. Sarmiento de Gamboa, *Segunda parte de la historia general llamada inca* [1572] (Berlin: Weidmannsche, 1906).

12. I will spare the reader a description of the tedious procedure and offer only these highlights: Cobo had already told us that ceque 8 of the Chinchaysuyu quadrant passed over the hill of Carmenga and terminated at Sicllabamba. Today about half of the huacas on its ceque can be found, as they retain their old names. Urcoscalla, for example, was a place "where those who travel to Chinchaysuyu lose sight of Cuzco" (Cobo, *Historia del Nuevo Mundo,* pp. 173–174). Based upon these sightings of Cuzco made from the hills west of Cerro Picchu, we equated the place where the city disappears from view with a locale that bears the modern name "Arco Punco." Continuing outward from the Coricancha along the same ceque, we discovered Poroypuquio, or the well of Poroy, its twelfth huaca. Cobo says that the Spanish built a water mill there. The ruins of the mill can still be seen near the modern village of Poroy. We found Collanasayba, the terminal huaca, "the principal *mojón,*" or marker, eight miles out from the Temple of the Sun. It is a rock outcrop about an acre in size at a prominent

bend in the river that flows in from Poroy. Original Inca walls were found there when the modern road to Chinchero was constructed, and the hacienda there still bears the name mentioned by Cobo, "Sicllabamba." Today the hill is still called Collanasayba, which belonged to Sicllabamba. The house of that hacienda stands adjacent to it, the last huaca of its ceque. This would have been an ideal place for the ritual purpose of throwing offerings brought from Cuzco into a river at the end of a ceque, a practice referred to often by the chroniclers.

13. Garcilaso de la Vega, *Royal Commentaries of the Inca* [1609], trans. H. Livermore (Austin: University of Texas Press, 1966), vol. 1, pp. 116–118.

14. The anonymous chronicler mentions a chain of four pillars, presumably running perpendicular to the ceque lines, but why does Cobo's description include only two of them? Probably because he was interested only in those towers on the ceque whose huacas he was delineating (as he had done for the case of the solstice pillars). The visual line from the ushnu to the pillars on Cerro Picchu turned out to be the tip of a rather large iceberg. Zuidema thinks it was derived from a reversal of observations taken in the other direction, that of the rising sun on the day of its passage across the zenith. Archaeologist Bauer and astronomer Dearborn, while accepting the notion that the Incas used zenith sun observations, find the evidence for an antizenith solar alignment wanting, as does archaeologist Katharina Schreiber.

15. Hesiod, *Works and Days,* trans. R. Lattimore (Ann Arbor: University of Michigan Press, 1972), lines 561–564.

16. The Inca also discovered an association between planting, the irrigation schedule, and the appearance and disappearance of the Pleiades star group. The 40-day absence of the prominent little star cluster from the sky coincided almost perfectly with the time from the end of the harvest to the beginning of the next planting season. Like the Aztecs of Mexico, the Inca built this particular sky orientation into their principal temple. They aligned the west wall of Coricancha and its principal doorway with the Pleiades rise position. When the compact little jewel box reappeared in the sky along this line, about June 6–9, it formally signaled the commencement of the month of planting. They even named it collca, or storehouse, where the harvested crop of the previous season is kept. This direction is also traced by a ceque that goes northeast from the Coricancha. There is a western orientation incorporated into the ceque system as well, to mark the point of disappearance of the Pleiades 40 days earlier.

The celestial llama is yet another important astronomical construct that turned up in ceque alignments. Its body is formed by the dark cloud called the Coalsack, near our constellation of the Southern Cross (R. T. Zuidema and G. Urton, "La Constelacíon de la Llama en los Andes Peruanos," *Allpanchis Phuturinqa* 9 [1976]: 69; G. Urton, *At the Crossroads of the Earth and the Sky* [Austin: University of Texas Press, 1981]). Its eyes are represented by the bright stars Alpha and Beta Centauri. This llama in the sky also has been intimately associated with the agricultural calendar in contemporary highland Peru. Each month of the year, the Inca sacrificed 100 llamas of different color categories (white, brown, and multicolored). The animals were brought to Cuzco in great numbers for this ritual. For example, the chronicler Molina tells us that in September (the month of planting), large numbers of animals due to be sacrificed in the next year were brought in from the fields, where they had grazed after the harvest. Another schedule of llama sacrifices was timed by the sky llama's disappearance and reappearance, as well as the dates when it stood at its highest and lowest sky positions at twilight. In the ceque system, the rising and setting points of the llama's eyes are neatly framed by the boundary ceques of the southernmost suyu. These stars and only a few other bright stars visible from Cuzco have the special quality of being visible at one time or another during the night year round, a characteristic called quasicircumpolar (R. T. Zuidema, "Catachillay: The Role of the Pleiades and the Southern Cross and Alpha and Beta Centauri in the Calendar of the Incas," in *Ethnoastronomy and Archaeoastronomy in the American Tropics,* ed. A. Aveni and G. Urton, *Annals of the New York Academy of Sciences* 385 [1982]: 203–229). Even though they are not circumpolar, these stars can be employed as time markers throughout the year. Such stars may have been recognizable as a unique class of celestial objects in the astronomy of ancient Cuzco.

17. Nobody knows why it should work, but one researcher thinks it may have to do with restoring balance and harmony between the internal state of the body and its outer surroundings. Malady is caused by what you consume, what you take in from the outside; urine that passes out of the body restores some of the imbalance. Collecting the urine and bathing the stomach in it amplifies the restoration to balance, a feedback effect—so theorizes Sarah Lund Skar ("The Role of Urine in Andean Notions of Health and the Cosmos," *Etnologiska Studier* 38 [1987]: 217–284).

18. The azimuth is the angular distance along the horizon measured in degrees from the north to the east; thus 90 degrees equals east, 180 degrees equals south, etc.

19. W. Marston, *Sciences,* July–August 1992, p. 7.

20. In early Nasca times the habitation sites were all well upstream. By late Nasca times they appear lower in the valley but not quite low enough to be adjacent to the pampa.

21. Clarkson and Dorn also used cation ratios to obtain both relative and numeric ages for the sample. For details see P. Clarkson and R. Dorn, "Nuevos datos relativos a la antigüedad de los geoglifos y pukios de Nazca," *Boletín de Lima* 13, no. 78 (1991): 33–45. Recently, some of Dorn's colleagues have noted that they were unable to replicate his results, largely because Dorn's samples contained contaminants. Dorn counterargues that such contaminants are known in other investigators' samples and that any failure to reproduce his results stems from a failure to follow his techniques. On the other hand, Dorn has admitted that his method does have some flaws, because samples can hold materials of different ages. At this time the issue, which has a profound effect on our knowledge of the age of the Nasca lines, remains unresolved. By Dorn's own admission, the method of desert varnish dating must be viewed with some skepticism, but its dates are consistent with dates derived by other methods, e.g., iconographic typology, archaeological associations, and demographic surveys. See *Science* 280 (26 June 1998): 2041–2042 and 2132–2139 and 286 (29 October 1999): 884–885.

22. P. Clarkson and R. Dorn, "New Chronometric Dates for the Puquios of Nasca, Peru," *Latin American Antiquity* 6 (1995): 56–69.

23. See K. Schreiber and J. Lancho, "The Puquios of Nasca," *Latin American Antiquity* 6, no. 3 (1995): 229–254. Having studied 35 puquios in the Río Grande drainage, these authors conclude that they were "almost certainly in use by the time of the Inka conquest."

24. Qanats are horizontal wells, tunnels up to 20 miles long punctuated by vent shafts about every 50 yards. Thousands of them can be found in Iran and North Africa.

25. J. Hyslop, *The Inka Road System* (New York: Academic, 1984), pp. 261–262 (translation by Hyslop).

26. So wrote the philosopher Marcel de Certeau in *The Practice of Everyday Life* (Berkeley: University of California Press, 1984). He is quoted in full and discussed in C. Tilley, *A*

Phenomenology of Landscape, Places, Paths, and Monuments (Oxford: Berg, 1994), p. 28.

27. J. Reinhard, *The Nazca Lines: A New Perspective on Their Origin and Meaning* (Lima: Los Pinos, 1987).

28. D. Wallace, "Ceremonial Roads in Chincha," presented at the 42nd Society of American Archaeology Meeting, New Orleans, 1971 (manuscript).

29. Hyslop, *Inka Road System,* p. 313.

30. G. Urton, "Astronomy and Calendrics on the Coast of Peru," in *Ethnoastronomy and Archaeoastronomy in the American Tropics,* ed. A. Aveni and G. Urton, *Annals of the New York Academy of Sciences* 385 (1982): 244–245.

31. M. Douglas, *Purity and Danger* (London: Routledge, 1966). This cleansing theme is common to many religions; e.g., A. Ortiz, in *The Tewa World* (Chicago: University of Chicago Press, 1969), describes how the sacred kivas of the Pueblo must be continually swept to be kept pure.

32. G. Urton, "Andean Social Organization and the Maintenance of the Nazca Lines," in *The Lines of Nazca,* ed. A. Aveni (Philadelphia: American Philosophical Society, 1990), p. 181.

33. "Repartimiento" [1772], translated by Gary Urton, in *Ethnoastronomy and Archaeoastronomy,* ed. Aveni and Urton.

34. Ibid., p. 190.

35. Many archaeologists don't like the idea of interpreting ancient Nasca lines through comparisons with later cultural behavior. Not only does it get away from the material evidence they depend on to back up their ideas, but also it's too big a stretch in space and time from the Nasca to the Inca, they argue. For example, archaeologist Bill Isbell complained that there was nothing at Nasca like the Inca ceques, which radiate from a central temple and link real water sources with agricultural fields and the tombs of the ancestors. So too, we might argue, was there nothing like experimental science in ancient Greece, and Greece (which was responsible for the form of science we practice today) is as remote in time from the Renaissance as Nasca is from Cuzco. No one will doubt that the Incas had reworked and rethought ancient patterns of Andean behavior. As Isbell and Schreiber have shown, they often reused Huari roads and other constructions (W. Isbell and K. Schreiber, 1978, "Was Huari a State?" *American Antiquity* 43, no. 3 [1978]: 372–389). Of course water was a part of the Nasca ray system, and the clustering of lines about the great Cahuachi pyramid resembles the tight focusing of ceques about the Coricancha of Cuzco. We still think the argument by analogy is a lot stronger than do some of our critics. For more on Cahuachi, see H. Silverman, *Cahuachi in the Ancient Nasca World* (Iowa City: University of Iowa Press, 1998).

36. E. Phipps, "The Great Cloth Burial at Cahuachi, Nasca Valley, Peru," in *Sacred and Ceremonial Textiles,* Proceedings of the Fifth Biennial Symposium of the Textile Society of America (1996), pp. 111–120.

37. A. Craig, "Final Report: Marine Desert Ecology of Southern Peru" (Boca Raton: Florida Atlantic University, 1968), p. 98. The map in question is Figure 6.1.

38. Reinhard, *The Nazca Lines.*

39. These quotes are cited and discussed in detail with reference to the orientation problem in A. Aveni and G. Romano, "Orientation and Etruscan Ritual," *Antiquity* 68 (1994): 545–563.

40. D. Johnson, "The Relationship between the Lines of Nasca and Water Sources," and D. Johnson et al., "The Relationship between the Lines of Nasca and Groundwater Resources," unpublished manuscripts, n.d.

41. R. C. Murphy, *Bird Islands of Peru: Oceanic Birds of South America* (New York: Macmillan, 1936), p. 872.

42. J. Bastien, *Mountain of the Condor* (New York: West, 1978), p. 63.

43. Reinhard, *The Nazca Lines,* p. 41. E. Cajon, "El hombre y los animales en la cultura quechua," *Allpanchis* (Cuzco) 3 (1971): 125–162.

44. Reinhard, *The Nazca Lines,* p. 42.

45. G. Urton, *At the Crossroads of the Earth and the Sky: An Andean Cosmology* (Austin: University of Texas Press, 1981), p. 170.

46. G. Hawkins, "Ancient Lines in the Peruvian Desert," *Smithsonian Astrophysical Observatory Special Report* 906-4 (1969), p. 36.

47. Reinhard, *The Nazca Lines,* pp. 34–37.

48. Ibid., p. 50.

49. B. Grzimek, ed., *Animal Life Encyclopedia* (New York: Van Nostrand, 1972), vol. 6, p. 23. I owe the latter observation to Gary Urton.

50. A. Woolfson, ed., *Recent Studies in Avian Biology* (Urbana: University of Illinois Press, 1955).

51. T. H. White, ed. and trans., *The Book of Beasts* (New York: Putnam, 1964).

52. *Chronicle of Higher Education,* 24 February 1988, pp. A4–5.

53. Ibid., p. A5.

54. M. Rostworowski, "Origen religioso de los dibujos y rayas de Nasca," *Journal de la Société des Américanistes* 79 (1993): 189–202.

6. Ley Lines to Labyrinths

1. M. Bridges, *Planet Peru: An Aerial Journey through a Timeless Land* (New York: Aperture, 1991), p. 107.

2. B. Oakes, *Sculpting the Environment* (New York: Van Nostrand, 1995), p. 181. Oakes also profiles several of the aforementioned works. In addition, see S. Herd, *Crop Art and Other Earthworks* (New York: Harry Abrams, 1994), and Jim Robbins, "A Tractor Instead of a Brush, Seeds Instead of Paint," *Smithsonian* 25, no. 4 (1994): 71–77.

3. Oakes, *Sculpting the Environment,* p. 7. I have only scratched the surface of the subject of contemporary earth art. *Art Journal* saw fit to devote an entire issue (Fall 1982) to this form of expression.

4. *Natural History,* July 1996, pp. 16–17.

5. R. Morris, "Aligned with Nazca," *Artforum* 14 (1975): 31.

6. H. Kern, "Labyrinths: Tradition and Contemporary Works," *Artforum* 19, no. 9 (1981): 60–68. At this writing a labyrinth-walking movement seems to have taken root across America; for relaxation, stress relief, or spiritual awareness, people walk church and homemade labyrinths, barefooted, blindfolded, or in deep meditation. The fad is particularly popular on the West Coast. See, e.g., "Winding toward Wisdom," *San Francisco Examiner Magazine* 13 December 1998, p. 22.

7. Kern, "Labyrinths."

8. W. H. Matthews, *Mazes and Labyrinths: Their History and Development* (New York: Dover, 1970), Ch. 5.

9. E. Mâle, *Chartres* (New York: Harper & Row, 1983), p. 3.

10. Matthews, *Mazes and Labyrinths,* p. 98.

11. For an interesting debate on this subject, see S. Coleman and J. Elsner, *Pilgrimage: Past and Present in the World Religions* (Cambridge: Harvard University Press, 1995), especially the epilogue.

12. B. Lepper, "Tracking Ohio's Great Hopewell Road," *Archaeology,* November–December 1995, p. 56.

13. N. Pennick and P. Devereux, *Lines in the Landscape* (London: Robert Hale, 1989).

14. Quoted in C. Chippindale, *Stonehenge Complete* (London: Thames & Hudson, 1993), p. 236.

15. See N. Pennick, *The Ancient Science of Geomancy* (London: Thames & Hudson, 1979), for a discussion of geomancy.

16. Chippindale, *Stonehenge Complete,* p. 236.

17. For example, P. Devereux, *Symbolic Landscapes* (Glastonbury: Gothic Image, 1992).

18. Wherever the astronomical alignment theory arises, the geometrical hypothesis is usually not far behind. What do all those spiral, circular, and rectangular carvings incised in the megalithic tombs of Great Britain signify? "An unequalled feat of visual communication," argues explorer Martin Brennan, concerning the marks on stones in Boyne Valley, Ireland, whose secret message he claims to have decoded. This isn't simple rock art. It's a system of geodetic measurements that reveals a giant map of the 15 square miles between the Boyne and Mattock rivers. Correctly understood, it locates the positions of the mounds, Brennan contends. The sinuous lines carved on the stones give the ground plan of the route to each burial chamber within. Brennan, "The Boyne Valley Vision," *Ireland* 29, no. 2 (1980): 10–15.

19. J. Michell, *The Old Stones of Land's End* (Bristol: Pentacle, 1979).

20. For a catalog of forms and their descriptions, see B. Johnson, "Earth figures of the Lower Colorado and Gila River Deserts: A Functional Analysis," *Arizona Archaeologist* 20 (1985).

21. Ibid., p. 17. The 1886 visitor quoted is T. J. Waterman. The Chemehuevis and other names mentioned here are all subgroups of the Mojave.

22. Ibid., p. 18.

23. My nomination for the most unusual of all the geoglyphs on the deserts of the Southwest is the Topock maze, a series of parallel gravel windrows covering ten acres. Near Needles, California, it isn't strictly a labyrinth because the ends of each row are open to the outside. The Mojave say the maze was an area where they conducted purification rites for their traders. Before traveling to the west coast, merchants were required to run the depressions between the low walls to cleanse themselves of any impurity they might encounter from contact with non-Mojave coastal people. See also F. Setzler, "Seeking the Secret of the Giants," *National Geographic* 102 (1952): 393–404.

24. Unfortunately, mudslides in the aftermath of hard rains caused by the record-breaking El Niño of 1997–1998 severely damaged a number of trapezoids. The figure of the lizard was among the fatalities. Since the death of Maria Reiche, who paid guards to patrol the pampa periphery, thoughtless tourists crisscrossing the pampa in vans and on motorcycles, often leaving refuse in their wake, have helped erase more of the pampa markings, as have looters in search of Indian graves.

25. J. Hawkes, "God in the Machine," *Antiquity* 41 (1967): 174.

INDEX

Acosta, José de, 71

Adaptive dispersal, 45–46

Agriculture, 48, 70, 90–92, 94–97, 115, 126, 131, 177, 185–186, 242–243n.16. *See also* Irrigation

Alexander the Great, 10, 15

Alexandria Lighthouse, 16–17, 19

Almagro, Diego de, 72, 74

Alpha and Beta Centauri, 121, 242–243n.16

Amun Temple, 17

Anasazi, 84

Ancestors, Temple of the, 62–63, 64

Anhingas, 3

Animal geoglyphs, 27, 30–35, 38, 39, 96, 97, 101–102, 104, 136, 137, 185, 191–193, 195–202, 204–205, 230, 239n37, 246n.24

Anthropogeometry, 109

Anthropology, 80–81, 135, 174

Antipater, 9–10, 17

Apachetas, 165

Aqueducts, 6, 166–167, 185, 187. *See also* Irrigation; Water

Archaeoastronomy, 106, 125–135, 209. *See also* Astronomy

Ariadne, 218

Art. *See* Ceramics; Earth art movement; Textiles; Wonders of the world

Artemis: Temple of, 9, 13–14, 17

Artemisia, Queen, 14

Arthur, King, 228

Astroarchaeology. *See* Archaeoastronomy

Astrology, 115, 118

Astronomy: and agricultural calendar, 242–243n.16; Andean constellations, 141, 174–175, 198, 205; archaeoastronomy, 106, 125–135; astronomy-geometry explanation of ancient ruins, 98, 101–102; Maya, 119; and

Monte Albán buildings, 122–123; and Nasca lines, 90–92, 96–97, 101–102, 114–155, 206, 209–210, 239n.50, 246n.18; as science, 118–119; and Stonehenge, 92, 102–103, 151

Aswan Dam, 22

Atahualpa, 3, 58–59, 76

Atlantis, 77–78, 107–108

Atwater, Caleb, 77

Aveni, Lorraine, 53, 127, 135

Avila, Francisco de, 60, 111, 198

Ayllus, 125, 175, 177, 179, 208, 240n.4

Aymara, 172

Aztec culture, 75, 77, 107, 120, 134, 181, 242n.16. *See also* Mexico

Babel, Tower of, 80

Babylon, 2, 9, 10, 12–13, 68, 108

Barnes, Monica, 166–167

Bartholdi, Frédéric, 19

Bastien, Joseph, 198

Bauer, Brian, 69, 128, 129, 241nn.9–10, 242n.14

Bayou Macon, 224–225

Bellerophon, statue of, 17

Betanzos, Juan de, 132

Bingham, Hiram, 85, 136, 237n.10

Bird geoglyphs, 3, 30, 31, 33, 34, 38, 97, 137, 195–198

Blythe, Calif., intaglios, 230–233

Bolivia, 6, 57, 160, 172, 173

Borglum, Gutzon, 19–20, 22, 23

Boyne Valley, Ireland, 246n.18

Brennan, Martin, 246n.18

Breunig, George von, 110–112, 239–240n.54

Bridges, Marilyn, 87–88, 212

Britain. *See* England; Stonehenge

Brooklyn Bridge, 21
Browne, David, 186
Buddhism, 222
Bushnell, Geoffrey, 89

Cahuachi, 42, 55, 181–184, 204, 209
Cairns, 144, 146, 150, 164, 165, 168, 172
Calancha, Antonio de, 85, 152, 220
Calendars: agricultural, 70, 131, 242–243n.16;
    astronomical, 90–97; and ceque system,
    125–126; Maya, 92–93; Nasca lines as, 91,
    96–98; Reiche on, 96; seasonal, 130, 174–
    175, 177; Stonehenge as, 102–103, 154;
    "subsistence," 174–175
California, 21, 83, 230–233, 246n.23
Callimachus, 10
Campos barridos, 186
Cané, Ralph, 26, 144
Cantalloc, 88, 110, 137, 165
Capella, 123
Capitolium, 17
Capra, Fridtjof, 215
Carr, Joe, 122–123
Carroll, Lewis, 202
Carter, Howard, 84–86
Caso, Alfonso, 120, 122
Ceques: and archaeoastronomy, 125–135, 208;
    and Chincha Valley roads, 173; Cobo on,
    70, 88, 124–126, 128, 241–242n.12,
    242n.14; description of, 67; design of,
    104–105; and irrigation, 126, 209; map of,
    69; as mnemonic device, 125; Nasca lines
    as, 88, 90; and pillars, 242n.14. See also
    Inca empire
Ceramics, 44, 45, 48–50, 56, 57, 111, 163–164,
    193, 236n.2
Cerne Abbas Giant, 229
Cerro Blanco, 186, 188
Cerro Picchu, 130–134, 242n.14
Certeau, Marcel de, 243n.26
Chancas, 62
Chan Chan, 81, 82
Charroux, Robert, 113

Chartres Cathedral, 218–220
Chemehuevis, 231
Cheops Pyramid, 23
Chhiuta, 175, 177, 179, 208
Chicago 1893 Exposition, 22
Chichén Itzá, 120, 123
Child sacrifice, 134, 181
Chile, 6, 25, 45, 47, 61, 200, 203
Chillicothe road, 226, 233
Chimú. See Chan Chan
China, Great Wall of, 18, 22
Chinchincalla mountain, 126, 128
Chinchorros culture, 47
Chipaya Indians, 170, 173
Chippindale, Christopher, 228
Christianity, 75, 173, 182, 190, 218–220, 222
Chrysler Building, 19
Chuquimarca, 129
Chuquimarcu, 71
Churchward, James, 78–79
Cieza de León, Pedro, 60, 62, 71–72, 73, 111
Clark, William, 83
Clarkson, Persis, 29, 42, 56–57, 90, 144, 148,
    161–167, 185–186, 188, 193, 200, 201, 205,
    210, 243n.21
Cleansing rituals, 175, 176, 181, 184, 208,
    244n.31, 246n.23
Clement VI, Pope, 182
Clottes, Jean, 216
Cobo, Bernabe, 60, 66–67, 70, 71, 75, 88,
    124–126, 128–130, 132, 178, 241nn.7–8,
    241–242n.12, 242n.14
Coca leaf, 114–115
Colosseum, 17
Colossus of Rhodes, 14–16, 17
Compound animals, 33, 35, 202
Con (god), 205–206
Condor geoglyphs, 30, 32, 137, 197, 198
Condor One, 110
Conklin, Barbara, 127
Conklin, Bill, 127
Con-Titsi (Kon-Tiki), 82
Cortés, Hernán, 58, 59

Cousin, Jean, 18
Craig, Alan, 185
Crazy Horse Monument, 22, 235n.12
Creation legends, 61–62, 73–74, 134, 232–233
Crete, 217–218
Crystal Palace, 22
Cuzco: and ceque system, 70, 104–105, 207; and horizon pillars, 128, 130–132, 241n.10, 242n.14; and Huanuco Pampa, 237n.13; as Inca empire capital, 3, 86; layout and description of, 62, 65–66; painting of, 132, 133; religious organization in, 125–126, 240–241n.6; social organization in, 66–67, 177; Spanish in, 58, 59, 60. *See also* Inca empire

Dance circles, 231–233
Daniken, Erich von, 5, 112, 157
Danzantes, 122
Darwin, Charles, 82
Dating techniques, 3, 46, 165–167, 193
Dearborn, David S. P., 128, 241n.10, 242n.14
Death, 47, 48–49
D'Ebneth, Maria Scholten, 109
Dégerando, Joseph-Marie, 80, 237n.4
Demetrius the Besieger, 15
Desert: Mojave, 217; Peruvian—*see* Pampa
Devereux, Paul, 227
Diana. *See* Artemis
Diequeno, 231
Dillehay, Tom, 45
Diodorus, 11, 17
Diseases, 74, 182
Dog geoglyphs. *See* Fox geoglyphs
Donnan, Christopher, 220–221
Donnelly, Ignatius, 78
Dorn, Ronald, 166, 243n.21
Douglas, Mary, 175
Dowsing, 190

Early Intermediate Period, 50, 236n.2
Earth art movement, 212–217
Earthwatch, 127–128, 135–136

Ecuador, 61, 199
Egypt, 2, 10–12, 23, 47, 68, 81, 107, 108, 113, 206–210
Eiffel, Gustave, 19, 21, 22, 23
Eiffel Tower, 19, 21, 22
El Niño, 30, 235n.14, 246n.24
El Tajin, 120
Empire State Building, 19
Engel, Frederic, 48
England, 80, 101, 226–229. *See also* Stonehenge
Erie Canal, 83–84
Estrada Monroy, 132, 133
"Ethnographic analogy," 181
Etruscans, 190
Extraterrestrial theories, 5, 112–113, 114
Ezekiel, 112–113

Farming. *See* Agriculture; Irrigation
Fertility, 111, 184, 185, 188, 199–200, 207, 229
Fish geoglyphs, 30, 199
"Fishing-rod" geoglyphs, 36, 99–101, 110–111, 140
Fleming, David, 167
Flower geoglyphs, 199, 200
Ford, James, 224
Fox geoglyphs, 30, 198
France, 80, 218–220, 237n.4

Galerías filtrantes, 185
Garcilaso de la Vega, 60, 67, 71, 111, 132, 135
Geller, Uri, 114
Geoglyphs. *See* Animal geoglyphs; Geometric geoglyphs; Nasca lines; Trapezoid geoglyphs, Triangle geoglyphs
Geometric geoglyphs, 39–42, 98. *See also* Trapezoid geoglyphs; Triangle geoglyphs; Zigzag lines
Geometry: anthropogeometry, 109; astronomy-geometry explanation of ancient ruins, 98, 101–102; geometric geoglyphs, 39–42; and Hopewell geoglyphs, 222–224; and Nasca lines, 37, 246n.18; and Native

American culture, 222–225; Poverty Point site, 224–225. *See also* Mathematics; Trapezoid geoglyphs; Triangle geoglyphs
Giants, 229, 232–233
Gold, 62–63, 83, 85
Golden Gate Bridge, 21
Great Britain. *See* England; Stonehenge
Great Pyramid of Khufu, 10–12, 47
Great Temple at Cahuachi, 55
Great Wall of China, 18, 22
Great White Horse, 7, 229
Gregory of Tours, 17
Guacas, 67
Guaman Poma de Ayala, Felipe, 60
Guatemala, 181
Gutiérrez de Santa Clara, 170, 171

Hadingham, Evan, 199, 221
Haeckel, Ernst, 78–79
Hall, H. Tom, 29
Hanging Gardens of Babylon, 2, 9, 12–13
Hartung, Horst, 124
Harvest (Herd), 214
Hawkes, Jacquetta, 114, 205, 238n.22
Hawkins, Gerald, 5, 56, 76, 102–106, 115, 119, 144, 151–152, 163, 199, 238n.22, 239n.44
Heads. *See* Trophy heads
Healing, 231. *See also* Cleansing rituals
Hemming, John, 62, 74
Herd, Stanley, 214
Herodotus, 10, 12
Heyerdahl, Thor, 110, 187
High Bank Works, 224
Hinduism, 221–222
Hodgen, Margaret, 76
Hollis, Douglas, 214
Holt, Nancy, 212, 215
Hoover Dam, 22
Hopewell octagon, 7, 98, 215, 222–224, 226, 233
Hopi Indians, 212, 232
Horkheimer, Hans, 89–90, 115
Huaca de la Luna, 52

Huaca del Sol, 52, 81. *See also* Temple of the Sun
Huaca Moxeke, 48
Huaca Prieta, 37, 52
Huacas, 70, 126, 127–131, 135, 241n.8, 241–242n.12, 242n.14
Huanuco Pampa, 237n.13
Huaqero, 54, 144
Huari empire, 51, 57, 61
Huáscar, 58–59
Huayna Capac, 58, 178–179
Huayna Picchu, 85
Humanoid geoglyphs, 200–201, 230
Humboldt, Friedrich Heinrich Alexander von, 81, 93
Hummingbird geoglyphs, 33, 97, 137, 197
Hyslop, John, 72, 156, 165, 167, 170, 173

Illinois, 215
Imhotep, 10–11
Inca empire: agricultural calendar of, 242–243n.16; archaeoastronomy used in study of, 125–135; and cleansing rituals, 175, 176; communal work activity organization in, 70; and construction, 3–4; creation legends of, 61–62, 73–74, 134; and Cuzco's layout, 65–66; discovery of, 3; and gold, 62–63, 83, 85; history of, 58–59, 61–70; and horizon pillars, 128, 130–132, 134–135; lost cities of, 85–86; mathematical knowledge of, 67; and Nasca lines, 4, 181, 244n.35; and radial division of space, 180; religion of, 62–63, 70, 76, 125–126, 240–241n.6, 242n.16; and ritual plowing, 126, 177; roads of, 3–4, 72, 73, 86–87, 148, 151, 167–170, 173; runners of, 111; social classification in, 63–65, 124–125, 175, 176, 177. *See also* Ceques; Cuzco; Nasca culture; Nasca lines; Pampa
Infanticide, 48
Infertility. *See* Fertility
Insect geoglyphs, 30, 33, 35. *See also* Spider geoglyphs

Intaglios, 230–233
International Congress of Americanists, 78
International Explorers Society of Miami, 110
Intihuatanas, 94
Iowa effigy mounds, 98
Ireland, 246n.18
Irrigation, 3–4, 6, 12–13, 33, 48, 89–91, 126,
    152–153, 161–173, 180, 184–190, 207, 208,
    243n.24. *See also* Water
Isbell, Bill, 53, 244n.35
Isidorus, 190
Islam. *See* Muslims
Island of the Sun, 241n.10
Israelites, lost tribes of, 76–77
Italy, 80

Jefferson Memorial, 20
Jewish diaspora, 76–77
Jik'illita, 172
Jívaro, 199
Johnson, Bill, 156
Johnson, Boma, 231, 232
Johnson, David, 190
Johnson, George, 88
Johnson, Gerry, 156–159

Kansas, 214
Kern, Hermann, 217
Khufu, 10–12
Kollo, 185
Kon-Tiki, 82
Kón Viracocha, 205–206
Kosok, Paul, 88–96, 109, 115, 141, 153, 206
Kosok, Rose, 90, 91, 96
Kroeber, Alfred Louis, 86–89, 140
Kuala Lumpur, 19

Labyrinths, 36, 217–222, 245n.6, 246n.23
Lacco, 129, 134
Lake Titicaca, 57, 61, 82, 134, 241n.10
Lancho, Josué, 53, 95–96, 101, 115, 160, 166,
    187, 204, 238n.32
Landa, Diego de, 77

Land of the Giant Trapezoids, 41
Las Haldas, 47
Leaning Tower of Pisa, 18
Lehner, Mark, 11
Lemuria, 78–79
Leonardo da Vinci, 99, 216
Lepper, Brad, 224, 226
Lévi-Strauss, Claude, 22, 174, 177, 210
Lewis, Meriwether, 83
Ley lines, 227–228
Lighthouse of Alexandria, 16–17, 19
Linsley, Bob, 120
Lithic Period, 45
Little Girl in the Wind (Herd), 214
Lizard geoglyphs, 137, 197, 199, 201, 246n.24
Llama, 242–243n.16
Lockyer, Norman, 92
Looting, 53–55, 62–63, 74–75
Lost continents, 5, 77–78, 84, 107–108, 187
Louis XIV, King, 22
Louisiana, 224–225
Louisiana Purchase, 83
Low-altitude surveys, 156–160
Lumbreras, Luis, 115

Machu Picchu, 84–86, 237n.13
Mâle, Emile, 218
Mallku, 6, 172
Manco Inca, 59
Marching Bear Group, 98
Maria, Walter de, 217
Markas, 165
Mars, 118, 119
Marston, Wendy, 161
Martial, 17
Martínez de Campañon, Bishop, 81
Masson, Duncan, 27, 144
Mathematics, 37–38, 67, 99, 108–109. *See also*
    Geometry
Matthews, W. H., 220
Maudslay, Alfred Percival, 120
Maussollos, King, 9, 14
Maya culture, 77, 92–93, 107, 119, 120, 123–

124, 163, 181. *See also* Mexico

Medenos, 83

Meisner, Doug, 156, 159

Mejía Xesspe, Toribio, 4–6, 88–90, 94, 115

Métraux, Alfred, 170

Mexico, 22, 84, 108, 120–124. *See also* Aztec culture; Maya culture

Michell, John, 228

Middle Horizon Period, 51–53, 184, 236n.2

Minos, King, 217–218

Minotaur, 217–218

Mississippi River Valley, 224–225

Mit'a system, 126

Moche culture, 51–53

Mojave Desert, 217

Mojave Indians, 231–232, 246n.23

Molina, Cristóbal de, 60, 209

Monkey geoglyph, 30, 34, 39, 96, 136, 191, 193, 198

Monte Albán, 120, 122–123

Moon Temple, 52

Moors, 59

Morris, Robert, 216

Morrison, Tony, 76, 94–95, 106, 155, 170, 172–173

Moseley, Michael, 46, 48, 51

Motolinía, Toribio de, 134

Mountain gods, 198

Mount Rushmore, 19–21

Mu, 78–79

Muhammad, 221

Müller, Rolf, 94

Mummification, 47, 49, 60, 94, 198–200

Mumtaz Mahal, 18

Murphy, Robert, 197

Murra, John, 64

Murúa, Martín de, 60

Muses Temple, 16

Muslims, 190, 221

Mutu mountain, 132

Mythology: arrival myth of Kón (Con) Viracocha, 205–206; and compound animals, 202; of Con-Titsi (Kon-Tiki), 82; creation legends, 61–62, 73–74, 232–233; and explanation of ecological disasters, 206; fertility myth, 111; of lost continents, 5, 77–78, 107–108; and modern interpretations of Nasca lines, 109, 112; of rain, 186, 188, 198, 204; Theseus and the Minotaur, 217–218. *See also* Religion

Napoleon, 81

Nasca, Don García, 74, 177

Nasca culture: and adaptive dispersal, 45–46; archaeological discoveries on, 53–55; architecture of, 44, 55; dates of, 26; in Early Intermediate Period, 50; Huari influence on, 51, 57; Inca domination of, 58, 71; introductory comments on, ix–xi; in Lithic Period, 44–45; in Middle Horizon Period, 51–52, 184, 236n.2; Moche influence on, 51–53; remains of, 50–58; settlement patterns of, 166, 243n.20; social hierarchy of, 124–125, 175, 176, 177; Spanish conquest of, 58–61, 71–75; spelling variations of "Nasca," 235n.15. *See also* Ceramics; Inca empire; Nasca lines; Pampa; Textiles

Nasca lines: aerial study of, 87–88, 109–113, 136–137, 143, 206; as art, 216–217; and astronomy, 90–92, 94–97, 101–102, 141–155, 206, 209–210, 239n.50, 246n.18; books about, 108; calendrical theories about, 90–92, 94–97; as ceque lines, 88, 90; construction of, 28–30, 38–39, 99, 101, 137–139; cult of the dead theory of, 88–90; dating of, 165–167, 193, 243n.21; description of, 2–4, 89; destruction of, 30; discovery of, 4–5, 94; as Eighth Wonder of the World, 23, 233; extraterrestrial theories of, 5, 112–113; features shared with Nasca roads, 167–170, 171; and fertility, 184, 188, 199–200; and geometry, 37, 246n.18; and Inca culture, 4, 181, 244n.35; and irrigation, 3–4, 6, 89–91, 152–153, 161,

162–173, 184–190; labyrinthine qualities of, 196; and lost continent theory, 5; low-altitude surveys of, 156–160; mapping of, 144, 239n.44; and mathematics, 37–38, 99, 246n.28; modern attempts at creating, 238n.33; order of, 141–155; parallels with ancient Egypt, 206–210; photographs and drawings of, 25–27, 29, 32, 36, 38, 101, 138–139, 145–148, 150, 168–169, 171, 183, 193, 194, 195; physical training site theory of, 5, 110–112, 239–240n.54; protection of, 115, 160–161, 240n.64, 246n.24; and ray centers, 143–148, 158, 159, 184–185, 191, 207–208; and relationship between animal and man, 202; and religion, 110, 115, 181–182; theories about, 4–8, 38–39, 87–96, 101–102, 109–113, 115, 141–155, 188, 206–210, 216–217; and topographical landscape, 24–37; unfinished lines, 29–30; walking on, 6–7, 143–144, 149–150, 160, 162, 206; and water cult theories, 33, 95–96, 162–173, 184–190, 208–209. *See also* Ceques; Cuzco; Inca empire; Nasca culture; Pampa

Nasca town, 136, 140–141, 143, 160, 177
National Geographic Society, 85, 103, 156
National Institute of Culture (INC) of Peru, 115, 143, 156, 160
National Museum of Anthropology and History (Mexico), 120
National Science Foundation, 156
Native American culture, 212, 217, 224–225. *See also specific tribes*
Nebuchadnezzar, 12
Needle and ball of wool geoglyphs. *See* "Fishing-rod" geoglyphs
New Age, 107–115
New Mexico, 212
New York state, 214
Ngo, Viet, 214–215
Nickell, Joe, 238n.33
Niles, Susan, 241n.9
Noah's Ark, 17, 79

North Dakota, 215

Oaxaca, 120–124. *See also* Mexico
Ohio earthworks. *See* Hopewell octagon; Serpent Mound
Ollantaytambo, 40
Omotoyanacauri mountain, 132
Oregon Trail, 83
Orion, 175, 191
Owl Man, 7, 200–201

Pacariqtambo, 175–177, 180, 181, 208
Pacatnamú, 220–221
Pachacamac, 86
Pachacuti Inca Yupanqui, 61, 71
Pachacuti Yamqui, Joan de Santa Cruz, 63, 64
Pacha Mama, 65–67
Pacific Ocean, 25
Paddock, John, 121–122
Palestine, 9
Palmer, George, 230
Pampa: and animal geoglyphs, 26, 30–37; black rock of, 28; ecology of, 208–209; names of sections of, 26; Pampa Cantalloc, 36; photographs of, 25, 26, 36; protection of, 115, 160–161, 240n.64, 246n.24; Silverman on, 44, 240n.64; soil fertility on, 185–186; stone circles on, 164; surveys of, 56–57, 90; and tourism, 56; walking on, 143–144, 149–150, 160, 162, 170, 172–173, 240n.64; water table on, 144, 148. *See also* Inca empire; Nasca culture; Nasca lines
Panacas, 125, 240n.4
Panama Canal, 21
Pan-American Highway, 25, 56, 72, 73, 94, 104, 115, 137, 143, 158
Papua, 112
Paracas, 49, 50, 94
Parcialidades, 177
Parker, David, 143
Paul, Apostle, 14

Pausanias, 13
Pelican geoglyphs, 33, 35
Pericles, 13
Peru. *See* Cuzco; Inca empire; Nasca culture; Nasca lines
Petronas Towers, 19
Pharos, 16–17, 19
Pheidias, 13
Philo of Byzantium, 16
Physical training on Nasca lines, 5, 110–112, 239–240n.54
Pictographs, 47
Pilgrimages, 6, 14, 55, 56, 132, 134, 181–182, 209, 217–222. *See also* Religion
Pillars, 128, 130–135, 241n.10, 242n.14
Piri Réis map, 113
Pisa, Leaning Tower of, 18
Pitluga, Phyllis, 204–205
Pizarro, Francisco, 3, 58, 59, 72, 74, 76, 132, 220
Plague, 74, 182
Plant geoglyphs, 194, 199, 200
Plato, 77
Pleiades, 152, 174, 242–243n.16
Pliny, 14
Plutarch, 217–218
Polo de Ondegardo, Juan, 60
Pontius, A., 240n.54
Pottery. *See* Ceramics
Poverty Point site, 224–225
Power circles, 232
Prescott, W. H., 82
Protestant Reformation, 80
Prussia, 19, 20
Pueblo Indians, 212, 217
Puquios, 70, 136, 243n.23
Purification. *See* Cleansing rituals
Pyramids, 2, 10–11, 23, 47, 77, 84, 108, 113, 119, 120, 173, 181–184

Qanats, 167, 243n.24
Qollur R'iti highland pilgrimage, 182
Quebrada de la Vaca, 178–180

Quebradas, 25, 26, 41, 165, 185
Quechua language, 60
Quetzalcoatl, 58, 205
Quiangalla, 126, 128–129
Quipus, 67–68

Radiocarbon dating, 3, 46, 166, 243n.21
Rain legends and rituals, 181, 186, 188, 198, 204
Rameses II, 22
Ravines, Rogger, 143, 160
Ray centers, 143–148, 158, 159, 184–185, 191, 207–208
Raymond, Scott, 235n13
Reiche, Maria: author's meeting with, 140–141; biography and early career of, 5, 93–94, 115; on calendar, 96; death of, 204, 246n.24; on Nasca lines, 2, 5, 38–39, 96–99, 101–102, 109, 115, 140–142, 144, 155, 191, 200; and news media, 94–95; and pampa, 56, 115, 160–162; photograph of, 39; relationship with other professionals, 110–111, 140–141, 155–156, 160–161; successor to, 204–205
Reiche, Renate, 160, 161
Reinhard, Johan, 33, 173, 184, 188, 198, 200, 204, 205
Religion: Andean, 181–183; Aztec, 134, 181; Buddhism, 222; and ceque system, 125–126; ceremonial walking, 170, 172–173; Christianity, 75, 173, 182, 190, 218–220, 222; cleansing rituals, 175, 176, 184, 208, 244n.31, 246n.23; and control of populace, 92–93; direction to face when worshipping, 190; and ecological disasters, 206; and extraterrestrial visitations, 112–113; and forced conversion, 75; and Great Pyramid of Cahuachi, 55, 181–184; Hinduism, 221–222; of Inca empire, 62–63, 70, 76, 125–126, 240–241n.6, 242n.16; Islam, 190, 221; Jewish diaspora, 76–77; Maya, 181; of Mojave Indians, 231–232; and mountain gods,

172; and Nasca lines, 88–89, 110, 115, 181–
182; and origin of life, 81–82; Protestant
Reformation, 80; purification rites,
246n.23; rain legends, 186, 188; sacrifices,
134, 181, 242n.16; staff deity, 203; and
Stonehenge, 154. *See also* Mythology;
Pilgrimages
Rhodes. *See* Colossus of Rhodes
Richards, Peter, 214
Río Grande de Nasca, 25, 53, 185, 243n.23
Ritual cleansing. *See* Cleansing rituals
Roads: and ceque system, 173; in Chincha
Valley, 173; Inca, 3–4, 72, 73, 86–87, 148,
151, 167–170, 173; and Nasca lines, 3–4,
88–90, 167–170; stone-paved, 86
Robinson, David, 53
Rocks, 28. *See also* Cairns; Stone circles
Romans, 190
Romantic movement, 77–79
Rope bridges, 83, 85
Rosborough, Brian, 127
Ross, Charles, 212, 213, 215
Rossel Castro, Alberto, 33, 95, 185–186
Rostworowski de Diez Canseco, Maria, 205–
206
Rousseau, Jean-Jacques, 77
Rowe, John, 45, 56
Ruggles, Clive, 154–155, 210
Running figures, 111
Rushmore. *See* Mount Rushmore

Sacrifices, 134, 181, 242n.16
Sacsahuaman, 65
Salomon, Frank, 73
São Paolo Tower, 19
Sarmiento de Gamboa, Pedro, 60
"Savage" morals, 76, 237n.4
Savoy, Gene, 237n.13
Sawyer, Alan, 51
Schama, Simon, 19
Schreiber, Katharina, 50, 53, 72, 166, 187, 190,
238n.19, 242n.14, 244n.35
Scotland, 101, 154

Sears Tower, 19
Sechin Alto, 47
Semiramis, 17
Sendero Luminoso, 115–116
Serpent Mound, 98
Seven South Dearborn, 19
Shah Jahan, 18, 22
Shark geoglyph, 192, 200
Shining Path, 115–116
Shipper, Robert, 88
Silverman, Helaine, 6, 42, 44, 55–56, 107,
114–115, 143, 181–184, 186, 193, 205, 209,
210, 240n.64
Skar, Sarah Lund, 243n.17
Sky Mound (Holt), 212
Smallpox, 74
Smithson, Robert, 7–8, 213, 217
Smithsonian Institution, 82
Snake intaglios, 230–231
Sneferu, 10
Société des Observateurs de l'Homme, 80
Solomon Temple, 17
Solstices, 94, 128–130, 132, 134, 151, 152, 214,
215, 241n.10, 242n.14
Southern Cross, 121, 123, 175, 242–243n.16
Spain, 58–63, 74–75, 167
Spence, Lewis, 78
Spider geoglyphs, 30, 101–102, 185, 191, 193,
199, 204–205
Spiral Jetty (Smithson), 213, 217
Spirals, 38, 39, 137, 159, 199, 201
Spring (Richards), 214
Squier, E. G., 82–83, 224, 237n.8
Staff-bearing gods, 111
Staff deity, 203
Star Axis (Ross), 212, 213, 215
Statue of Liberty, 15
Stephens, John Lloyd, 82
Stiebing, William, Jr., 113
Stone circles, 164, 232
Stonehenge, 5, 92, 99, 102–103, 114, 115, 151,
154, 226, 228, 234, 238n.22
Strabo, 16

Strauss, Joseph, 21
Strong, William Duncan, 53–55, 166
Suárez, Pedro, 74
Sucanca, 130, 131
Suez Canal, 21
Sun, Temple of the, 52, 62–63, 66–67, 81, 85, 128
Sundials, 135
Suyus, 65–66
Swedenborg, Emanuel, 77

Tahuantinsuyu, 65, 75. *See also* Cuzco
Taj Mahal, 18, 22
T'aki, 172
Tambo, 165
Tambo Colorado, 40
Tello, Julio C., 88, 94
Temple of Amun, 17
Temple of Artemis, 9, 13–14, 17
Temple of Solomon, 17
Temple of the Ancestors, 62–63, 64
Temple of the Moon, 52
Temple of the Muses, 16
Temple of the Sun, 52, 62–63, 66–67, 81, 85, 128
Tenochtitlán, 181
Teotihuacan, 22, 56, 84, 120, 124
Texas, 44
Textiles, 33, 37, 44, 48, 49, 53, 111, 200
Theseus and the Minotaur, 217–218
Thom, Alexander, 97, 99, 101, 154
Thomas, Saint, 219
Tiahuanaco empire, 57–58, 61, 82, 203
Tinkuy, 65
Tipi rings, 164
Titu Cusi, 85
Toltec, 120
Tompkins, Peter, 109
Topock maze, 246n.12
Tourism, 56–57, 116, 143
Tower of Babel, 80
Trapezoid geoglyphs, 5, 27, 38, 40–41, 89, 90, 106, 136–137, 147, 149, 163, 169, 188–190,

246n.24. *See also* Geometric geoglyphs
Trell, Bluma, 14
Triangle geoglyphs, 66, 89–90. *See also* Geometric geoglyphs
Trophy heads, 51, 198–200
Truel, Lorenzo Rosselló, 239n.50
Tudor, Guy, 197
Tula, 120
Tupac Yupanqui, 71
Turkey, 113
Turner, Frederick Joseph, 23–24
Tut, King, 84
Tylor, Edward, 81, 82
Typhus, 74

Uffington Great White Horse, 7, 229
UFOs. *See* Extraterrestrial theories
Uhle, Max, 86
Urine, 136, 243n.17
Urton, Gary, 53; and Andean constellations, 141, 174–175, 198, 205; and ceque system, 70, 126; and code of quipu, 67; and Don García Nasca's will, 74; on legend of Cerro Blanco, 186; on Nasca lines, 6, 42, 141–155, 179–180, 210; on Pacariqtambo, 175–177, 208; on Quebrada de la Vaca, 178–180; and rectangular walled structures, 165; and Reiche, 155–156, 160–161; and seasonal calendar, 174–175, 177; and Silverman, 181; on water in Nasca valley, 185
Ushnu, 65, 131
Utah, 213, 217
Uxmal, 120, 123–124

Vaiont Dam, 22
Van den Bergh, Sidney, 118
Van Heemskerck, Maarten, 18
Ventilla, 55–56
Ventura i Ballbé, Joan, 238n.33
Venus, 118, 119
Versailles, Palace of, 22
Vilcabamba, 85, 86, 237n.13

Viracocha, 82, 134, 186, 188, 205–206

Vision quest rings, 232

Von Erlach, Johann Fischer, 18

Vulture geoglyphs, 185

Walking: ceremonial, 6–7, 170, 172–173, 207; in labyrinth, 217–221, 245n.6; on Nasca lines and pampa, 6–7, 143–144, 149–150, 160, 162, 170, 172–173, 206

Wallace, Dwight, 173

Warfare, 50, 199–200

Wari Wilka, 51–52

Washington Monument, 20, 21

Washington state, 212

Water: dowsing for, 190; Incas and water rights, 180; and Nasca lines, 33, 95–96, 162–173, 184–190, 208–209; pampa water table, 144, 148. *See also* Aqueducts; Irrigation; Rain legends and rituals

Watkins, Alfred, 227–228

Whale geoglyphs, 192, 200

Whately, Richard, 81

White Horse at Uffington, 7, 229

Wisconsin, 98

Wonders of the world, 2, 9, 10–18, 23, 233

Woodman, Jim, 109–110, 157

Woolfson, Albert, 201

World Trade Center, 19, 212

Yung, Susan, 195–196, 199

Zapotecs, 120–121, 124

Zeus, statue of, 13

Zigzag lines, 31, 33, 36, 37, 110–111, 190, 201. *See also* Geometric geoglyphs

Ziolkowski, Korczak, 235n.12

Zoos, 80

Zoser, 10

Zuidema, Tom, 67, 69, 70, 99, 124–126, 129, 130–156, 210, 242n.14